PRAISE FOR *PROJECT FEAR*

'Explosive.'
Daily Mail

'Brilliant.'
Sunday Times

'A racy eye-witness account.'
The Independent

'Remarkably revealing, and often amusing too.'
Andrew Sparrow, *The Guardian*

'Fabulous … Seriously, read it.
It's fascinating and beautifully written.'
Isabel Hardman, *The Spectator*

'[An] adrenaline-fuelled, blood and guts account.'
Prospect

'The best (and most entertaining) account yet of the Scottish
referendum … Lots of lessons for the EU referendum.'
(Lord) Andrew Cooper, former director of strategy to
David Cameron

'A great read and very well written.'
Nicola Sturgeon MSP, First Minister of Scotland

'Shocking, riveting and hilarious. The Scottish *Thick of It*.'
Owen Jones

PROJECT FEAR

HOW AN UNLIKELY ALLIANCE LEFT A KINGDOM UNITED BUT A COUNTRY DIVIDED

JOE PIKE

Biteback Publishing

For Mike, Claire, Jess & Gordon

CONTENTS

AUTHOR'S NOTE

I was walking across Lambeth Bridge after two interviews in Westminster: the BBC's *Daily Politics* followed by *The World at One*. My phone buzzed, signalling the arrival of what turned out to be a furious text.

It was 18 September 2015, the one-year anniversary of Scotland's independence referendum – and the day *Project Fear* was first released. While attempting to launch this book, I was having to contend with the barrage of reactions it provoked from those involved.

Some were far from delighted with the stories uncovered and the often farcical truth behind the political spin. Many more revelled in the details of their enemies' errors. The consensus, however, was encouraging. Among those mentioned in the following pages, the vast majority admit that although they might rather *Project Fear* had never been written, it succeeds in being a fair depiction of a transformative time in UK politics.

The idea for this book came soon after the referendum. It had been a unique and thrilling period. And, for me, the unlikely alliance of the three pro-UK parties in a Better Together coalition had been particularly intriguing.

Yet, despite the campaign capturing global media attention, no one had fully uncovered and documented what was happening behind the scenes. The more I talked to politicians, advisers and staffers, the more I was convinced that there was a fascinating tale to be told.

Project Fear starts with an account of the referendum's No campaign, and later covers how the three pro-UK parties fared in the general election that followed. With Scottish Labour the best-represented at Westminster – at least back then – its affairs dominate.

In this revised and updated edition, we explore the striking parallels between the Scottish and the EU referendums, the impact on Scotland of Jeremy Corbyn's extraordinary rise, and what the SNP's continuing dominance means for politics both north and south of the border.

This book is neither an exhaustive history of events nor an assessment of the merits of arguments on either side.

The majority of the content is based on sixty interviews with key players, almost all conducted in person, with many speaking for the first time. Every interview – from junior staff to leading politicians – was conducted on the same off-the-record basis. Only a handful of people refused to be involved.

When quotation marks are used, the source was someone directly involved, a witness to a conversation, or a transcript. Quotes without quotation marks merely summarise the thrust of what was said. Many interviewees have kindly provided emails, internal documents, polling information, contemporaneous notes and the content of text messages.

I hope this is a pacy, entertaining read, full of fresh insight, and of particular interest to those keen on understanding contemporary UK politics, campaigns and referendums.

Ahead of the EU referendum – and perhaps even a second Scottish referendum – there is clearly much to learn.

I have kept analysis to a minimum, allowing those at the centre of events to provide their own contrasting interpretations, and allowing readers to make up their own minds.

My then partner, now husband, Gordon Aikman worked for Better Together until being diagnosed with the terminal neurodegenerative condition motor neurone disease in early 2014. To avoid any conflict of interest, I have steered clear of his involvement.

I am, above all, extremely grateful to my sources. They have been generous with their time and candid in their contributions. I realise some have not enjoyed depictions of themselves in print, but I hope that participants in the process will recognise the care taken to be both empathetic and balanced.

Iain Dale kindly took a punt on this, my first book, and has championed it ever since; I am indebted to him for his continued encouragement and advice. Olivia Beattie and Melissa Bond at Biteback Publishing have done sterling work getting the project into shape and turning the text around in record time. Victoria Gilder, Sam Deacon, Sam Jones, Ashley Biles and James Stephens all ensured the first edition was a commercial success, paving the way for this updated publication.

Edward Durnall at Opal deserves credit for fixing my laptop (and saving the text) when it came into contact with a cup of coffee.

I am grateful to Catherine Houlihan for her support, and to my colleagues at the Scottish Parliament: Paul McKinney, Peter MacMahon, Kathryn Samson, Kerry Plummer and Alistair McKenzie.

Dr Helen O'Shea, Dr Mike Pike, Dr Claire Burns, Dr Gerard Cummins, Giles Winn and Isobel Salmond have all provided invaluable feedback on early drafts. However, any errors remain mine and mine alone.

Finally, Gordon Aikman has been a constant source of encouragement and support. His fearlessness, kindness, reassurance and patience have made me a far better person.

Joe Pike
@joepike
Edinburgh, February 2016

DRAMATIS PERSONAE

GEOFF ABERDEIN: Chief of staff to Alex Salmond.

GORDON AIKMAN: Director of research, Better Together.

DANNY ALEXANDER: Chief Secretary to the Treasury, 2010–15. Liberal Democrat MP for Inverness, Nairn, Badenoch & Strathspey, 2005–15.

DOUGLAS ALEXANDER: Labour's 2015 chair of general strategy. MP for Paisley South, 1997–2005, and for Paisley & Renfrewshire South, 2005–15.

PHIL ANDERTON: Board member, Better Together. Business consultant.

MICHAEL ASHCROFT: Businessman. Conservative peer. Pollster.

JACKIE BAILLIE: Board member, Better Together. Labour MSP for Dumbarton, 1999 to present day.

ED BALLS: Shadow Chancellor of the Exchequer, 2011–15. Labour MP for Normanton, 2005–10, and for Morley & Outwood, 2010–15.

EDDIE BARNES: Director of strategy and communications, Scottish Conservatives.

GREG BEALES: Director of strategy to Ed Miliband.

TORSTEN BELL: Director of policy to Ed Miliband.

NATALIE BENNETT: Leader, the Green Party of England and Wales, 2012 to present day.

GORDON BROWN: Prime Minister, 2007–10. Labour MP for Dunfermline East, 1983–2005, and for Kirkcaldy & Cowdenbeath, 2005–15.

DAVID CAMERON: Prime Minister, 2010 to present day. Leader, Conservative Party, 2005 to present day.

ALASTAIR CAMPBELL: Journalist. Author. Director of communications and strategy to Tony Blair, 1997–2003.

GLENN CAMPBELL: Political correspondent, BBC Scotland.

ALISTAIR CARMICHAEL: Secretary of State for Scotland, 2013–15. Liberal Democrat MP for Orkney & Shetland, 2001 to present day.

MARK CARNEY: Governor, Bank of England.

SCOTT CHISHOLM: Media trainer. Former Sky News anchor.

NICK CLEGG: Deputy Prime Minister, 2010–15. Leader, Liberal Democrats, 2007–15.

ANDREW COOPER: Director of strategy to David Cameron, 2011–13. Co-founder, Populus.

LYNTON CROSBY: Campaign consultant to Conservative Party, 2012–15.

MARGARET CURRAN: Shadow Secretary of State for Scotland, 2011–15. Labour MP for Glasgow East, 2010–15.

JOHN CURTICE: Professor of politics, Strathclyde University. President, British Polling Council.

SUSAN DALGETY: Director of communications, Scottish Labour, 2015.

ALISTAIR DARLING: Chair, Better Together, 2012–14. Chancellor of the Exchequer, 2007–10. Labour MP for Edinburgh Central, 1987–2005, and for Edinburgh South West, 2005–15.

MAGGIE DARLING: Former journalist. Married to Alistair Darling.

RUTH DAVIDSON: Leader, Scottish Conservatives, 2011 to present day.

DAVID DINSMORE: Editor, *The Sun*, 2013–15.

MIKE DONILON: Debate coach to Ed Miliband.

KEZIA DUGDALE: Deputy leader, Scottish Labour, 2014–15. Leader, Scottish Labour, 2015 to present day.

ANDREW DUNLOP: Special adviser to David Cameron on Scotland, 2012–15. Scotland Office minister, 2015 to present day.

NIGEL FARAGE: Leader, UK Independence Party, 2006–09 and 2010 to present day.

MURRAY FOOTE: Editor, *Daily Record*.

JIM GALLAGHER: Adviser, Better Together. Visiting professor of government, University of Glasgow. Former director-general for devolution, UK government.

GEORGE GALLOWAY: Former Labour MP. Respect Party leader, 2012–15.

ANNABEL GOLDIE: Member of the Smith Commission. Leader, Scottish Conservatives, 2005–11. Conservative peer.

IAIN GRAY: Member of the Smith Commission. Leader, Scottish Labour Party, 2008–11.

STAN GREENBERG: Debate coach to Ed Miliband. Chairman and CEO, Greenberg Quinlan Rosner.

HARRIET HARMAN: Deputy leader, Labour Party, 2007–15.

CRAIG HARROW: Board member, Better Together. Convener, Scottish Liberal Democrats.

PATRICK HARVIE: Member of the Smith Commission. Co-convener, Scottish Green Party, 2008 to present day.

PATRICK HENEGHAN: Executive director of elections and stakeholders, Labour Party.

BLAIR JENKINS: Chief executive, Yes Scotland, 2012–14.

RAMSAY JONES: Special adviser to David Cameron on Scotland, 2012 to present day.

PETER KELLNER: President, YouGov.

CHARLES KENNEDY (1959–2015): Leader, Liberal Democrats, 1999–2006. Liberal Democrat (formerly SDP) MP for Ross, Cromarty & Skye, 1983–97, for Ross, Skye & Inverness West, 1997–2005, and for Ross, Skye & Lochaber, 2005–15.

JOHANN LAMONT: Leader, Scottish Labour, 2011–14.

TIM LIVESEY: Chief of staff to Ed Miliband.

ED LLEWELLYN: Chief of staff to David Cameron.

GREGG MCCLYMONT: Member of the Smith Commission. Labour MP for Cumbernauld, Kilsyth & Kirkintilloch East, 2010–15.

JACK MCCONNELL: First Minister of Scotland, 2001–07. Labour peer.

BLAIR MCDOUGALL: Campaign director, Better Together. Director of policy, Scottish Labour, 2015 to present day.

MARK MCINNES: Director, Scottish Conservatives.

HENRY MCLEISH: First Minister of Scotland, 2000–01.

CATHERINE MACLEOD: Journalist. Special adviser to Alistair Darling, 2007–10. Political editor, *The Herald*, 2003–07.

DAVID MCLETCHIE (1952–2013): Board member, Better Together, 2012–13. Leader, Scottish Conservatives, 1999–2005.

NICHOLAS MACPHERSON: Permanent secretary, HM Treasury.

JOHN MCTERNAN: Chief of staff to Jim Murphy, 2015. Adviser to Tony Blair, 2004–07.

ED MILIBAND: Leader, Labour Party, 2010–15.

MICHAEL MOORE: Member of the Smith Commission. Secretary of State for Scotland, 2010–13. Liberal Democrat MP for Tweeddale, Ettrick & Lauderdale, 1997–2005, and for Berwickshire, Roxburgh & Selkirk, 2005–15.

JAMES MORRIS: Pollster and debate coach to Ed Miliband. Partner, Greenberg Quinlan Rosner.

DAVID MUNDELL: Scotland Office minister 2010–15. Conservative MP for Dumfriesshire, Clydesdale & Tweeddale, 2005 to present day.

RUPERT MURDOCH: Chairman, News Corp, owner of *The Times*, the *Sunday Times*, *The Sun* and the *Scottish Sun*.

JIM MURPHY: Leader, Scottish Labour Party, 2014–15. MP for Eastwood, 1997–2005, and for East Renfrewshire, 2005–15.

SHEILA MURPHY: Veteran Labour Party organiser.

ROB MURRAY: Deputy director of operations (grassroots), Better Together.

CRAIG OLIVER: Director of communications to David Cameron, 2011 to present day.

GEORGE OSBORNE: Chancellor of the Exchequer, 2010 to present day.

BERNARD PONSONBY: Political editor, STV.

IAN PRICE: General Secretary, Scottish Labour Party, 2013–14.

KEVIN PRINGLE: SNP communications director, 2012–15. Special adviser to Alex Salmond, 2007–12.

WILLIE RENNIE: Leader, Scottish Liberal Democrats, 2011 to present day.

EUAN RODDIN: Special adviser to Michael Moore and Alistair Carmichael, 2010–15.

BRIAN ROY: General Secretary, Scottish Labour Party, 2015 to present day.

FRANK ROY: Labour MP for Motherwell & Wishaw, 1997–2015.

ALEX SALMOND: First Minister of Scotland and leader of the SNP, 2007–14.

TAVISH SCOTT: Member of the Smith Commission. Leader, Scottish Liberal Democrats, 2008–11.

MICHAEL SHEEHAN: Debate coach to Ed Miliband.

ROB SHORTHOUSE: Director of communications, Better Together.

PAUL SINCLAIR: Adviser to Johann Lamont, 2011–14. Adviser to Gordon Brown, 2008.

GORDON SMART: Editor, the *Scottish Sun*.

ROBERT SMITH: Chair of the Smith Commission. Cross-bench peer.

NICOLA STURGEON: First Minister of Scotland and leader of the SNP, 2014 to present day. Deputy First Minister of Scotland, 2007–14.

JOHN SWINNEY: Member of the Smith Commission. Deputy First Minister of Scotland, 2014 to present day. Cabinet Secretary for Finance, 2007 to present day.

BRUCE WADDELL: Editor, the *Daily Record*, 2003–11. Adviser to Gordon Brown.

KATE WATSON: Director of operations, Better Together.

LEANNE WOOD: Leader, Plaid Cymru, 2012 to present day.

PROLOGUE

'**O**h fuck,' said one aide as the news reached Downing Street. At 4.12 p.m. on Saturday 6 September 2014, Rupert Murdoch tipped off his half a million Twitter followers about an electrifying new poll appearing the following day in his British broadsheet, the *Sunday Times*. Even at eighty-three, the media magnate revelled in making mischief. A late convert to Twitter, he had developed a knack for using it to cause a stir. The 'reliable new poll on Scottish independence', he typed, 'will shock Britain … everything is up for grabs.'

Panic soon spread across Whitehall: independence, once perceived as an impossibility, was now a painfully real and present prospect. At No. 10, there was an attempt at decorum: 'When dealing with big issues, like the future of the country, there is no time to go into meltdown,' claimed one senior figure. There was, however, no way to control the frenzy.

Conservative MPs, many of whom had minimal contact with Scotland, did not help the volatile situation. Ministers – including the PM – and their advisers were inundated with text messages asking what was going on: 'Everybody under the sun had advice,' said one source in government. 'Sir Bufton phones his aunt in Pitlochry and she says, "I've only had a leaflet delivered from Yes." Then, suddenly, they contact the Prime Minister to say: "Everyone's telling me it's all falling apart."'

David Cameron was in Scotland, but cut off from the comfort of his usual team and the Whitehall machine. The Prime Minister was spending the weekend with the Queen at Balmoral Castle in the Highlands. The traditional summer visit dates back to the reign of Queen Victoria. John Major complained about not being able to think due to the morning bagpiper, and Tony Blair – whose youngest child Leo was conceived there – described the visit as 'a vivid combination of the intriguing, the surreal and the utterly freaky'. But Cameron was not to be distracted by royalty or protocol. He had to act – and fast. His nervousness over the referendum had increased sharply in past weeks, and he knew that, if his side lost, he would have to resign, being the Prime Minister responsible for the break-up of a once united kingdom.

Two weeks before, the Queen had been entertaining a different politician: Alex Salmond. Her reaction to the poll is said to have echoed that of her Prime Minister, and, a week later, she too would intervene, advising Scots to think 'very carefully' about their decision.

But, on this Saturday afternoon, just twelve days before the referendum, Scotland's First Minister was taking a break from campaigning and was enjoying a round of golf at the Castle Stuart course, overlooking the Moray Firth near Inverness. Alex Salmond was interrupted by a call from his chief of staff Geoff Aberdein with details of the impending poll. Salmond welcomed the progress but worried it had come a week too early – shocking his opponents into action and hampering Yes Scotland's final push to victory.

In the days running up to the YouGov poll's release, ana-
lysts at the pollster's HQ had picked up an intriguing shift in
opinion. Until this point, the No campaign had consistently
been ahead. However, sifting through reams of data at their
offices near Old Street Tube station in London, they noticed
Labour voters in particular were moving towards voting Yes.
As the race tightened, the markets were instantly spooked,
with the *Financial Times* prominently reporting how shares
in two banks with cross-border interests – RBS and Lloyds
Banking Group – were being hit.

Two or three quick-thinking hedge funds contacted
YouGov and intimated they would be willing to pay 'very
large sums of money' to have advanced sight of high-profile
polls, including the upcoming research for the *Sunday Times*.
Clearly, in a situation where investors with an hour's notice
could make a killing, newly delivered but as yet unpublished
poll results were solid gold. YouGov's response was terse:
'We told them to fuck off.'

The pollsters were acutely aware that the interest of the
powerful and the acquisitive had been piqued. With so much
at stake, with such unprecedented attention, there was a
danger that future polls might become public knowledge
before their embargoes were lifted. 'Shit. The last thing we
want is an accidental leak,' worried one senior player at
YouGov. Realising the potency of their research, the company
moved to tighten its internal security. Until referendum day,
all poll results were removed from shared files on YouGov's
computer system. Sight of the figures was restricted to a tight
group of staff.

In the sleek new London offices of the *Sunday Times*, on
the ninth floor of the 'mini-Shard', the results were also being
guarded closely. On the Friday, final figures were emailed to

Charles Hymas, the paper's managing editor. The numbers were then circulated only to the three-strong political team, responsible for the paper's coverage of the story, and a few senior executives. Editor Martin Ivens contacted Rupert Murdoch to share the scoop.

Ivens's team was aware the poll was, in essence, a one-fact story, and all too easy to leak. In their open-plan newsroom overlooking the River Thames, conversations about the results were minimised. A strict 10 p.m. embargo was put on the *Sunday Times* front page, which splashed with the headline: 'Yes vote leads in Scots poll'. Available internally in the newsroom from about 7.30 p.m., it was also circulated under embargo to broadcasters in advance so they would be able to make the strongest impact on the 10 p.m. television bulletins, maximising sales when the paper hit the streets.

In Glasgow, at Better Together's grubby Savoy Centre headquarters, the atmosphere was tense. By now, even at weekends, the No campaign's office was packed with tired, overworked staff. And although none had sight of the poll results, they knew it would show a lead for their rivals for the first time. A staff conference call was hastily arranged for 7.30 p.m. to include the organisers working in local offices across the country. As the pre-arranged call time came and went, eighty staff waited on their phones for the campaign's director Blair McDougall. It was his job to break the news and then issue a motivational, rallying cry. But the call never came. McDougall had lost his phone on the way home.

When the troops eventually reconvened at 9 p.m., the tone was calm. Uppermost in McDougall's mind was a concern for his organisers – many in their late teens and early twenties – who were likely working harder than they had ever done before. 'It will be a shit few days,' McDougall said, defiant.

'You'll read in the paper that this campaign is falling apart. Don't take the bait on Twitter from people who will wind you up saying we will lose. I am telling you: we will win.'

At the centre of this relentless, intense struggle was former Labour Chancellor Alistair Darling – a respected, experienced politician, in a role he never actually wanted. Responsible for keeping all the disparate factions working together, Darling was so drained he privately vowed never to take on a similar role in politics again.

As 10 p.m. approached, and the hysteria grew, with as yet no firm confirmation of the actual findings, YouGov's staff were all together, but not at the company's offices. Laurence Janta-Lipinski, a member of their political and social research team, had not expected his open-air wedding reception in Hackney to be quite so exciting. But, as the alcohol flowed, the story was erupting on Twitter, with many wedding guests glued to their phones.

Twenty-five minutes before the embargo, the result escaped onto social media: 51 to 49. For the first time, the pro-independence campaign was ahead. 'It was like flicking a switch,' said one party press officer. The Labour, Conservative and Liberal Democrat communications teams were suddenly inundated with calls. BlackBerrys and iPhones pinged repeatedly into the night as inboxes grew at a rate too fast to answer. The *Sunday Times* hoped it would boost sales – and it did: the paper's print and digital circulation jumped by 5,000. But the real impact was far greater.

Soon, it was even on the radar of the White House. In the offices of the National Security Council – effectively the US President's in-house foreign affairs team – advisers working closely with the State Department hurriedly wrote and circulated a series of briefing papers. For the Obama administration, the concern was not about maintaining a decades-old special relationship, or even Scotland's important strategic position in the North Sea. Instead, they worried that, if Scots voted for independence, during the subsequent two years – the rest of the presidency – the UK government would be preoccupied with constitutional wrangling.

Protracted negotiations between the Scottish government and Whitehall would leave little political will to assist the United States in a challenging foreign policy environment. It would mean no help combating the new threat of Islamic State, opposing the aggression of Russia and addressing the continuing threat posed by Iran. At one hastily convened White House meeting, an aide asked: 'What's the contingency if they vote Yes?' The reply was blunt: 'There is no contingency.'

This was one of those rare moments in history when the UK political establishment was caught utterly by surprise, shocked at the sudden realisation that they were failing to win what had at first seemed a deceptively simple fight. After two and a half exhausting, bruising years, Better Together had squandered its thirty-point lead. They had survived for much of this time on a shoestring budget – at one point close to bankruptcy – but now, with big donations coming in fast, the challenge was not money, but time. Supposed allies were anonymously briefing newspapers about internal chaos. Accusations from all quarters of an overly negative campaign were overshadowing the key messages and demoralising staff. Outwitted and under pressure, every tactic was now scrutinised not just by the UK media, but by journalists swarming to Edinburgh and Glasgow from across the world.

Saturday 6 September 2014 was to be a game-changer in the referendum race. With just twelve days of campaigning left, YouGov's poll acted as a warning of looming defeat, shattering complacency and galvanising many pro-UK businesses to finally speak out. It provided a stark message to No supporters that each of their votes really mattered. It was a catalyst for Westminster's three main party leaders to take the unprecedented step of cancelling Prime Minister's Questions in favour of travelling north to campaign in Scotland.

The poll also marked the beginning of a turbulent transformative period in British politics: Scotland would dominate the 2015 general election, destroy the careers of some of the country's most senior politicians, and leave political parties facing near wipeout north of the border.

Yet, on that evening, neither David Cameron nor Alistair Darling nor Alex Salmond realised that the shift in public opinion was so significant. None of them had any idea what would happen in the next fortnight, let alone the following year. *Project Fear* tells the inside story of how an unlikely alliance kept a kingdom united but left a country divided.

PART 1

REFERENDUM

CHAPTER 1

BETTER TOGETHER

As one Glasgow result was read out in the BBC studio, Labour MP Margaret Curran let out an audible gasp. 'That's a shock. That's a loss,' she said. Scottish Labour had a rolling media plan for Holyrood election night 2011. Flow charts directed the party's spokespeople, who appeared on TV and radio to a series of scripts with sound bites to use as the results came in. There were examples of how to respond to Labour gaining seats, to there being little change, and to a loss of party support. 'But', said one of the team, 'we had no script for getting completely screwed.'

Politicians of all parties were touring the BBC and STV studios at Glasgow's Pacific Quay, and it was becoming increasingly clear the SNP would do the seemingly impossible, and win a majority. The Additional Member System of electing the Scottish Parliament's 129 members was not designed for majority rule. Rather, it encouraged consensus-building, embodied in either a coalition or minority government. But the SNP won an astonishing 45.4 per cent of constituency votes and 44 per cent of votes on the regional list, giving them sixty-nine MSPs out of the total

129 seats. No one – least of all First Minister Alex Salmond – had expected *this* result.

Two UK ministers, one Liberal Democrat and one Conservative, had been lumbered with much of the media duties. Michael Moore, by then Scottish Secretary for nearly a year, was one of only five Liberal Democrats in David Cameron's Cabinet. As Moore sat under the heat of the studio lights watching his friends lose their jobs, the BBC's overnight anchor Sally Magnusson asked, almost pityingly: 'What is happening to your party?' The Lib Dems were in the process of losing eleven of their sixteen Scottish seats. Across the UK in local council elections, it was the party's worst electoral performance in almost thirty years. The next day, their Scottish leader, Tavish Scott, resigned.

Moore's deputy, the Scotland Office minister David Mundell, was searching hard for a Conservative spin. As one of the party's few politicians not facing re-election, and the only Tory MP north of the border, he was in constant demand. But it was a challenge to find anything positive to say: they were in the process of losing five of their Scottish Parliament seats. Within three days, Scottish Conservative leader Annabel Goldie announced her resignation.

But the real agony of the night was reserved for Scottish Labour. Scotland's establishment party – the architects of devolution – was being comprehensively supplanted at Holyrood. In Labour's worst election defeat in Scotland since 1931, four former ministers were out of a job. And most insiders had failed to see it coming. On polling day, plans were still being finalised for a four-strong team to lead coalition negotiations. Scottish Labour had even drawn up a grid of the party's first 100 days in government, mapping out policy announcements, speeches and ministerial visits. But, on the day set aside for power brokering, the party's belea-guered Scottish leader Iain Gray announced his resignation.

It had been a difficult few weeks for Gray, whose most disastrous campaign moment involved being chased into a Glasgow branch of the sandwich shop Subway by a group of shouting, placard-wielding, anti-cuts protestors. TV crews and photographers climbed onto tables to capture the full confrontation. The Labour leader was eventually ushered outside and delivered into a taxi. Later, a Labour activist mischievously texted one of Gray's team: 'What did you order at Subway?'

The reply was brief: 'A 12-inch clusterfuck.'

Michael Moore was now one of the few senior non-SNP Scottish politicians still with a job. And that job was about to be transformed in a way he had never expected. As dawn broke after what Liberal Democrats privately admitted had been 'a train wreck of a night', he knew that there would be a referendum on Scottish independence.

Scotland had hardly appeared on Downing Street's radar during the first year of the Conservative–Lib Dem coalition. The topic occasionally arose in Cabinet when the Strategic Defence Review and spending plans were being discussed, but Scottish affairs were never – perhaps unsurprisingly – a priority. The SNP's extraordinary victory in the Holyrood election changed the game entirely. Suddenly, ministers who had never been granted audiences with either the Prime Minister or Chancellor were summoned to advise on the gov-ernment's response. Within days of Alex Salmond's victory, Michael Moore and David Mundell were asked to appear in front of the most powerful body at the core of government: the Quad.

The complications of coalition meant key policy decisions

were made not at Cabinet, but in meetings of the Quad –
the four-strong group composed of the Prime Minister,
the Deputy Prime Minister, the Chancellor and the Chief
Secretary to the Treasury. The last of these – Highlands Lib
Dem MP Danny Alexander – held great sway over his colleagues on matters north of the border.

They met around the Cabinet table in the usual formation
designed to engender consensus: David Cameron sat with
Alexander on his left and opposite his deputy Nick Clegg;
Chancellor George Osborne sat diagonally across. Moore
and Mundell were ushered in. It was a testosterone-fuelled,
alpha-male environment.

Cameron swiftly attacked the cautious strategy set out
by the Scotland Office ministers. The Prime Minister was
insistent his government must 'seize the initiative', 'take control' and look at 'all options'. George Osborne duly outlined
the possibilities. They could, he said tokenistically, replicate
Spain's attitude to Catalan separatists and declare any referendum illegal. This was swiftly ruled out: all agreed it would
guarantee Scottish secession.

All four members of the Quad were loath to underestimate Alex Salmond. Yes, the UK government's ace was the
legal power to grant or block any referendum. But Salmond
had won a mandate and the coalition accepted they would
need to facilitate a vote. Scots, they believed, would reject
independence. Around the Cabinet table, Cameron and
Osborne were never complacent. Both recognised the dangers, however small they seemed. Neither wanted to have the
break-up of the United Kingdom in their political obituary.

Ed Llewellyn, David Cameron's chief of staff, knew there
was an expertise gap at No. 10. Danny Alexander's dominance
on Scottish matters was also a danger for the Conservatives:

the Liberal Democrats could not be allowed to control the government's work on the referendum. If the No side won, part of the victory must be the Prime Minister's. After all, he had most at stake. To ensure the government was up to speed, to take control and to continue in a more aggressive style, two special advisers were recruited between winter 2011 and spring 2012: one specialising in press; one in policy.

Ramsay Jones's career in the media had started somewhat unexpectedly in Scottish women's rugby in the 1990s, where he was the team manager. His tentative efforts to raise the squad's profile in print and on air helped forge good contacts with journalists, and soon he was a radio pundit. He was approached in 2000 by Scottish Conservatives leader David McLetchie to lead the party's press operation at Holyrood. Jones agreed, and worked for McLetchie until his resignation in 2005, when the *Sunday Herald*'s Paul Hutcheon exposed the leader's £11,500 taxi expenses, some of which broke the Parliament's rules. Jones then continued to work for McLetchie's successor Annabel Goldie. In the leadership election sparked by Goldie's resignation in 2011, Jones was accused of inappropriately supporting the young Cameroon candidate Ruth Davidson, and suspended from his job. Yet he was soon secretly being lined up for a much bigger position with the Prime Minister, using his expertise with Scotland's political press pack.

Alongside him, another old hand was recruited. Andrew Dunlop had risen fast through Conservative ranks in the 1980s and early 1990s. Starting as head of research for the Scottish Conservatives, before moving to Conservative Central Office in London, he was later the Scotland Office's first ever special adviser, working for Secretary of State George Younger. The Westland affair – a complex dispute in

Margaret Thatcher's Cabinet that ended in the resignation of Defence Secretary Michael Heseltine – led to Younger's promotion to the MoD. Dunlop followed him there, before being headhunted by Downing Street's policy unit, working under both Thatcher and John Major. Back then, only a small team worked on policy, allowing Dunlop to develop a broad range of expertise stretching from defence procurement to employment, training and social security.

For the next twenty years, Dunlop ran his own public affairs company, Politics International. Just as he was stepping down after selling the business, an old Conservative colleague got in touch. Decades before, Ed Llewellyn had been working in the party's research department when Dunlop was employed at Downing Street. The seniority was now reversed, but Dunlop was keen to help.

The brief for both Andrew Dunlop and Ramsay Jones was to get inside the mind of Alex Salmond. 'He is thinking 24/7 about nothing else but independence,' they were told. The referendum was one of the Prime Minister's three big challenges – alongside ending the recession and lancing the boil of Europe – and it could define his premiership.

Dunlop was a smooth operator, used to Whitehall's idiosyncrasies. He would be the 'point person' in No. 10, acting as the key contact for what would become the Better Together campaign. Dunlop and Jones would work on David Cameron and George Osborne's behalf, mobilising and guiding the government machine. As a signal of his seniority, out of Cameron's top team of twenty-six special advisers, Dunlop was the tenth best paid, on a salary of £74,000. Ramsay Jones was not far behind on £65,000. Both would be powerful players in the pro-UK campaign, but who would front it?

On moving out of No. 11 Downing Street after the 2010 general election, Alistair Darling knew he needed a break. His three years as Chancellor of the Exchequer under Gordon Brown had been utterly draining. The 'pressure cooker' of responding to the global financial crisis and preventing the collapse of the UK's banking system had exhausted him, as had working – and living – within the 'permanent air of chaos and crisis' of Brown's government. Relations between the two had deteriorated rapidly, and, from 2009 onwards, almost broke down completely.

After being elected as Labour leader in September 2010, Ed Miliband sounded out Darling as to his future plans. Would he be interested in a plum role in the shadow Cabinet? 'Before you get going, I'm probably not standing again,' Darling told him. 'So proceed on that basis.' Nonetheless, speculation about the former Chancellor replacing Ed Balls as Labour's shadow Chancellor continued for months. Darling was happy keeping a low profile on the back benches, and working on the well-received account of his time at the Treasury, *Back from the Brink*.

Once that was published in September 2011, however, Darling's focus was to turn elsewhere. A referendum was now on the horizon and there seemed to be little being done by the pro-UK parties to challenge the SNP's well-oiled political machine. Someone needed to step up and lead. Jim Murphy and Douglas Alexander – two of Labour's most senior Scots – were not keen. 'If we win, you'll get your reward,' Darling told them. But neither was prepared to relinquish their weighty shadow portfolios: defence and foreign affairs, respectively. Various politicians approached John Reid, but Tony Blair's fourth and final Home Secretary did not fancy the job either. Now in the House of Lords, Reid had made

London his home and was staying put. He also did not have a close relationship with Ed Miliband.

Gordon Brown was never seriously considered. After all, at this point, as one minister observed, 'he was in hiding' and never seen in the House of Commons. Scottish Labour's leader, Iain Gray's successor Johann Lamont, was approached in case the party in Scotland might be able to take charge. However, that organisation was still in convalescent mode following its drubbing at the 2011 Holyrood elections, and in no fit state to take on further challenges. The few Conservative politicians left in Scotland still contributed a certain toxicity to the Scottish political weather, so there was no chance they would take charge. And, although the only possible leader from the much-weakened Liberal Democrats – former party leader Charles Kennedy – was a strong media performer, he was also a recovering alcoholic, and thus seen as unreliable.

Soon, Darling came to the conclusion that, as nobody else would do it, he might just have to. On 25 November 2011, at a lunch in Glasgow for the Journalists' Charity, his frustration became publicly evident. Darling gave a speech that included a passionate defence of the union, prompting the charity's West of Scotland branch chairman David Dinsmore – then *Scottish Sun* editor, later the paper's UK editor – to comment that it 'sounds like a bid for the job'. It was not a conscious pitch to lead the campaign, but Darling's long-term friend and adviser Catherine MacLeod told him he had certainly given that impression. His wife was resigned to the prospect: she knew the couple's late-discovered calmer pace of life would never last.

Maggie Darling – only her husband calls her 'Margaret' – had sacrificed much over past decades. In 1982, before the couple married, the ambitious young journalist lost her job when the newspaper she worked for closed down. Her redundancy money was spent not on her own future, but on paying for her then boyfriend's legal training. Later, her successful career in journalism at the *Daily Record* and the Glasgow-based *Herald* was wound down as Alistair climbed the Westminster ladder. Her supporting role has been far more than just an emotional one. Maggie Darling is deeply political and was a member of the Labour Party before her husband. When living at No. 11, she supported Alistair at a time of supreme criticism, including when the 'forces of hell' were unleashed by the Prime Minister next door. Michelle Obama called her a 'true firebrand'. It was the best training for the stresses of the referendum race. Alistair Darling recognised that going through such an intense battle with a non-political partner would have been especially difficult.

The campaign's name was decided over a glass of whisky between Darling and Brian Wilson – a close friend and former Labour MP who was instrumental in the 1979 campaign opposing Scottish devolution. An alternative slogan, 'Scotland United', was considered but discounted: it sounded like a football team, and it was also patently untrue. 'Better Together' could, however, be slipped naturally into a conversation about independence, without seeming forced – in contrast, for example, to the oft-used but indigestible Conservative buzz phrase 'long-term economic plan'. In focus groups, participants repeatedly struggled to explain why they opposed independence, but then said: 'We're just better together.' It tripped off the tongues of ordinary Scots. Further research into the name's effectiveness found that, although it failed to provoke much enthusiasm, Scots were equally not put off by it.

Meanwhile, in Whitehall, discussions were continuing over quite what form the referendum would take. The Scottish Parliament did not have the powers to organise a vote, and detailed legal advice was commissioned to understand whether the UK government could hold one. Cameron and Michael Moore had differences of opinion, but both realised they could not give Salmond a blank cheque over the terms. The Prime Minister also realised that, if he was not proactive, he could be bounced into a referendum to Alex Salmond's specifications. The precise referendum question and referendum date were absolutely key variables that needed to be pinned down.

Almost lost in this constitutional wrangling was the 2012 Scotland Act. Although decidedly unsexy, the new law was significant. 'It's the biggest transfer of fiscal power from London since the creation of the UK,' declared Michael Moore, who had spent much time and energy conceiving and delivering the act. When the bill's second reading passed unopposed, the Scottish government was keen to play down its importance. After all, they were campaigning for a far more radical change: independence. In contrast, Moore was determined to celebrate its arrival.

On Tuesday 15 May 2012, an evening reception was held at the Scotland Office in Dover House on Whitehall. Members of Westminster's small Scottish press pack were invited, and the Prime Minister agreed to pop along to say a few words. Cameron's off-the-cuff comments surprised everyone.

The faces of his Scotland Office ministers and special advisers dropped as he told the assembled crowd he was not 'too fussy' about the timing of the referendum. No one had had any forewarning of this astonishing – and unplanned – *volte-face*. Attendant prime ministerial advisers tried to hide their bewilderment. In fact, they were equally shocked. Close aides insisted it was certainly 'not the plan' to talk about the timing, and no one understood what was going through the Prime Minister's mind. But, with journalists present, the gaffe could not be reversed.

Instead of injecting momentum and urgency into the referendum fight, Cameron had suddenly punctured the government's case for a speedy vote. At that point, few had the foresight to realise how far-reaching the proximity of the referendum to the general election – just eight months between the two – would be. It remains a key regret of Cameron's colleagues: 'We should have forced it sooner,' conceded one government source. 'We didn't grasp how close it would be to the general election build-up. There was no period of consolidation or reflection.' As he left the room that February evening to return to his Downing Street flat, Cameron turned to Michael Moore and said breezily: 'I realise I may have over-stretched my brief in terms of the timing.'

In that moment, the government's negotiating position was lost. Both Cameron's Scottish Conservative counterparts and ministers at Whitehall had been arguing the opposite for months, and now the Prime Minister had accidentally conceded that the referendum could be exactly when the nationalists wanted: two and a half years away in the autumn of 2014.

CHAPTER 2

TWO GUYS IN GLASGOW

Maggie Darling had, as ever, produced a vast amount of food. It was hoped her copious culinary delights would help to smooth over the vast political differences between guests. The Darling family home, on a quiet street in Edinburgh's leafy Morningside, was intended to be a relaxed setting for what would be a pivotal meeting. For the first time, representatives from Labour, the Conservatives and the Liberal Democrats were gathering to discuss how they would form a campaign to keep Scotland in the United Kingdom.

It was April 2012. Welcomed into the Darlings' large sitting room, among piles of books, colourful art and a grand piano, was a curious collection of cross-party talent, brimming with ego and mutual suspicion. Underlying this awkwardness was the reality that many summoned to attend had never worked together before – and likely never wanted to.

Andrew Cooper, the Prime Minister's director of strategy, had been sent up from London – a bold statement of intent from the UK government. He was, according to the late New Labour strategist Philip Gould, 'without doubt the best political pollster of his generation, and one of the few who knows how to fuse polling and strategy'. Cooper stressed to the assembled political grandees that proper polling needed to be commissioned, including a big segmentation study – dividing voters into groups so those with similar attitudes were together – to build up the key principles behind a campaign strategy.

Andrew Dunlop and David McLetchie also attended, as did Mark McInnes, director of the Scottish Conservatives. Craig Harrow – convener of the Scottish Lib Dems and another board appointee – and Euan Roddin – Scottish Secretary Michael Moore's special adviser – were also present. A company would be set up to facilitate the campaign, with a board of directors consisting of representatives from each of the parties.

The Tories, it was swiftly established, would provide the funding, and Labour the campaigning machine, while the Liberal Democrats would concentrate their efforts on their eleven Westminster constituencies across the country.

It was, however, the Labour representatives at this early meeting who provided the most revealing insight into the campaign's future tensions. MPs Douglas Alexander and Jim Murphy, both with senior roles in Ed Miliband's shadow Cabinet and elected in neighbouring constituencies near Glasgow in 1997, might have been presumed to be solid friends, yet they were anything but. Colleagues even likened – perhaps melodramatically – their intense, deep-seated rivalry to the breakdown in relations between Tony Blair and Gordon Brown. 'You'd need to be a psychologist to understand their relationship,' joked a friend of the pair. 'They're chalk and cheese,' explained another colleague. 'Douglas over-intellectualises everything like a politics professor, whereas Jim is a man of the people.'

At this cross-party meeting, the dysfunctional duo seemed semi-detached from the discussions, which were principally concerned with recruiting someone to run the campaign. The Tories and Liberal Democrats wanted a director they could trust, but conceded it would have to be a Labour figure. Paul Sinclair – a former *Daily Record* political editor and a Brownite special adviser, who was attending in his role as Scottish Labour's director of strategy – argued the campaign could not be seen to be run by Scots at Westminster.

There were also various personal prejudices and conflicting interests that meant name after name was discounted on the grounds they would not be able to work with some section of the party, or had burned their bridges with an influential figure. 'It got to a stage when we couldn't think of anybody who could be director,' complained one person present. The unwritten conclusion from this prickly meeting was that the least controversial candidate was likely to be chosen. One observer said: 'It was a first insight into the extraordinary un-fathomable factionalism of the Scottish Labour Party.'

Soon after the event, the first internal poll was carried out by the research company ORB International, and the first focus group by another organisation, BBM Campaigns. But Andrew Cooper suggested a third company could also help. 'I declare the obvious conflict of interest,' he told Douglas Alexander, 'but you should go to Populus.' Cooper had founded the research and strategy consultancy with fellow Conservative Michael Simmonds in 2003, but was now on a 'leave of absence' working at Downing Street. The company had an enviable reputation in the field and, more importantly, Alexander trusted Cooper: the two had developed a solid relationship, connected through their mutual friend, Philip Gould.

Over the next two and a half years, Better Together would spend around £232,000 on research from Populus. Most considered it a worthwhile investment, because the level of detailed data harvested was invaluable, and its research was to be carried out regularly right into the final weeks of the referendum race.

One of the most important pieces of research Populus undertook for the No campaign was the 'segmentation' of the Scottish electorate in 2013. This involved identifying key voter groups through a combination of a far larger sample and more penetrating questioning than most opinion polls.

'By asking between fifty and sixty questions, each with numerous variables,' explained one of the team, 'it was possible to get a more subtle and nuanced picture.' Participants were not just asked how they felt about Scotland and the United Kingdom, but were invited to explore their personal aspirations and values in depth.

Soon, six discrete groups emerged. These were not pre-defined by geography, gender or social class, but shared key attitudes. Each group was given a memorable name, although these were never publicly discussed. The six segments, in their order of commitment to support for the union, were:

- Mature Status Quo
- Hard-pressed Unionists
- Comfortable Pragmatists
- Uncommitted Security Seekers
- Blue Collar Bravehearts
- Scottish Exceptionalists

Two of the six groups were strongly pro-independence (29 per cent of the electorate) and two groups were committed to staying in the UK (37 per cent of voters), which left two undecided groups (amounting to 34 per cent) in the middle. There was, therefore, more support for remaining in the UK than leaving it, but to nowhere near the degree that many had expected. And a third of voters were undecided on the future of their country. Over the following months and years, staff would repeatedly be reminded that their attentions should only be directed at 'the million in the middle' – the Don't Knows who had the power to swing the referendum.

The two segments sure to vote Yes – imaginatively labelled 'Blue Collar Bravehearts' and 'Scottish Exceptionalists' by the strategists – were 'de-prioritised'. Respectively, 93 and 94 per cent were likely to choose independence, and it was deemed that time spent trying to dissuade them was time wasted.

Equally, the 'Hard-pressed Unionists' and 'Mature Status Quo' were 98 and 99 per cent likely to vote No, respectively. It was recognised they needed to be reassured and motivated, although the campaign would never put much effort into this.

All of Better Together's work became ruthlessly focused on developing an intimate understanding of the two undecided groups. Who were the Don't Knows? What made them tick? What were their values? And how could the campaign convince them to vote No?

The first group was the 'Comfortable Pragmatists'. They were often male and young, and sometimes Labour or Lib Dem voters. They were fairly likely to vote, but sceptical about independence. Although warm to the concept of the United Kingdom, many credited the Scottish government – and therefore the SNP – with significant successes.

The second undecided group was the 'Uncommitted Security Seekers'. These voters were more likely to be female, young and from the C2DE (working-class) social demographic. They were often public sector workers, sometimes Labour voters, likely to be critical of the European Union and anxious about immigration. Voters in this section were concerned about the state of their personal finances, and feared both losing the pound and any threat to UK jobs. Most saw independence as a risk, but were also uncertain about their own financial future.

This research, and the subsequent strategy, evolved over many months, but, back in spring 2012, the immediate and pressing requirement was for a campaign director working to back Alistair Darling as figurehead and chair of the Better Together board. Scottish Labour's unerring ability to fight against itself, rather than its opponents, made the decision of whom to recruit tricky at best. After much discussion – and some disagreement – Blair McDougall was appointed campaign director. The top job was never advertised, and there was no formal interview, just a few conversations with Labour politicians, concluding with a meeting with Alistair Darling.

McDougall had caught the campaigning bug working for Jim Murphy as a teenage activist in the 1990s and, while still at university, helped Murphy set up his constituency office after the 1997 general election. McDougall progressed to become chair of Scottish Labour Students, but it was his election as youth representative on the UK party's National Executive Committee (NEC) that was to prove critical to his future career.

With members of the NEC seated alphabetically, McDougall was always next to Ian McCartney, who was to become his first boss in Westminster. As a serial special adviser, after working for McCartney at the Cabinet Office,

Foreign Office and Department of Trade and Industry, McDougall was recruited by James Purnell to support him in his role as Secretary of State for Culture, Media and Sport, and later at Work and Pensions.

McDougall left Gordon Brown's government in dramatic fashion in June 2009, when Purnell resigned minutes after polls closed in the local and European elections in an attempt to topple the Prime Minister. Purnell's plan to install his close ally David Miliband in Downing Street in time for the 2010 general election failed spectacularly when no one else jumped ship.

After leaving Whitehall, McDougall worked for Tony Blair's Governance Initiative in Rwanda, and was part of the team behind David Miliband's failed bid for the Labour leadership, before joining Miliband's Movement for Change – a community-organising charity – as chief executive.

The links to Murphy, Miliband and Blair, as well as McDougall's role in the Purnell putsch, meant he was considered right wing, certainly by the standards of Scottish Labour. Very much a Jim Murphy loyalist, and unlikely to be able to form any working relationship with Gordon Brown, McDougall had been out of Scottish politics for nearly a decade. And he had never run a campaign on anything like this scale. However, Blair McDougall's experience of Whitehall would prove invaluable when working so closely with the Conservative–Liberal Democrat coalition government. A creative thinker with expertise in opinion polling and speechwriting, he was also a self-starter and used to working alone.

This final attribute was to prove most useful in the first months in the job. McDougall quit his job, sold his house and moved north to Glasgow with his wife, Mary, then eight

months pregnant with their first child. He launched Better
Together using his own credit card, making orders without knowing when there would be money to pay for them.
McDougall mainly worked out of his mother-in-law's front
room, hardly sleeping and using coffee shops for meetings.

This frenetic start was due, in part, to pressure from
Better Together board members to hold a launch event as
soon as possible. The pro-independence movement had publicly kicked off their campaign on 25 May at the Cineworld
cinema complex in the west of Edinburgh. But while Salmond
launched Yes Scotland in Screen Seven, commentators had
a field day pointing out that the Sacha Baron Cohen film
The Dictator was being shown in Screen Three. A poster
in the cinema lobby promoting Ridley Scott's *Prometheus*
had the tagline: 'The search for our beginning could lead to
our end.' And marketing ahead of the release of the fourth
Ice Age film was headed 'Wild and Woolly' and 'Cranky
and Clueless'.

Inside the dark cinema, Alex Salmond told his supporters: 'We unite behind a declaration of self-evident truth. The
people who live in Scotland are best placed to make the
decisions that affect Scotland.' Yet among the long list of
speakers were actors Alan Cumming and Brian Cox, neither
of whom lives in Scotland and were, therefore, ineligible to
vote. Even the celebrity endorsements were not enough to
prevent a barrage of criticism from the media.

Exactly a month later, on 25 June, Better Together held
their equivalent event in an egg-shaped lecture hall at
Edinburgh Napier University. Having learnt lessons from the
exploits of their rivals, movie stars were nowhere to be seen.
Instead, 'ordinary Scots' were interviewed by two female
MSPs, and Alistair Darling gave the first of hundreds of

speeches for the campaign. Each paragraph of Darling's ora-
tion was packed with tried and tested campaign messages,
although he had not quite mastered the autocue.

The unintended – but perhaps inevitable – focus of the
launch was the novelty of the three Scottish party leaders
together: Labour's Johann Lamont and the Conservatives'
Ruth Davidson sat side by side, smiling.

There had been much speculation about how the rival political parties would work with each other during the referendum. Internal research suggested the electorate liked seeing
politicians uniting for a common cause. Johann Lamont and
her advisers agreed, without much internal opposition, that
Labour should join the cross-party effort, while still agreeing
to run its own distinctive campaign. It was only after the
referendum that the SNP's message of Labour being 'hand-
in-glove, shoulder-to-shoulder with the Tories' would start
to prove damaging.

In the next day's papers, the No campaign's launch received a far warmer write-up than their opponents' had. The
Daily Record's Magnus Gardham described it as 'down-to-
earth', with Darling's performance 'thoughtful rather than
barnstorming'. The *Sunday Herald*'s Tom Gordon sum-
marised the speech as: 'I love Scotland, scary out there, big
gamble, RBS, Iceland, jobs, Better Together.'

After the stress of launching what was, at that point, a non-
existent campaign almost single-handedly, Blair McDougall
started to build a team. But his first recruit would also prove
to be one of his most controversial hires. McDougall decided
to form a top team of directors, and the most pressing need
was for an in-house expert in communications.

Rob Shorthouse did not have a background in journalism, and he had had little involvement in big election

campaigns. But the Glasgow-based PR man had a glittering CV. He had advised former First Minister Jack McConnell, been part of the team behind Glasgow's bid to host the 2014 Commonwealth Games, and later headed up communications for the Scottish Football Association and then Strathclyde Police, Scotland's biggest force. But not everyone was inspired by the planned appointment. One Labour figure suggested that former *Scotsman* editor John McLellan or ex-editor of the *Daily Record* Bruce Waddell would each be a far better fit. 'They have contacts books that could choke a horse,' Darling was told. But these recommendations did not fly. Michael Crow – a former STV presenter, and RBS's public affairs chief – was also considered, but 'his Tory background was a problem', according to one board member.

Shorthouse's proposed salary of £100,000 – far more than his boss McDougall was being paid – concerned some of the board, who were tasked with making the final decision. David McLetchie and Craig Harrow were also sceptical of appointing anyone who had not experienced the 'crazy intensity' of a full-scale election campaign. However, senior Labour MSP Jackie Baillie was far more enthusiastic: 'If he can work with [Strathclyde chief constable] Sir Stephen House, he can work with anybody,' she told colleagues. Eventually, the appointment was approved and Shorthouse joined Better Together on 1 July as employee number two. His salary would later rise to £105,000.

McDougall and Shorthouse spent much of summer 2012 establishing relationships with key politicians and advisers across the parties. They developed the campaign's web and social presence, and also found an office. Better Together's new base was to be on the ground floor of a Georgian town-house in the city's expensive Blythswood Square. Mackintosh

House had stained-glass windows, chandeliers and original art, but no space to extend into as staff numbers expanded. And its cream carpets were not installed with the tramp of weary, muddy activists in mind.

With little of the pollster Populus's research available, there was an air of confidence about the fight ahead, and naivety about quite how tough and relentless it would be. In a conversation with one senior Labour figure, Shorthouse remarked: 'To think when this is all done, it'll have been down to two young guys in an office in Glasgow.' The response was fury. This campaign was about far more than gaining credit, he was curtly told. And it would not be an easy ride.

Summer 2012 was also an opportunity for McDougall and Shorthouse to form links with the UK government, especially Andrew Dunlop and Ramsay Jones. Unlike Better Together, Downing Street and the Scotland Office had already been working for over a year on the legal basis for a referendum and this was about to be formalised.

On Monday 15 October 2012, David Cameron was travelling in a motorcade across the Forth Road Bridge, passing above the sleepy village of North Queensferry – the home of his predecessor Gordon Brown. To the Prime Minister's left, as his limousine crossed the estuary towards Edinburgh, was the iconic Forth Rail Bridge, with its distinctive red paint. Cameron had just left Rosyth dockyard in Fife – where he had been inspecting a more contemporary marvel of Scottish engineering: the construction of HMS *Queen Elizabeth*, a new aircraft carrier – and he was now being driven towards Edinburgh to meet Alex Salmond at the headquarters of the Scottish government. It was the start of a new week and an opportunity to get an important formality out of the way.

The Prime Minister was wary of meetings with Scotland's

First Minister. On a previous visit to the same offices at St Andrew's House in February 2012, Cameron had been confronted by a group of anti-cuts protesters. He had been forced to enter the building through the garage. At the time, Salmond insisted privately: 'It's a free country and I can't keep them from protesting.' Yet those present from the UK government disagreed: they thought it outrageous that police had failed to hold the demonstrators back for such a high-profile visit.

This time – eight months later – the contrast was clear. No sign of trouble and a well-sited police cordon. Cameron and Michael Moore were due to sign the Edinburgh Agreement, alongside Salmond and his deputy Nicola Sturgeon. After many months of negotiation, these four signatures would confirm the legal basis for the referendum on Scottish independence.

International media were, for the first time, interested in the story of Scotland's future. UK broadcasters also sent teams up from London, with the BBC anchoring their six and ten o'clock network news programmes from Edinburgh.

Moore and his team from the Scotland Office had set up base at the Apex Hotel on Waterloo Place. Although perfectly situated – just a two-minute walk from St Andrew's House – it was decided that, for the benefit of the TV cameras, Cameron and Moore should arrive together.

The Secretary of State set off in his ministerial car. The plan was to loop up and join the Prime Minister's convoy. However, on this ridiculously short journey, the car broke down and the panic began. Helen, Moore's quick-thinking government driver, thought she would be able to get a rolling start, and so turned the vehicle downhill. This attempt backfired, leaving the car broadside across a deserted street, as police had cleared the whole area of vehicles. Within minutes, two uniformed officers in the distance spotted the accidental roadblock and started running on foot.

Scotland Office staff and Moore's special adviser grappled with the car, moving it to the side of the road. A call was made to the Prime Minister's team: 'Tell him we'll see him there.' After spending all day just 150 yards from the site of this carefully choreographed piece of political history, Moore was now far further away, and minutes from missing it.

He rushed up the road, and, on approaching St Andrew's House, did his best to look relaxed and breezy as he walked in, to the evident surprise of Nicola Sturgeon. 'Change of plan', he said.

The Prime Minister soon arrived, posed outside with Salmond, the two men shaking hands, before being taken into to the First Minister's office. Always keen to stage-manage set-piece events, Salmond had requested the permanent secretary's grand wooden table be moved in for the four politicians to sit around.

Previous visitors recall the First Minister's delight in pointing to his map of Scottish Parliament constituencies: the SNP's success in 2011 had ensured this was a sea of yellow. For the Lib Dems, it was the wrong shade. In advance of the meeting with Cameron, the First Minister had insisted this map be moved behind his seat so that it would appear in the background in photos as the two leaders signed the Edinburgh Agreement.

This document gave the Scottish Parliament the power to hold a referendum, including responsibility for setting the question, choosing the date and deciding who would be allowed to vote. The UK and Scottish governments had, however, agreed there should only be a single question – no second one on whether further powers should be devolved – and the referendum would take place before the end of 2014.

After the formalities were completed, the four politicians each added their signatures to further copies of the agreement, so each could take home their own record of the day. Keen to ensure his visit was not too brief, and preventing journalists outside from sensing any *froideur*, Cameron made polite conversation with Salmond and asked about progress for the Glasgow Commonwealth Games, before saying, 'Thirty minutes seems reasonable,' and making his departure.

The UK government's formal role as an impartial referendum facilitator was largely complete. Cordial relations were over, and now both sides could get stuck into the referendum proper. Armies of civil servants in the Scottish and UK governments, who had been liaising constructively, would now, with the flick of a switch, turn on each other. The starting gun had effectively been fired. Watching the coverage of the Edinburgh Agreement on TV, one senior Better Together figure turned to a colleague: 'Shit just got real.'

CHAPTER 3

ALEX IN WONDERLAND

On Friday 4 October 2013, Michael Moore had just returned from a family holiday visiting his sister in Florida. After some rare downtime, he quickly realised his focus would now need to return to work. He had just seven weeks to prepare the UK government's strategy for responding to the Scottish government's White Paper on independence. Tuesday 26 November was an important date in the Scotland Office diary: Alex Salmond was due to launch a detailed blueprint of how Scotland would, he believed, be stronger as an independent nation.

Back in his Scottish Borders constituency, Moore's phone buzzed. It was a text from Joanne Foster, Nick Clegg's deputy chief of staff: 'Are you available for a call from Mr Switch?' This was code for the Downing Street switchboard. Soon the Deputy Prime Minister was on the line, and thirty seconds of obligatory holiday chit-chat followed.

Clegg then interrupted: 'Hey, Mike.' This was his well-trailed mannerism for moving a conversation onto business. But, at the same time, the Deputy Prime Minister's tone unexpectedly changed, and Moore knew he was being prepared for bad news. After deftly negotiating the new

Scotland Act – which devolved further powers to Scotland – and agreeing terms for a fair referendum, Moore was being sacked from the Cabinet. And he had not seen it coming.

After the 2010 general election, Michael Moore had not even been appointed to a junior ministerial role in the coalition. It was only after the resignation of Liberal Democrat MP David Laws as Chief Secretary to the Treasury, upon which Danny Alexander left the Scotland Office to replace him, that Moore got his chance. A year into the job, his position as Scottish Secretary had been far from secure. But now, after three and a half years of delicate, conscientious – if not high-profile – service, he was confident of his record. He had secured a number of successes, and built consensus with key SNP ministers.

In Nick Clegg's six years as Liberal Democrat leader, this was the third time he had demoted or sacked Michael Moore. And Moore was seething: 'It's a funny way to treat a bloody loyal ally,' he told his boss. The Tories are having a reshuffle on Monday, Clegg explained. 'If you want to, you can resign.' This did little to calm the conversation: 'Why the hell would I resign?' Moore responded. 'If you want to sack me, sack me. I'm proud of what I've done. And, anyway, nobody would believe me.'

Two days later, with Moore's imminent departure still unannounced, the outgoing Secretary of State realised reading the Sunday papers that the Conservatives would not be reshuffling any of their Cabinet members, just junior ministers. Nick Clegg had omitted to mention this key fact. Aware that his was to be the most high-profile sacking, and would lead news bulletins, Moore decided to take charge of the situation.

On Monday morning, before the Tory changes had been announced, he tipped off BBC Scotland's Westminster correspondent Tim Reid who broke the story on Twitter. Soon, Moore received a call from a Liberal Democrat colleague in government: 'I'm really sorry, Mike. There's been a leak.'

It had been nearly a year since David Cameron and Alex Salmond had signed the Edinburgh Agreement. In the intervening months, the technicalities of the referendum had been finalised. There would be one question: 'Should Scotland be an independent country?' Sixteen- and seventeen-year-olds would be able to vote, the referendum would take place on 18 September 2014, and each official campaign would have a spending limit of £1.5 million during the formal 'referendum period'.

At Yes Scotland, where chief executive and former BBC manager Blair Jenkins had appointed five directors 'of the highest calibre', director of operations Jacqueline Caldwell and director of communications Susan Stewart had already left the organisation for unknown reasons. Within months, the other three directors would also be casualties of the campaign.

In contrast, Better Together continued as a small team of fewer than ten staff. The mood was positive, although one office joke had proved very damaging. 'Project Fear' was the tongue-in-cheek name members of the No campaign used to describe the nationalists' response to their operation. It was a knowing nod to the negativity of many of Better Together's key messages – the risks and uncertainties of independence – and to the relentless accusations of scaremongering from their opponents. Director of communications Rob Shorthouse coined the phrase, and another member of the team let it slip to the *Sunday Herald*'s Tom Gordon. In June 2013, Gordon briefly mentioned the term towards the end of a long article in his paper. But the Yes Scotland team spotted it and seized upon 'Project Fear' as evidence the unionists were trying to scare Scots from voting for independence.

'Is this going to be a thing?' colleagues asked Shorthouse, concerned the phrase would continue as a caricature of the campaign for months. 'Nah. Don't worry,' was the reply. But, from then on, as one Labour source admitted, 'It was impossible to shake off.'

Lack of fundraising was a growing problem for Better Together and prevented the campaign staff growing. When news reached their Blythswood Square office that Michael Moore was to be turfed out of the Scotland Office, the reaction was one of bafflement and irritation, not least because of the timing – the referendum was just eleven months away.

Moore's removal, as with all Lib Dem Cabinet ministers, was Nick Clegg's decision not that of David Cameron. It was a move strongly supported by Willie Rennie, the Lib Dems' Scottish leader, and Chief Secretary Danny Alexander, whom many suspected of briefing the media against Moore. Not part of the Cleggite clique, Moore was always, to some extent, under threat. His talent for calm, methodical, face-to-face negotiations had been valuable when legislation was the focus of the Scotland Office's work. However, his party's leadership believed a new phase was starting; the fight needed to be taken to nationalists, and that required a less polite type of politician.

After the 2010 general election, Alistair Carmichael had taken what some in government saw as the most difficult of Liberal Democrat posts: the party's Chief Whip. Without power at Westminster for nearly 100 years, the Liberals had never before needed a serious whipping operation. Suddenly, the member for the most far-flung constituency in the UK – Orkney & Shetland – was forced to spend much of his week in the Commons bars and tearooms, twisting the arms of potentially recalcitrant fellow MPs. One Conservative colleague sympathised with the challenge of 'herding cats' such as Mike Hancock MP, who was accused of (and denied) sexually assaulting a constituent, and David Ward, MP for Bradford East, who made controversial comments criticising Israel that some perceived as anti-Semitic.

One advantage of Carmichael's role was the opportunity to regularly visit his leader's offices in the Palace of Westminster and in Whitehall, which afforded ample opportunity to lobby for promotion. But discussion of the change was kept within a very tight group. Some of Clegg's advisers were not even told: 'We didn't know. We were shocked,' said one.

Because Moore refused to resign, Nick Clegg's team had to accentuate the reasons for wanting to replace him with Carmichael. Journalists were briefed that the latter was a bruiser, who would use his natural aggression to thwart the nationalists and 'shake up' the referendum debate. One paper claimed Carmichael was the 'hell-raising streetfighter' the No campaign needed. Yet, by promoting the new Scottish Secretary's supposed talents, the Liberal Democrats were also forcing Alistair Carmichael to prove the wisdom of their strategy. And this proved difficult.

Within weeks of taking over at the Scotland Office, Carmichael was floundering. First, he was monstered in an STV debate by Deputy First Minister Nicola Sturgeon: 'It was catastrophically bad,' remembered one campaign chief. Carmichael's appearance the next day on the BBC's *Question Time* programme was widely criticised. Colleagues in government considered his performance before a Holyrood committee equally weak.

With hindsight, the Liberal Democrat consensus is now that Moore should have stayed, especially to assist in responding to the independence White Paper. 'We expected Alistair Carmichael to be better,' said one at Downing Street. 'He doesn't prepare well enough.' Others were even more scathing: 'We were told he'd be a Rottweiler, but he was more like a Bichon Frise.' Soon, Carmichael was sidelined, by both his Conservative colleagues in government and the Better Together campaign: 'There was a car crash. And then he disappeared.'

As Alistair Carmichael attempted to cram the complex policy details of his new brief, the rest of the No campaign was preparing for the most unpredictable challenge of the whole referendum race. The Scottish government's long-awaited White Paper on independence had been many months in the planning, and Better Together would have to respond fast when the raft of policy positions were announced.

The conference call was brief, but there was one big revelation: 'Henry McLeish has come out for Yes,' declared Jim Gallagher, policy adviser for Better Together. On both ends of the call, among the campaign team in Glasgow and Treasury and Scotland Office civil servants in Whitehall, there was a sharp, collective intake of breath. *How the hell are we supposed to respond to that?*

Securing support from a former Labour First Minister – and an ex-Labour MP and MSP – was a coup for Yes Scotland. It was guaranteed to shore up support for the independence campaign from the all-important working-class Labour voters. And Better Together needed to react fast. Should they retaliate with their own big-name endorsement? Could they rubbish McLeish directly as Scotland's shortest-serving, least successful leader? (He had resigned after a year

in office following a financial scandal.) Press officers immediately started hammering away at their keyboards.

However, this dramatic moment in the campaign was all
pretence. McLeish never came out in support of the Yes campaign. It was a game, albeit one played utterly seriously. At
the centre, Professor Jim Gallagher – until 2010, Whitehall's
most senior civil servant responsible for devolution – had set
the hare running.

Gallagher had written a 150-page-long fake White Paper
entitled 'Scotland's future in Scotland's hands'. Hidden inside
were graphs and tables, as well as announcements on childcare
and taxation, that the Better Together team needed to spot,
analyse and react to fast. Even less noticeable were sections of
comedy drivel: 'Scottish innovators have pioneered penicillin,
television, the ATM, Dolly the Sheep, MRI scanning, Irn-Bru
and many other world-renowned inventions and discover-
ies.' A later section detailed how: 'Our history, our enterprise,
education, science and technology, but perhaps especially our
whisky, mean that we have punched above our weight in international affairs for many decades and centuries.'

Jim Gallagher was in a room in the Cabinet Office,
and in his element, throwing more scenarios into the mix.
Drip-fed throughout the process were: a fake transcript
of an interview with Alex Salmond on the BBC's *Good
Morning Scotland* radio programme; a fake blog by the
corporation's Scottish political editor Brian Taylor; a fake
statement to the Scottish Parliament from Alex Salmond; a
fake record of a press conference with Nicola Sturgeon at
Edinburgh Castle; and even a fake media request from the
Scottish Sun as to how much the UK government would be
spending on direct communication to voters in Scotland.

The point was to anticipate likely and less likely lines of

attack, and to identify and streamline the response. Both Better Together and the UK civil service understood acutely the importance of responding to a developing story with unity. Once the key document was released, there would likely be more random announcements, supplementary pieces of policy, as well as individual endorsements from unexpected people. Knowing the flaws of Whitehall, Gallagher was also keen to test the response if one team were to unexpectedly veer off message. Some of those who took part claimed, 'It was far more testing than the real thing.'

A three-level plan was put in place to respond to the White Paper. First, establish the core facts. Second, analyse them. In both these roles, the Whitehall machine was superb. But the UK government was not able to assist with level three: political marketing and communications were the responsibility of Better Together.

Their strategy was simple: rubbish the White Paper, partly through ruthless dissection of the facts, partly through painting it as a work of fiction. Wacky stunts were conceived to catch the imagination of those voters less engaged in politics. One plan was to disguise copies of the White Paper as fairytale stories, using fake book covers, and leave them in bookshops and libraries, as well as in public places. Possible titles included 'The Lying, The Which and the Holyrood', 'Lord of the Lies' and, most popular, 'Alex in Wonderland' – the cover of which was mocked up with the First Minister depicted as a colourful Mad Hatter.

Another idea was to project a blue plaque – usually used to mark the houses of great historical figures – outside Bute House, the First Minister's official residence in Edinburgh. It would say: 'Alex Salmond, fiction writer. Lived here 2007 to present.'

A similar concept was to imitate the fourth plinth at London's Trafalgar Square. A plastic Salmond statue would be erected in Edinburgh, with a plaque commemorating him as 'Author of the White Paper' and 'Scotland's greatest ever fiction writer'.

None of these ideas were ever put into practice. Without knowing the content of the Scottish government's document, it was deemed too risky to spend significant sums commissioning stunts that might later be impossible to execute. And money – or rather the lack thereof – was becoming a serious problem.

As Better Together's board met in mid-October 2013 in the grand boardroom of their Blythswood Square offices, the campaign was at financial crisis point. Although backed by the three UK parties, big donors had not materialised. Over past months, the increasingly frustrated board members had asked accountants Chiene + Tait to present a financial statement at each meeting. Now, interrogating the figures, there was a dawning, shocked realisation that, in two months, Better Together would be bankrupt, unable even to afford to pay redundancy for its staff.

The campaign's only significant income had been £500,000 from oil tycoon and Conservative Party donor Ian Taylor. This had transformed the organisation, but, due to early investment in expensive polling and the high salaries of the small team, that money had all but been spent. 'Chronically underfunded', according to one senior figure, Better Together's only chance at changing this situation seemed to be 'mad Tories in castles wanting to run pointless fundraising events'.

In an effort to solve the campaign's funding problems in early 2013, Alistair Darling had recruited Phil Anderton, former CEO of Heart of Midlothian Football Club and the Scottish Rugby Union. He was widely known as 'Firework Phil' – a nod to the pre-match pyrotechnics he introduced before Scotland matches at Murrayfield.

Yet, while the rest of the board gave their time *pro bono*, Phil Anderton was being paid a monthly fee of £5,000, plus expenses. When details of Anderton's 'consultancy fees' eventually trickled out to a few of his colleagues, it provoked considerable resentment. 'He talks an excellent game, is as smooth as anything, but did very little,' according to one on the board. 'He fooled a lot of people for a long time.'

In fact, when Anderton – a talented corporate fixer – joined the board, the campaign had no staff member focused on fundraising, let alone a fundraising strategy. Using his personal contacts in business, and his experience in pitching for investment, the former CEO slowly amassed donations, but they were usually in the region of £7,500 – the limit above which donations needed to be publicly disclosed. The campaign desperately needed cheques of ten times that value.

When attempting – alongside Alistair Darling – to persuade millionaires to contribute, Anderton personalised the referendum with an emotive argument: 'Imagine waking up on 19 September and we've lost by one vote. Could we all look in the mirror and say we'd done our best? For the sake of £50,000, the union would be lost.'

His performances in boardrooms and at private members' club were well honed. Yet, significant funds failed to materialise for three key reasons.

Principally, the statistics did not back up investing. Businessmen and -women were aware of Better Together's significant poll lead, giving little compulsion to invest. For philanthropists, the choice might be between leaving a

legacy by funding something tangible – a new medical research laboratory or hospital ward – or pouring funds into
a campaign for which victory was never questioned, and
the biggest success for which would literally be securing no
change at all: the status quo.

Secondly, there seemed very little to gain from coming out
publicly and supporting either side. Businesses risked alienating a significant proportion of their own customers, and,
after a boycott of the union-supporting Barrhead Travel and
a backlash against the Confederation of British Industry due
to its unionist (albeit confused) position, the dangers for many
were too much. Others suggest there was a 'real element of
bullying', citing threatening phone calls. One potential six-
figure donor in the end never donated: 'I can't do anything
while this planning application is coming up.'

Thirdly, there was a misunderstanding among potential donors about the funding of political campaigns. Some
assumed the UK government would assist; others under-
estimated the scale of the funding required to run complex
campaigns, especially the marketing costs. Unlike a general
election, when the focus is solely on a select few marginal
constituencies, with the referendum, every vote was worth the
same, and therefore every constituency had to be treated as a
marginal.

Eventually, at the suggestion of the Conservatives, investment banker Andrew Fraser was brought onto the board
– never formally a director, but with access to more wealthy
donors than the rest of his colleagues combined. Since
2004, he has given £1 million to the Tories, and, in early
2014, would give £100,000 to Better Together. Fraser was a
decent, gentlemanly understated presence who transformed
the campaign's fortunes: 'He did most of the fundraising,

would write a cheque when we were short of money, and never took the credit,' according to one board member.

£120,000 was spent on Better Together's response to the White Paper, including, at its core, the much-hyped 'war room'. Key campaign staff were decamped from their Glasgow base to a soulless meeting room in Dynamic Earth, a futuristic visitor attraction and conference centre next to the Scottish Parliament. However, the publication the No campaign were reacting to was not to be launched from Holyrood, or even from Edinburgh, but back in Glasgow. To make things worse, there were flaws in the technology. 'There was no TV and just one phone line,' said one person involved. 'We were as far away from the action as possible. Almost incommunicado.'

The Scottish government allowed the three opposition parties to send a representative to view the White Paper at the Scottish Parliament, one hour ahead of its official publication. The Scottish Conservatives and Liberal Democrats sent their leaders Ruth Davidson and Willie Rennie, while Scottish Labour's talented young MSP Neil Bibby was tasked with extracting the most important details for both his party and Better Together.

At 9 a.m., they convened in Minister for Parliamentary Business Joe Fitzpatrick's office – a glass box on the top floor of the building. Mobile phones were confiscated. The three were allowed only a pen and paper, and they could not take the document away with them. Davidson argued against the exam-like conditions, but to no avail. Unable to read anything like all 650 pages in an hour, Bibby was briefed to focus on the expected childcare announcement.

Support for independence was consistently lower among women, and both Alex Salmond and Nicola Sturgeon – neither

of whom are parents – were seen by some as having little understanding of the challenges many families face. In an effort
to tackle this perception, the White Paper promised a 'childcare revolution'.

At 10 a.m., the 170,000-word blueprint for independence was released to the world. Each of Scotland's 129 MSPs
were allocated one hard copy. The government was not in
the business of making life easy for the No campaign; no
copies were provided to them. One junior staffer was tasked
with running with a box of copies from the Parliament to
the war room for analysis. Weighing 1.4 kilos per copy, he
arrived red-faced and glistening with sweat.

As the Better Together team started frantically flicking
through trying to find holes, Alex Salmond was taking to
his feet at the Glasgow Science Centre to unveil his 'pro-
spectus for an independent Scotland'. His approach was
deliberately sober and serious. The BBC's Nick Robinson
observed: 'Scotland's First Minister and his deputy behaved
today less like excited midwives and more like low-key, well-
briefed company executives launching a corporate rebrand-
ing exercise.'

Entitled 'Scotland's Future: Your guide to an independent
Scotland', it cost over £1.2 million to print and distribute.
In Glasgow, Mr Salmond claimed the document was: 'The
most comprehensive blueprint for an independent country
ever published, not just for Scotland, but for any prospective
independent nation.'

Across the country, in Edinburgh, the Better Together
team was on edge, hurriedly leafing through the document.
With the substantial might of the Scottish civil service, it was
assumed the SNP would use the White Paper to answer the
considerable number of questions surrounding independence,

absorbing uncertainties over the economy and Europe. This would allow them to change gear and focus on creating an emotional connection with voters – arguing for democracy and self-determination to bring about a more prosperous and fair country.

Among the team of advisers, researchers and press officers at Dynamic Earth, Jim Gallagher leaned over to Alistair Darling: 'There's not a lot in this.' Puzzled, staff continued to search the 650 pages for financial data, before realising there was just one page of costings. Page seventy-five gave projections for the first year of independence, but the No camp believed such a lack of detail gave them an easy line of attack. 'It was neither an analytical piece nor successful political rhetoric,' said one old hand. 'There were pages of complete guff on how the time zone and Eurovision Song Contest would stay. What a load of mince.'

Better Together had been anxious about the White Paper, expecting to take a hit in the polls. Yet they ended up surprised that more had not been done to clear up the unknowns of independence. The SNP chose not to set out an alternative plan for keeping the pound under a currency union – a key weakness.

However, alongside the childcare offer, the Scottish government did include pledges to scrap the controversial bedroom tax, remove Trident nuclear weapons from the Clyde by 2020 and protect state pensions. At 10.40 a.m., a conference call between Edinburgh and Whitehall began, and it was agreed that Alistair Darling would give the first reaction on the BBC News channel at 11 a.m., one hour after publication. He branded the document a 'work of fiction, full of meaningless assertions … a wish list with no price list'. The strategy was simple: to raise doubts in voters' minds – and so Darling posed endless questions. What currency would we use? Who would set our mortgage rates? How much would taxes have to go up? How would we pay pensions and benefits in future?

The SNP government later made a statement in the chamber of the Scottish Parliament, but the exchanges were 'a sideshow', according to one person involved. The real spin war was outside, at the extensive media village set up on Holyrood's front lawn.

All was not going smoothly in the war room. The conference phone that Blair McDougall had ordered specially for the event failed to connect. Instead, an old handset was found and switched to speakerphone. The one landline that connected the campaign in Edinburgh with the room of key civil servants in Whitehall was the sole channel underpinning the exchange of information, the dividing-up of analysis and, crucially, the co-ordination of messaging.

A strict schedule of calls was drawn up in advance, with minutes and action points to be circulated as soon as each call ended. But most of the calls ended up being rather farcical, with staff crowded around the one cheap phone, and shouting into it. The team knew speed was of the essence. A rapid but credible reaction was essential if they were to stand a chance of winning the spin war.

However, it was not the White Paper launch, but rather the following day that would be critical. The atmosphere in Dynamic Earth on Wednesday morning, where the war room was still in operation, was one of relief. The No team was particularly pleased with the front page of the *Daily Record*: 'Forget about the price tag?'

Seeking to capitalise on their perceived advantage, and with the world's media still in town, Darling held a press conference attacking the fiscal credibility of the White Paper – a line he knew was resonating, and ground on which the former Chancellor was comfortable. One researcher was tasked with locating a copy of the 'red book': the extensive analysis paper produced by the Treasury to accompany the UK Budget. In front of a room full of journalists and cameras, Darling held up in one hand the single page of fiscal projections contained in the White Paper – and, in the other, the red book, eliciting laughter from the assembled press.

On the next day, 28 November 2013, tourists at the gates of Downing Street might have spotted a Saltire on the building's roof, and some pro-independence protestors handing out leaflets to those arriving at the Prime Minister's home. St Andrew's Day had never been a highlight of the social calendar at No. 10, but David Cameron's Scotland advisers – Andrew Dunlop and Ramsay Jones – decided that, with the referendum on the horizon, this was a valuable opportunity for some soft diplomacy.

Securing celebrity endorsements was a constant challenge for both campaigns. High-profile support could boost the campaign and allow a new voice to articulate the central arguments. As well as adding credibility, a sprinkle of stardust could help appeal to those less engaged in politics, allowing access to a difference audience.

Earlier in the year, Better Together had undertaken research with the help of pollsters Populus to find out who the best 'message-carriers' for the campaign were. This was done through investigating who 'best represents Scottishness'. Celebrities from entertainment, the arts and sport, as well as politicians, were included. Although different Scots spoke to different segments of the population, overall, the best representatives of Scottishness were comedian Billy Connolly, tennis player Andy Murray and Olympic champion cyclist Chris Hoy. Alex Salmond was also a powerful representative of Scottishness, but only to those highly likely to vote Yes. Salmond polarised opinion, as did Nicola Sturgeon, but to a lesser degree.

However, the SNP leadership far outshone their pro-UK counterparts. In fact, the research was so damaging that No campaign chiefs vowed it would never be released to the public. Researchers found that those least likely to 'represent Scottishness' were rock star Rod Stewart, Gordon Brown and Alistair Darling – two of whom would, in time, become campaign figureheads. Perhaps most galling was the finding that the third of voters who were most likely to vote No thought Alex Salmond represented Scottishness better than the leader of the No campaign.

Recruiting famous faces was a delicate operation. Both the central campaign and the UK government agreed it was better to make a personal approach through friends of the respective celebrity, rather than a formal one via an agent.

There were attempts to recruit Andy Murray through former Manchester United manager Alex Ferguson. A Scot and long-time Labour supporter, Ferguson had become one of the tennis player's most high-profile supporters, with Murray describing their private sporting conversations as 'gold dust'. Murray was reluctant to commit to either side, although many at Better Together believed his family to be nationalists. Alex Salmond had also been working hard to court Murray's mother, Judy, inviting her to the First Minister's official residence in Edinburgh.

Chris Hoy was approached in a similar way, although he was seen as far more pro-UK than Murray. 'You just have to see him going round that cycle track waving a Union Flag,' said one source in government. However, Hoy had already been partially coopted by the Scottish government because he was an ambassador for the 2014 Commonwealth Games in Glasgow, and would need to keep clear of politics.

TV presenter Lorraine Kelly had the ability to communicate with the female working-class voters both sides desperately wanted to convince. However, her role working on news coverage prevented any involvement. As with the unwillingness of many in business to get involved in the referendum, celebrities realised that, in such a polarising debate, there was very little to be gained.

Better Together's director of communications Rob Shorthouse spent much time trying to recruit what his colleagues termed 'the Edinburgh luvvies'. But he started from a challenging position: the majority of creative types had already endorsed the nationalists, and there was a limited pool of people to choose from.

Guests walking through the iconic doorway of No. 10 on St Andrew's Day never got to meet David Cameron that night. The Prime Minister had been diverted to an EU summit in Lithuania to discuss the continuing conflict between Ukraine and Russia. Nick Clegg and George Osborne were left to host the party, alongside Samantha Cameron. Many of the politicians and advisers attending were still on a high after the UK government's successful response to the White Paper two days earlier.

Most of the famous faces at Downing Street were not Scots who had made the trip down, but those who were based in London. Guests included businessman Duncan Bannatyne, comedian Ronnie Corbett, entrepreneur Michelle Mone and actor John Barrowman.

Stand-up comedian Kevin Bridges turned down an

invitation, tweeting to his 644,000 Twitter followers: 'My heart is saying "Fuck that" and my head is saying "Aye, fuck that".' Scottish celebrity chef Nick Nairn also boycotted the event, deciding it was a 'cynical ploy by a government conducting a hearts and minds campaign'. However, a rival Scottish chef, Tom Kitchin, did attend, providing Michelin-starred canapés to the great and good.

The mood was happy, rich with laughter and the clink of wine glasses, but the jollity was not to last. The No campaign's seemingly secure position riding high in the polls would later shift, with internal battles and secret briefings leading Alistair Darling to threaten to quit.

CHAPTER 4

TAKING A POUNDING

A s the sun rose over Edinburgh on Wednesday 29 January 2014, the Governor of the Bank of England was arriving on the north side of the city's historic Charlotte Square wearing a long brown coat and clutching a folder of papers under his left arm. A pack of photographers and TV cameras were poised to capture his much-anticipated arrival at No. 6. Mark Carney was in town to meet Scotland's First Minister.

What currency an independent Scotland might use had proven to be the single most contentious issue of the referendum so far. With just one matter on the agenda, Carney and Salmond were on a collision course. Salmond knew it was going to be a difficult day for the Yes campaign.

Carney, an economics graduate of both Harvard and Oxford, had travelled north to discuss whether the pound could be used in an independent Scotland. Salmond's plan was to form a currency union with the rest of the UK, and continue to use the pound sterling – an approach greeted with scepticism from many in business and academia. Better Together's critique of his plan was entitled: 'Taking a Pounding'.

The previous afternoon, at a public event with the Scottish

Cabinet in Bathgate, West Lothian, Salmond decided to disclose details of a private discussion he had had with Carney's predecessor. The First Minister claimed that the first thing Mervyn King had said when he met him back in June 2013 was: 'Your problem is what they' – meaning the Treasury – 'say now and what they say the day after a Yes vote in the referendum are two entirely different things.'

Revealing details of a closed-door conversation was a breach of protocol, but Salmond knew the stakes were high. Both campaigns were acutely aware that the issue of currency loomed large for undecided voters. 'Salmond's strategy was obvious,' argued one senior campaigner. 'He was attempting to undermine the Governor before he even opened his mouth.' But Carney was determined not to be played by the First Minister. According to journalist Alan Cochrane, Carney told Salmond: 'I'm only here for one day, Alex, but don't fuck with me or I'll be up here a lot more often.'

After posing for photographs on the steps of Bute House, Salmond welcomed Carney inside for breakfast. On the menu was a Scottish classic: porridge. In a bid to sweeten up the Canadian Carney, maple syrup had been provided. 'I thought it was a nice touch,' the Governor admitted.

From the start, Alistair Darling felt currency was the critical issue. 'If we can't kill them on the economic argument, we'll never win,' he told his team. The UK government realised it would be dangerous for the Bank of England to be drawn into the pre-referendum political scrimmage. But Mark Carney – described by one at Better Together as 'the financial George Clooney' – hardly needed to be told. It was rare to find a brilliant economist who also possessed political nous. Having lived through the 1980 and 1995 Quebec independence referendums, Carney also intimately understood the separatist sentiment. Some close to him claim he had little time for it: 'I know his views. He's aware of Quebec. He's not a separatist.'

However, with combined annual earnings of over £870,000, the Governor's role was above politics both in salary and, more literally, in avoiding any perception of political interference. In advance of his visit to Scotland, the Governor's team stressed he would not make any judgement on the merits or otherwise of an Anglo-Scottish currency union. Travelling to Edinburgh to clarify the Bank's role had been Carney's own idea. 'I know he did it off his own bat,' claimed a source close to deliberations. 'But it had been cleared by the Treasury.'

For newspapers and TV stations who had sent their economics editors to Edinburgh, the best opportunity to hear (and interpret) Carney's carefully worded views came after his meeting with Salmond during a lunchtime speech hosted by the Scottish Council for Development and Industry. After a two-course meal in the opulent King's Hall at Edinburgh's four-star George Hotel, the Governor spoke for forty minutes to an audience of 200 business and banking industry figures. Alistair Darling and his team had no advance notice of what he would say. But, they argued, they did not need to. Months earlier, delight swept through the Better Together HQ when the text of a speech Carney had given in 2013 as Governor of the Bank of Canada was unearthed. In it, he made clear that an effective currency union requires fiscal union – precisely what would likely end in the event of independence. The No camp felt sure they were onto a winner.

Furthermore, Alistair Darling and Mark Carney knew each other far better than many ever realised. The two never overlapped in their roles at the Treasury and the Bank of

England, but, in his previous job as Governor of the Bank of Canada, Carney would attend all G7 meetings and, throughout the financial crisis, he and Darling met regularly at the Financial Stability Forum, which co-ordinated much of the international regulatory response. Darling joked that he saw more of Carney than many of his own Treasury officials. The former Chancellor also rated him far more than his own central banker Mervyn King, whose response to the global financial crisis of 2007–08 had, he felt, been significantly slower.

In his speech in Edinburgh, Carney set out to his audience the pros and cons of currency unions, while continually emphasising that any decision would be a matter for the UK and Scottish governments. However, the Governor did warn of 'clear risks', highlighting examples 'in the euro area over recent years'. He also emphasised that 'a durable, successful currency union requires some ceding of national sovereignty', implying that Scotland might not become quite as independent as many nationalists desired. Former SNP deputy leader Jim Sillars would later describe the SNP's currency plans as 'stupidity on stilts'.

Unsurprisingly, both Yes and No claimed the Governor's speech was a win for them. The SNP's John Swinney argued Carney had given 'a serious and sensible analysis of how a currency union can work in practice'. In contrast, the UK Treasury claimed Carney had highlighted 'the principal difficulties of entering a currency union'.

The next morning, the UK government and Better Together were delighted with newspapers' responses. It was front-page news. 'Bank's pound threat to Nats' was the *Scottish Sun*'s headline the next morning. 'Carney in currency warning to Scotland' was the *Financial Times*'s take. 'Don't bank on it' thundered the *Scottish Daily Mail*. Yet, despite what seemed a clear victory for the No camp, pro-UK campaigners soon realised the Governor's visit had done little to convince their target voters. Any backslapping had been premature.

The Populus team held focus groups in Edinburgh and Glasgow on the evening of Carney's visit and the day after. Participants were shown clips of the visit, including the Governor and First Minister shaking hands. 'Salmond was beaming ear to ear, saying he had confirmed that "technical discussions" with the Bank of England would continue,' explained one strategist. 'And Carney was talking about confusing things in an enigmatic way.'

With few voters in the focus group grasping the Governor's macroeconomic message, they looked instead to body language for an understanding of who had come out on top in the encounter. And the First Minister was grinning. 'That's a huge win for Salmond,' concluded one participant. 'It's a big risk for No,' commented another.

'Carney was so Delphic,' complained a Better Together source. 'He said it so obliquely no one understood.' This reflected a wider problem in explaining the core economic message. 'We were doing focus groups throughout, which consistently found that most of our target voters actually believed the Salmond assertion that the pro-UK parties were bluffing,' said another on the research team.

Alistair Darling had been discussing with Downing Street when best to take the currency debate up a gear. Because the issue was potentially very tricky for the Yes campaign, Better Together knew they had to make sure it remained a central issue. A high-profile but high-risk strategy for setting the agenda was for the UK government to publicly rule out a currency union. But timing was key. 'It needs to be done early, not like a panic in August,' he told his team.

Darling had phone conversations with George Osborne, Ed Balls and Danny Alexander. It was essential any intervention was carefully co-ordinated and choreographed, so there was no speculation as to what each of the three candidates for Chancellor thought.

As an architect of the five economic tests for the UK joining the euro, Ed Balls was well aware of the strengths and weaknesses of currency unions. Proportionally more dependent on oil, Scotland had a different economic structure to the rest of the UK. As such, a drop in oil price could mean a sudden drop in revenues, and knock-on consequences for the economy. 'Why would you want a currency union?' Balls asked privately.

Explaining that a monetary union would mean an economic policy partially set by someone else was critical – but difficult to explain. 'If there was another banking crisis, Scotland would be bankrupt', said one Conservative. But the campaign could not be so blunt, for fear of talking Scotland down – something they knew did not play well with undecided voters.

The onslaught of unionist economic rhetoric began on 11 February 2014, just a fortnight after Carney's speech. The methods were far from orthodox. A letter written by the Treasury's top civil servant to George Osborne was made public – not leaked, but published on the UK government's website. Over three pages, Sir Nicholas Macpherson warned that currency unions were 'fraught with difficulty'. The permanent secretary wrote: 'There is no evidence that adequate proposals or policy changes to enable the formation of a currency union could be devised, agreed and implemented by both governments in the foreseeable future.'

Such a rare civil service intervention was clearly significant, but so unprecedented that it led to criticism. The SNP claimed the civil servant had bowed to political pressure – something Macpherson denied.

Echoing the advice of his permanent secretary two days before, on Thursday 13 February, George Osborne told a packed room of reporters at the Point Hotel in Edinburgh: 'The SNP says that if Scotland becomes independent there will be a currency union and Scotland will share the pound. People need to know – that is not going to happen.' Hammering his point home, he concluded: 'If Scotland walks away from the UK, it walks away from the pound.'

And, as planned, Labour and the Liberal Democrats swiftly joined in, with Ed Balls telling the media: 'Scotland cannot keep the pound and the Bank of England if it chooses independence.' Danny Alexander, who was central to the coalition's referendum campaign, said: 'It is clear to me that a currency union wouldn't work for Scotland if it was independent; it wouldn't work for the rest of the UK.'

It was recognised that the planned series of currency interventions were always going to be tough for the No campaign. 'It turned out to be a long burst of pain, not short', conceded one person involved. A Conservative central to discussions added: 'We needed to explain the flaw in Salmond's argument; that a currency union was not in the interests of the rest of Britain. But it's hard to do without a politician being seen as threatening. We never succeeded.'

Secret Cabinet Office polling carried out by Ipsos MORI's Mark Diffley backed this up: 55–60 per cent of all Scottish voters thought the UK government was bluffing. One frustrated pro-UK campaigner complained: 'It was all contested. The Yes campaign's entire strategy was based on things not being true. And the pain was there's no way of knowing what would happen until after you leave.'

Many on the No side believe the currency interventions were misjudged. 'They talked about it so much they neutralised their own argument,' argued a senior source. 'We had a strong hand, but we overplayed it,' admitted another.

Soon, Better Together's strategy on currency would change. 'We stopped trying to persuade people about certainties, but instead emphasised risk. It's much easier. All we needed to do was persuade voters we just wouldn't know and couldn't be sure.'

Translating this research into political messages was a complex process and a team effort: core Better Together directors worked alongside Andrew Cooper, Douglas Alexander, Andrew Dunlop and Alistair Darling. It was an iterative process; getting the balance of key messages correct was difficult and it became clear that positive arguments about the UK would not be effective. If undecided voters could be reassured about independence, they would vote Yes; if not, they would vote No. 'With the burden of proof on the Yes campaign,' explained one senior strategist, 'it became clear that the strongest case for voting No was, in fact, the risk of voting Yes.'

Based on the evidence, negative messages would therefore be central to the Better Together campaign, but it needed to not look that way. 'We struggled from the start and never really succeeded in creating a positive frame for the campaign,' admitted one senior figure.

This rethink and adjustment to the campaign's strategy was a result of the ever-growing mass of research data. The Better Together team aimed to distil a potent tonic to persuade undecided voters to vote No. There were two ingredients.

First was a mixture of irreversibility and patriotism. 'By accepting that independence was irreversible,' explained one strategist, 'voters would perceive the step towards voting Yes as being larger and the risk more significant.' Stressing that voting No could be a 'patriotic' decision was vital. Undecided voters would make up their minds by trying to work out 'what's best for Scotland', and Better Together had to strongly counter any perception that voting No was a 'vote of no confidence' in the country.

The second ingredient in this political elixir was a combination of risk and uncertainty. In focus groups, undecided voters were unsettled by what they termed 'Alex Salmond's "it'll be alright on the night" approach'. However, attacking the First Minister himself – for being arrogant or obsessed with independence – did not work with the two target segments: 'Comfortable Pragmatists' and 'Uncommitted Security Seekers'. 'They respected Salmond,' admitted a senior adviser. 'They might not agree with him, but they honestly believed he wanted what's best for Scotland.'

So instead of attacking Salmond's motives, the No campaign was forced to argue that the First Minister was so passionate about independence that he would not face up to the risks or uncertainties. Better Together depicted Salmond as blinded by his separatist spirit, and unwilling to set out what would happen if everything did not go his way.

The detailed analyses of these one million undecided voters were turned into colourful graphs, tables, diagrams, briefing documents and PowerPoint presentations. The research was so extensive that Populus spent considerable time investigating which words and phrases in the English language the No campaign needed to 'own' in the minds of voters.

Research found that Yes Scotland, and the wider independence campaign, already 'owned' positive words like 'change', 'pride', 'patriotism', 'ambition' and 'brave', but also negatives such as 'uncertainty' and 'risk'. Voters associated the concept of voting No with words like 'security', 'reassurance', 'peace of mind', 'job security' and 'financial security', but also the negative phrase 'more of the same'.

In the middle, the Yes and No campaigns would have to fight for control of 'the future'; they both attempted to do this using 'young people', and endlessly couching the referendum decision in terms of what it would mean for 'our children'. Both sides also wrestled for control of 'hope' and 'opportunity'. Better Together attempted to neutralise the 'more of the same' attack from their opponents, and, equally, Yes Scotland intended to neutralise 'uncertainty' – but, ultimately, neither succeeded.

With such a thorough understanding of the messages needed to influence their target voters, Better Together's key strategists now started trying to frame the argument to their advantage. They also needed to get into the heads of their opponents. A frequent question at team meetings was: 'If you were sitting around the table at Yes Scotland today, what would you be planning?' It was vital they understood the mindset of the independence campaign and the tactics they were likely to deploy.

It was only in early 2014, during a series of sessions with Douglas Alexander, Andrew Cooper and Spencer Livermore (Labour's general election campaign director), that much of the strategy was written down. They deduced that the Yes campaign would attempt to frame the choice facing Scots as:

'Independence is the normal state of affairs. An independent Scotland will be richer and fairer.' *versus* 'Westminster is holding Scotland back.'

They predicted the pro-independence campaign would have five key aims: firstly, to delegitimise the No campaign as being a combination of 'London Labour' and the 'English Tories'; secondly, to de-risk independence; thirdly, to blame all Scotland's grievances on 'broken Westminster'; fourthly, to appeal to patriotism and offer a chance to 'shape our own destiny'; and, fifthly, to inspire participation with the offer that Scots could 'make history' by being part of something great.

In contrast, Better Together would attempt to frame the debate as:

'Staying in the UK is the best of both worlds: security and more powers guaranteed.' *versus* 'An irreversible leap into the unknown, with independence being just too risky.'

It was decided the No campaign would have four key aims: firstly, they would need to make voting No a vote for change, instead of being a vote for the status quo; secondly, they needed to make promises of further devolution credible; thirdly, it was important that undecided voters make the decision one of head not heart, preventing them from being blinded by passion; and, fourthly, the campaign's focus must always be on the big risks of independence in five policy areas (currency, jobs, pensions, the EU and public services), while stressing the lack of a Plan B, and the irreversibility of voting Yes.

As months went by, and criticism of Better Together being too negative really began to sting, the senior staff members would always return to their research. 'Is it negative to argue about the loss of something positive?' was Blair McDougall's regular refrain in TV interviews. The 'Project Fear' label had stuck, and, soon, the condemnation was coming not just from the campaign's opponents, but from its political allies. Anonymous briefings to the newspapers about internal chaos would overshadow the key messages and demoralise staff, pushing Alistair Darling to the brink of resignation.

CHAPTER 5

THE SPRING OF DISCONTENT

On 11 March 2014, Douglas Alexander, Blair McDougall, Rob Shorthouse and Andrew Cooper met in the wood-panelled shadow Cabinet Room at the House of Commons. The grand setting – with high windows and long wooden table – was chosen for both convenience and privacy. This was a last-ditch attempt to try to solve Better Together's marketing problem.

Described by a source intimately involved as 'a traumatic saga', the No campaign had already employed two successive advertising agencies, with little to show for the vast sums of money spent. Now, they were about to select their third.

At first, Grey London had been brought on board, but their work was 'so off-strategy, it was never really used', according to one adviser. Next, BD Network produced a memorable yet controversial advert, using the words 'Breaking Bad' – the title of an American crime drama. It featured a white background and a dark-blue outline of the UK with Scotland severed. At the bottom were the words: 'Divorce from the UK will cost us thousands of jobs.'

The concept was widely circulated among both staff and the board, prompting a mixed response. Some were enthusiastic, desperate to create an image that would go viral online – *Breaking Bad*'s recently concluded fifth and final hit season had confirmed its global popularity. But others were scathing. One board member called it 'ludicrous', another questioned whether a niche reference to the cult Netflix series would make any sense to the two target groups of undecided voters. For many, the programme's focus on the manufacture of crystal methamphetamine rendered it a risky reference point for a campaign message: 'This is about drugs, don't you understand?' one politician raged.

The advert also bombed in focus groups: 'It had bad grammar and strange phrasing,' explained one who saw the reaction from voters. 'People who did understand it thought it a sneering English caricature, a *Trainspotting* image of Scotland as a haven for drugs.'

After two agencies had failed to impress, Douglas Alexander intervened: 'We need grown-ups.' London agencies with international experience were invited to pitch for a contract with Better Together. With short notice, only two agreed: TBWA and M&C Saatchi.

Around the shadow Cabinet table, an articulate strategy expert from TBWA impressed with a clever comparison of the campaign's key risk message to the challenges of road safety. But the pitch took a turn for the worse when an account director from the agency admitted their real attraction was to win the Labour Party account back.

TBWA had handled advertising for the party under Tony Blair's leadership, and joked to the Better Together team that their name stood for 'Tony Blair Wins Again'. The account director then proceeded to criticise the work of the party's current agency Lucky General – unwise, since it was Douglas Alexander, the party's chair of general election strategy, who had signed them up. One concept TBWA presented was of Alex Salmond on a wrecking ball, like pop star Miley Cyrus in her suggestive 2013 music video. 'It was wrong and lazy,' said one witness.

Downhearted by the unimpressive pitch, the mood of the four No campaigners was soon boosted by the arrival of Moray MacLennan, worldwide CEO of M&C Saatchi. 'Douglas fell in love with him on sight,' said one person present. And, for a political geek like Alexander, this was a one-off opportunity: 'Douglas has always wanted to work with famous political people, and, because M&C Saatchi are Tories, he knew he would never get the chance again.'

MacLennan was smooth and plausible. The concept – 'No We Can' – was an incredibly literal interpretation of turning a negative into a positive. It impressed the team, and M&C Saatchi were duly hired – to the consternation of the Yes campaign. 'The fact that the No campaign has hired Margaret Thatcher's favourite PR people, who helped usher in eighteen years of Tory government that the people of Scotland rejected, shows just how out of touch they are,' a Yes Scotland spokesperson said, and, when tested in a focus group, M&C Saatchi's slogan went down badly.

This marketing debacle was symptomatic of wider problems in the campaign, many of which were blamed on two key members of staff: the campaign's director Blair McDougall and communications chief Rob Shorthouse.

'There was a general feeling after the first six months that Blair was not a strong enough figure to effectively manage the various voices,' said a senior Conservative. 'He had never run a campaign on this scale before.' Of course, few had, and the alternatives were never clear.

McDougall was disorganised, missed meetings and failed

to reply to emails – all of which slowed down the campaign machine. 'He was overstretched,' explained one Labour colleague, dismayed by McDougall's too frequent media appearances that distracted from his principal management role. 'He didn't know if he was the frontman, the chief executive or the office manager.'

Others were more supportive: 'Administratively, he's a fucking disaster, but he's the most creative, intelligent thinker out of everyone.' McDougall 'produced his best work at 3 a.m.' and his mastery of polling, messaging and speechwriting was invaluable. One colleague described him as 'a genius'.

McDougall needed a handler – a well-organised personal assistant – but the budget was tight, staff was scarce, and he was also reluctant. Regularly working through the night, he coped well with the high level of pressure and responsibility, but did consider quitting when what he saw as interference from Downing Street and Westminster got too much.

Frustrations with McDougall seemed minor, however, compared to the vitriol directed at Rob Shorthouse. 'I don't know how he slept at night,' said someone who watched the director of communications at work. 'He has a good CV. He's a great guy. But he took on a big job, was paid a lot of money, and utterly bullshitted his way through every second of every day. It was astonishing.' Shorthouse's creation of the term 'Project Fear' to describe the No campaign had been damaging. But he had strong contacts in the Scottish media, and put in the hours. 'He could pick up the phone to any journalist and be chatty, persuasive and full of banter,' said one colleague. 'He was definitely the most fun person to work with,' added another.

One downside of his thankless role was that all three parties and the campaign's board members had opinions – often contrasting – on the campaign's communications output. Not being in any political camp or faction, Shorthouse had few backers, and became, according to colleagues, a 'lightning conductor for internal bollocks'.

Much of the resentment was due to his salary, now at £105,000 and far above the £58,678 that MSPs – including the three opposition leaders – earned. Other senior figures outside the campaign were eyeing up his job. The three political parties found Shorthouse a useful scapegoat. Politicians irritated that they were not getting on the TV were told: 'Sorry, it was Rob's decision.'

'Rob lets a lot wash over him and only picks fights that are productive,' explained a close colleague. 'The art of cross-party politics is swallowing your pride and he did, putting up with a lot of shit a lot of the time.'

The relationship between the board and the campaign's senior staff had also broken down. Board meetings had soon changed 'from coffee and cake or tea and scones in Alistair's house' to a series of crisis meetings. 'People on the board were keen to get rid of Rob and Blair,' said one key figure. 'But the Labour directors [MSPs Jackie Baillie and Richard Baker] would never endorse it.' Alistair Darling also had an unofficial no-sacking rule. 'He tries to avoid confrontation,' explained a friend. 'He doesn't like it full stop. And he's also a decent person who knew both men had young families.'

Requests by the board for a 'war book' detailing the campaign's strategy were never fulfilled. 'It was like pulling teeth,' said one person involved. 'They would actively tell us little white lies because they hadn't done stuff.' Another complained: 'It was like dealing with treacle – you never got a straight answer. Even donors who got in touch, willing to give tens of thousands of pounds, were never replied to.'

The board tried to take charge by setting up sub-groups to manage the campaign's problematic areas. This went down badly with exhausted staff: 'We were not supported by the board when we really needed it. It was a horrible working environment.'

This growing frustration was echoed in Westminster. In the final six months, more decisions were wrested away from the central campaign, with Douglas Alexander pushing to take on a more prominent role. He had secured the confidence of David Cameron and would organise regular meetings with Andrew Dunlop and Danny Alexander in his House of Commons office. But not everyone was convinced that reverting to leadership by Scots based in London would work: 'Douglas was trying to get Danny Alexander, Miliband and Cameron to think he was the answer to all their prayers.'

In this period, there were three high-level meetings convened to help turn the campaign around – one between Cameron and Miliband, another between Darling and Osborne, and one involving Darling, Osborne and Cameron. The conclusion was always the same: Darling should focus on being the frontman and let Douglas Alexander take more control of the back-room operation. 'Osborne thought Douglas was overrated, but the only game in town,' said one Conservative. 'They told Alistair that Douglas could do the heavy work, like chairing the 5 a.m. conference calls, which, of course, never happened, because Blair wouldn't come in until half ten.'

'Alistair's not daft, he knew what was going on,' said one confidant. 'But he wouldn't just stand aside.' Darling had experience of attempts by No. 10 to sideline him under its previous occupant. He had also known Alexander for decades, and was wary of his and Jim Murphy's tactics. 'I want them where I can see them,' Darling told his staff.

The Scottish Liberal Democrat conference was traditionally not an event synonymous with anything even close to drama. That had changed over the past two years.

In 2013, a senior Better Together figure was thrown out of the gathering after screaming the word 'cunts' at activists who were questioning why they should vote No.

In 2014, in Aberdeen, the once pleasant gathering was again transformed. The front page of the *Scottish Daily Mail* on Friday 28 March 2014 was the first headache in what would turn out to be a diabolical weekend for Better Together.

'Campaign to save the UK in crisis' read the headline. Political editor Alan Roden had an exclusive story that began: 'Leaders of Scotland's No campaign are holding crisis talks today as they battle internal splits and rising support for independence.' The previous critical article from the *Mail* had been before Christmas, when 'senior Conservatives' described Alistair Darling as 'useless' and 'comatose'. This time, the paper's reference to 'Better Together board members' made them the focus of suspicion. Someone needed to track down the source and stem the flow of damaging leaks.

Later that day, Better Together's board met secretly in Glasgow's Jury's Inn Hotel, away from the campaign's HQ in order to avoid further press interest. 'In a testament to the Better Together way, the room hadn't even been booked properly,' complained one attendee. The meeting had been originally scheduled to discuss marketing strategy, but the morning's *Daily Mail* article transformed the atmosphere.

Alistair Darling surprised everyone. He was enraged: 'If this continues, I'm going,' he said. 'I don't need the hassle.

I don't need people inside this room briefing against me. If you do, I'm going to quit.'

'It was brilliant,' said one board member. 'Normally if you have insomnia, Alistair's your man, but, this time, he got really angry.' Darling had recognised the danger of any breakdown of trust at the top of the organisation, and knew he had to stamp it out.

Around the meeting table, nobody named the suspected leaker, but Rob Shorthouse had been tasked with tracking down the source. All fingers pointed to Craig Harrow, convener of the Scottish Liberal Democrats. 'We acted shocked,' remembered one board member. 'It's terrible! Who could do such a thing? But we all knew it was Craig. His views were correct, but a story in the *Mail* was hardly going to help.' The anger privately directed towards Harrow for his apparent indiscretion was palpable: 'He reminds me of Penfold in *Danger Mouse*, the bespectacled hamster,' said one colleague. 'And he's got more faces than the town hall clock.'

Part of the frustration was that Harrow was one of the most experienced and knowledgeable campaigners on the board, and, more importantly, Darling respected him. 'Alistair was furious,' claimed a close colleague, 'because Harrow wasn't in some loose orbit of the organisation. He had done a lot of the heavy lifting.'

To add to the difficulties, in Aberdeen, Liberal Democrat leader Willie Rennie was critical of the campaign's tone, and launched a 'sunshine strategy' for the referendum – a thinly veiled attack on the negativity of Better Together: 'People need to know there's something great about the United Kingdom,' he told reporters.

Rennie's predecessor as leader, Tavish Scott, was more direct in his criticism of the No campaign: 'I don't think

Alistair Darling is pulling that whole swathe of people back into definitely voting for the union,' he said.

That evening, the Better Together team had a rare night off. But it was soon ruined. David Ross, the campaign's head of press, was at a family party flicking through his phone when he spotted an article on the *Guardian* website that made him feel physically sick.

Nicholas Watt, the paper's impeccably connected chief political correspondent, had spoken to a UK government minister, who had said that 'of course there would be a currency union' if Scots voted for independence.

Watt had rung the Downing Street press office, instead of the No campaign in Scotland, for a comment in response to his story, so Better Together had no prior warning. Ross immediately phoned round his senior colleagues, who, in turn, were soon inundated with calls and texts from journalists. 'It's pish. I don't know who said it. It's not true,' was the exasperated response to media enquiries.

Meanwhile, the Yes campaign, long criticised for not putting forward a Plan B on currency, seized on the story as proof they could keep the pound. 'It was the worst moment by a million miles,' moaned one Better Together campaigner. 'Our whole argument was based on currency. If that fell, the whole thing could crumble.'

The *Guardian* story described the ministerial source as 'at the heart of the pro-union campaign', and someone who would play a 'central role in the negotiations over the breakup of the UK if there were a yes vote'.

With the Scottish Liberal Democrats conference taking place over 300 miles away in Aberdeen, fingers were soon pointed at 'moronic Lib Dem ministers'. Suspicions later turned on Cabinet Office minister Oliver Letwin – normally

kept away from the media – and Foreign Secretary Philip
Hammond. The latter claimed that as he was in the US, he
was innocent, to which the No campaign privately pointed
out that geographical distance in 2014 would not preclude
communication with journalists.

Alistair Darling was furious at such a serious lapse coming
from the UK government itself. Yet, having spent decades
in Westminster, he was well aware of Watt's beguiling technique: never asking questions, just chatting and waiting for
his next exclusive. The next day, Darling phoned the editors
of Sunday newspapers to try to talk down the story.

In such a sustained and unrelenting campaign, it was difficult to retain the confidence of all parties, particularly when
the polls were hesitant. And, more concerning, the media
view of the No campaign had also changed: 'Journalists were
bored with Better Together being ahead,' admitted a senior
staff member. 'It didn't matter what we did, the narrative
was we were rubbish.' Another campaign source added: 'The
fact is the tide had turned, the hacks were bored of writing
the same story and wanted to move on to something else.'

Better Together also found combating the Yes campaign's
mindset almost impossible. 'We were trying to put forward
facts to convince people who have ideologies with no interest in fact,' claimed one senior figure. 'It was infuriating.
Like whack-a-mole.' Another campaign chief argued, with
an equally inspired simile: 'It was like a monster horror film.
You plunge a stake through their heart but they sit up in the
coffin again and again.'

Over the first four months of 2014, even with the early
interventions on currency, opinion polls suggested Yes
Scotland increased their support base from 33 to 37 per cent
of the vote. In the same period, the No campaign slid from

48 to 45 per cent. Yes Scotland argued that this proved the manifesto for an independent Scotland in the White Paper was sinking in, and they were winning the arguments.

Adding to the challenges, Gordon Aikman, the Better Together campaign's director of research, had been diagnosed with the degenerative neurological condition motor neurone disease, and had to step back from many of his duties. Aikman had been the point of contact for many in the UK government, and his illness left McDougall even more extended.

'It was hard to keep motivated,' explained a senior campaigner. 'Everyone talked about how crap we were, many people were ill, Gordon being diagnosed upset a lot of people and had a profound effect on the mood.' With no money to expand the team, briefings against the boss, shifting polls and personality clashes, many were pushed to their limits. 'It really was so tough,' said someone involved. 'It was the hardest thing I've ever done.'

In another unexpected twist, when funds were finally found to recruit an extra staff member for the research team, the new employee – recently returned from working in Sierra Leone – became unwell and was put into isolation in hospital until Ebola was ruled out.

Yet, among the strain of spring 2014, there was one moment of sheer joy. It was long past midnight on Tuesday 29 April 2014 and Blair McDougall had just got to sleep at his home in Glasgow's Southside after checking the front pages of the Scottish first editions. That was until he was woken up by his heavily pregnant wife. Mary McDougall was starting to get contractions.

After making their way downstairs, the couple phoned the hospital. 'You've got a good bit of time yet,' they were told, 'so start thinking about coming in, but there's no hurry.' Blair McDougall returned upstairs to grab a couple of things and brush his teeth, but suddenly his focused calm turned into sheer panic. He heard his wife screaming and, all of a sudden, it started to happen.

He phoned 999. 'Wash your hands,' they said, 'take off your ring and get ready to deliver.' McDougall had one of the most high-pressure jobs in UK politics, without the added challenge of DIY midwifery.

'Our first child was a seventy-hour labour, so we were a bit complacent,' he later explained. An addition to the clan just before the start of the intense final summer months of the campaign was not intentional. 'Our first child was born with IVF and the result of long-term planning,' he told a reporter. 'The second one certainly wasn't,' he roared with laughter.

The ambulance arrived with just a few minutes to spare and at 3.15 a.m., Gus McDougall was born on the living-room floor. It was a rare moment of happiness in an otherwise arduous campaign: a reminder that Scots would be deciding not just their own future, but those of their children and grandchildren. And also a crashing illustration that life continued outside the bubble of the independence referendum.

CHAPTER 6

NON, MERCI

'One hundred days to go' was a major media milestone. After a difficult few months for the No campaign, at last there was a chance to recalibrate and get back on track. The eyes of the world were on Scotland more than ever before: the *Daily Record*'s front page read '100 days from destiny'. Monday 9 June 2014 had long featured on the No camp's forward-planning grid. For months, Better Together had been devising a big, noisy and, crucially, positive series of events.

Logistics were fine-tuned: Alistair Darling's gruelling schedule was to kick off with a rally in Glasgow, before heading east to visit a small business in the capital, then travelling north-west to Stornoway in the Outer Hebrides for a town hall meeting in the evening. With a packed timetable of interviews, a different press officer was assigned to handle media on each leg of the journey.

At 10.30 a.m., the Community Central Hall in Maryhill, Glasgow, was packed with hundreds of Better Together activists. The words 'We can have the best of both worlds for Scotland' glowed on a screen above the stage.

Delivering an assured speech, Darling called on voters to

reject independence. But the tone was different – more upbeat and confident, less focused on the weaknesses of independence. Darling spoke of 'Scotland's positive, possibility-rich future' as part of the United Kingdom, and stressed that voting No would still deliver 'substantially enhanced powers for the Scottish Parliament'. A series of 'ordinary' voters then spoke, urging their fellow Scots to join them in voting No.

This was also the moment 'Better Together' was rebranded as 'No Thanks'. 'I lost count of how many discussions we had about transitioning to "No". We couldn't have left it much later,' revealed one senior figure. Better Together had avoided using the word because of its intrinsic negativity. But, in the final period of campaigning, it was essential to emphasise that there would be no 'Better Together' option on the ballot: Scots were being asked to put a cross in a box marked 'No'.

Douglas Alexander was a political obsessive, and relished the challenge of trying to solve strategic problems, especially at the intersection between polling and messaging. The shadow Foreign Secretary had spent much of his free time over the winter studying the Québécois independence referendums of 1980 and 1995, seen as the closest western comparison to the vote facing Scots.

In the early hours of one morning, he found a YouTube video of Canadian Prime Minister Pierre Trudeau in 1980, giving his final address to a rally in a massive ice-hockey rink. A huge crowd were cheering Trudeau and waving Maple Leaf flags. Behind the podium was a vast red and white banner emblazoned with the words: '*Non Merci*'. In a flash, Alexander knew he had his slogan. The next week, the phrase 'No Thanks' was put to focus groups of voters. 'It tested out of the park,' said one person involved. 'It was polite and courteous with a hint of defiance.' 'No Thanks'-branded merchandise proved far more popular with activists than 'Better Together'. 'T-shirts and boxes of leaflets kept disappearing,' one campaign chief recalled.

Through his research into the politics of Quebec, Alexander also developed an understanding of the great rhetorical moments of the 1980 and 1995 campaigns. These came from Trudeau and Jean Chrétien, respectively. Both were Québécois Canadian prime ministers, both statesmen who could argue commandingly against separation, and both delivered powerful, emotive speeches on the eve of polling. Applying the principles from Canada, Alexander had a slow realisation that only one Scot could deliver a speech with the equivalent intensity. He knew Better Together needed Gordon Brown.

But with 100 days to go until the referendum, Alistair Darling was not thinking about his former Downing Street neighbour. The Better Together chairman was in a car approaching Edinburgh for his next event, delighted at the success of the campaign's launch that morning. He was blissfully unaware that, at that precise moment, Gordon Brown was sitting down for lunch at the Palace of Westminster with the UK's most influential political writers and broadcasters. No one in the Better Together campaign had been given any advance warning of his impending speech.

As Darling arrived at the offices of Smart PA, a small business on Edinburgh's Melville Street, the chairman of the Westminster press gallery – the BBC's James Landale – was introducing Brown with a witty speech, ribbing the former Prime Minister for his infrequent appearances in the House of Commons.

Brown stood up and began with a joke: he told journalists

he needed a 'guided tour' to find his way around the parliamentary estate. Brown had so far given only one speech in the Commons that year. But the tone soon became more serious as the former Prime Minister gave his analysis of the independence referendum.

He was critical of David Cameron's 'threats and ultimatums' over an independent Scotland's use of the pound – one of Better Together's central arguments. 'Last week, when the Scottish Office and the UK government put out that statement that Scots would be £1,400 better off without independence – and they gave the example of fish and chips you could buy, or holidays in Torremolinos – I thought that was patronising.' Brown also had a stark message for the media: 'If Britain does not wake up, there will be home rule for Scotland. You can lose a country by mistake,' he warned.

One person watching described the speech as 'amusing, passionate, persuasive'. Yet it was in the question-and-answer session afterwards that Brown was to cause most trouble: 'I think it would be a good idea if David Cameron could debate Alex Salmond,' he said, flatly contradicting the No campaign's argument for many months.

This was a big deal. Better Together strategists knew undecided voters were concerned that voting No would be seen as anti-Scottish or a vote of no confidence in their country. 'The visuals, the message, everything about a Cameron versus Salmond debate was wrong,' said one senior No staffer. 'The Yes campaign was desperate to frame the debate as Scotland versus England – this played right into their hands.'

Daily Telegraph commentator Dan Hodges described Brown's comments as 'bonkers'. Scottish journalist Euan McColm wryly tweeted: 'Better Together wheels out big gun. Big gun shoots Better Together in the bollocks.'

Relations between the three pro-UK parties remained perfectly cordial. It was internal ructions in the Labour Party that continued to hamper the campaign's best efforts. But at least one party welcomed the former Prime Minister's comments. SNP politicians were delighted, tweeting that 'for once' they agreed with Brown.

The Better Together team – who had, up until that point, been progressing through a well-choreographed agenda – were soon fielding calls from London reporters asking for a reaction to Brown's comments.

The impact was that Alistair Darling's TV interviews for the rest of the day were dominated by responses to Brown's words, instead of getting his campaign's key messages across. 'Gordon Brown's way off message today. Is that what you're saying?' asked Sarah Smith on the BBC's *Scotland 2014* programme. Darling duly dodged: 'Gordon is entitled to his own opinion.'

Alistair Darling was angry: he assumed Brown's intervention had been timed to cause maximum damage. But Blair McDougall, knowing how hard his staff had worked for the '100 days' event, was furious. 'Blair thought Brown was being a cunt and doing it deliberately,' said a No campaign source. McDougall phoned Brown's press adviser Bruce Waddell. If you do this again 'the gloves are off', Waddell was told.

Others were more sympathetic. Professor Jim Gallagher, who was close to Brown, attempted to argue on Brown's behalf: 'He's out of practice.' It had, after all, been the Q&A after the speech that had caused headaches, rather than the speech itself. But few in the No campaign were convinced.

'Gordon blew it all out of the water,' raged one of the campaign's press team. 'Our event was good, but the coverage the next day was all about Gordon.' The response from

Downing Street was incredulity. 'It helped no one,' said one source in government. 'But there was a lighter moment later: the explanation from Gordon was that he'd been misquoted, which was hilarious.'

Building any sort of relationship with Gordon Brown was a challenge. He had famously fallen out with Alistair Darling when they were, respectively, Prime Minister and Chancellor. Brown's team had issued a series of negative media briefings against Darling, which the Chancellor described as like the 'forces of hell' being unleashed. Blair McDougall was an even less likely Brownite ally. He was special adviser to James Purnell when the Work and Pensions Secretary had tried to oust Brown from power in 2009.

'Gordon didn't want to become involved,' said one Better Together chief. 'He's only involved when he can run something.' And Brown had already attempted that. In 2012, a few months after Better Together's launch, Brown met Johann Lamont. 'He slid across the table a letter he had drafted with Johann's name at the bottom,' claimed a senior figure. If signed, it would have empowered Brown to act on behalf of Scottish Labour. 'Johann slid it back.' But the pair remained close, with a member of the party characterising their relationship as 'Pygmalionesque'.

The former Prime Minister would have to forge links with Better Together because he had no other means of organising an audience. Scottish Labour's director of strategy Paul Sinclair, who had worked for Brown at Downing Street, acted as a conduit. Darling also tried hard to forge a truce, recognising the potential benefit. The pair had spoken briefly in the House of Commons towards the end of 2013, and in Glasgow in May 2014. 'You need to do more; people will listen to you,' Darling told his former boss.

The previous month, the UK government had also attempted to establish stronger links with Brown by sending Cameron's special adviser for Scotland, Andrew Dunlop, as an emissary to meet the former Prime Minister in his Commons office. 'It was like a trip to the court of King Philip of Spain or the Vatican,' one coalition minister joked of the encounter. 'A message is handed over, he takes it out, scrawls on it, and sends it back.'

David Cameron and his team recognised Brown's power to reach a cross-section of Scots no one else could. 'He has an authenticity and is seen as a guardian of Scottish values,' explained one Conservative.

Dunlop had been warned in advance that 'Brown doesn't like Tories. If he takes against you, it'll be a short meeting.' But the former Prime Minister was soon charmed by Dunlop's recollections of watching a hustings between Brown and Conservative Michael Ancram in 1979, when the pair was standing against one another to be the MP for Edinburgh South. Dunlop also delighted Brown with tales of being taught at Edinburgh University by Professor J. P. Mackintosh, a former Labour MP, who wrote seminal works on devolution. Brown and Dunlop soon hit it off, forging the way for a closer relationship between Brown and Cameron.

Eight days after his intervention at Westminster, Gordon Brown's personal take on the decision facing Scots was published. *My Scotland, Our Britain: A Future Worth Sharing* was not – Brown insisted – a 332-page political manifesto. Instead, it was a heartfelt and patriotic exploration of his connection to the country, his interpretation of its history and his take on its future in an increasingly interdependent global economy. He also called for further powers for Holyrood, UK-wide devolution and House of Lords reform.

'Gordon essentially gave a lot of people a playbook: an argument and a script,' explained one Labour adviser. Brown had talked to lots of Labour MPs, and had thought through the key arguments with an intellectual heft few others in Scottish politics possessed. It was a solidly Labour case for maintaining the union, with social justice and the UK's fostering of a 'moral community' – in which social and economic rights are pooled and shared – at the fore.

As the leader of Scottish Labour, Johann Lamont was responsible for making that distinctive Labour case for remaining in the UK. Yet she was also having to contend with rumbles of dissent about her own leadership.

Early signs of discord had followed a speech Lamont gave in Edinburgh in September 2012 (less than a year into her leadership), which famously attacked what she saw as Scotland's 'something for nothing' culture. STV's political editor Bernard Ponsonby described the speech as 'almost Blairite in substance'. Political commentator Iain Macwhirter called it 'an astonishing act of political self-harm'.

Lamont's relationship with Ed Miliband also deteriorated during the controversial selection of a candidate to fight the Westminster seat of Falkirk, when the trade union Unite was accused of trying to rig the outcome – something they consistently denied. Resistance to Lamont's leadership intensified when disagreements arose over further tax powers for Holyrood, which were being considered by the party's Devolution Commission.

Over Christmas 2013, Labour sent a booklet to all party members across the UK. There was no mention of the upcoming independence referendum, except in 'dates for your diary'. Lamont went ballistic, and apologies were soon forthcoming from London. But it was a sign Scotland was not wired into

authority and respect,' said one Labour source. Murphy took charge of the campaign, re-jigged the grid and, in two weeks, had not only understood the problem, but united the staff. Ian Price, Scottish Labour General Secretary, was not keen on a challenge to his leadership, but he could do nothing to oppose it. 'Shut up, this is happening,' was one blunt response.

It was not just in the Labour campaign that people were frustrated. Activists at the Liberal Democrats' Orkney office were getting increasingly tired of edicts from Better Together's 'grass-roots' team. One activist's heart sank as he answered the phone to yet another request: 'We need you to do a train-station leafleting session,' explained a member of staff in Glasgow. 'We're doing it across the country.'

'When's the train coming?' the campaigner asked. There was silence at the other end of the line. Orkney is 10 miles north of mainland Scotland. There is no train.

All three pro-UK parties had significant frustrations with the No campaign's broad-brush approach towards grass-roots campaigning in Scotland's distinct regions and communities. Few had confidence in the man first responsible for the ground operation.

Rob Murray was Better Together's third full-time staff member after Blair McDougall and Rob Shorthouse. A friend-ly, jokey figure, he was nicknamed 'Bertie' and, as national campaign organiser, responsible for co-ordinating teams of activists on the ground, was one of the few Conservative em-ployees. 'As soon as he was appointed, there was a problem,' said one experienced hand. 'No one from any party could work out who he was. And he was fundamentally useless.'

'He's a Boy Scout who got a job way above his station,' said one senior Liberal Democrat. Labour colleagues were equally scathing: 'Dyb dyb. That's what he did best. He was the token Tory in the room, recommended by the Tories, but they messed up.'

Murray's approach to Better Together's activists and volunteers was also widely criticised: 'He was patronising to old sages who've been campaigning for decades,' said one. 'He had a superiority complex and treated experienced organisers with utter contempt,' said another. At least two campaign staff quit Better Together in its early stages – one of whom had been asked to follow Alex Salmond around in a chicken suit when the First Minister was still refusing to debate Darling on television – though there is no suggestion these departures were directly linked to Murray's management style.

Rob Murray did, in fact, play a significant role under huge pressure with very little support. He first requested that funds were found for a team of eight organisers in 2012, but this basic demand was only fulfilled at the start of 2014. For much of the referendum race, Better Together was paralysed by a shortage of money, and employing campaign organisers was never a priority. 'We spent hundreds of thousands of pounds on polling, with no money to do anything with what we'd discovered,' said one board member. Senior figures were fascinated by marketing and strategy, but the basics of campaigning were rarely a focus.

'There was a complete lack of visibility on the street,' complained a senior adviser, citing Better Together's relentless focus on face-to-face canvassing when many volunteers are not keen on knocking on doors. 'Posters don't win votes,' explained another experienced campaigner, downhearted by the dominance of Yes signs on Scotland's streets, 'but they are good for morale.'

The No campaign's voter contact system – for gathering information on voting intention – was more successful.

Based on Labour's 'Contact Creator' tool, Better Together named their system 'Patriot'. A bespoke phone-canvassing programme called 'Blether Together', developed by Barack Obama's online strategists Blue State Digital at a cost of over £300,000, was also well received.

Greg Nugent, a branding expert from London 2012, was brought in over the summer to build a volunteer base to get out the vote. The campaign's database of activists had been 'completely mismanaged', according to someone involved: '150,000 people had signed up, were interested in helping, but were spammed so often that the messages went into their junk email. We could never communicate with them again.'

Unlike the Yes campaign, which developed a political movement with hundreds of grass-roots groups being set up in a spectrum of communities across the country, a decision was made in Better Together to keep control centrally. There were sound reasons for doing so: principally to avoid rogue supporters embarrassing the campaign. Yet, by trying to organise everything from one small headquarters, local enthusiasm was lost, leaving the energising force and a sense of momentum largely on the Yes side.

Mirroring Labour's recruitment of fixers to solve their campaigning problems, Kate Watson, a Labour organiser and former aide to Douglas Alexander, was brought in as director of operations, and, soon, grass-roots activity was added to her areas of responsibility. 'She's a bossy bastard, but knows what she's doing,' said one senior colleague. Watson would frequently fall out with McDougall, and considered quitting her job, but she remained a productive political powerhouse. 'She's brutally effective, but mad,' said one Labour source. 'She makes herself utterly indispensable and makes things happen.'

In April 2014, Alistair Darling also brought in Frank Roy – Labour MP for Motherwell & Wishaw – to be what he called his 'Super Agent'. 'Frank is like a foreman,' said one colleague, and, indeed, much of Roy's career had been in industry, as a steelworker at Ravenscraig. He was made redundant in 1992, went to university as a mature student, and was elected to Westminster in 1997.

Frank Roy had built up a reputation as Scottish Labour's go-to expert for by-elections and general elections. He was seriously respected by Alistair Darling, and had soon won the trust of the Conservatives. His appointment was the first step in a politicians' takeover of Better Together, which, for the intense 'short campaign', replaced the cross-party board of directors. 'The grown-ups were finally in charge,' one person involved commented. This did not please everyone: 'Blair was in a dark mood,' explained a senior adviser, 'with the daily frustration that he and his team were under attack as more chiefs came in.'

'Better Together stopped being a completely shambolic series of meetings at the point they brought in Frank Roy,' said one senior politician. 'There was a general feeling of relief. They brought in a hard-nosed campaigner – one who actually had done this before.' One close colleague described Roy's approach: 'He sits in a corner like a spider at the centre of his web and watches. When he's angry, he goes quiet and eats bars of Galaxy chocolate.'

Chief Secretary to the Treasury Danny Alexander joined at a similar time and, as the most senior Scot in the UK government, acted as the point of contact with Whitehall. One activist remembers giving the minister a lift in his car for an event in the Highlands. Towards the end of the meeting, Alexander asked to borrow the car keys under the pretence

that he had 'left something in the back seat'. It was a while
into the drive back alone to Glasgow that the campaigner
spotted a Tesco carrier bag on the passenger seat. Inside
were two bottles of Coke and a pack of Maltesers. Not all
Lib Dems were bad, he thought as he tucked into his gift.

Labour's shadow Foreign Secretary Douglas Alexander
took control of messaging, marketing and the grid, introducing a sign-off system for all leaflets and mail-shots. Senior
Labour MSP Jackie Baillie, who was on the campaign's
board, also joined the team, spending a considerable amount
of time smoothing over tricky relationships. Baillie would
occasionally disappear, returning with an order of sixty
cakes from the Savoy Centre bakery, all in an effort to allay
simmering tensions.

This top team of senior Scottish politicians was not based
in a 21st-century political nerve centre, but in a run-down
Glasgow shopping complex. A donor had given Better
Together free use of office space at the Savoy Centre. 'It was
bizarre. We were in the upstairs of a mangy shopping centre,
full of mobile-phone kiosks and discount shops,' said someone involved.

Ventilation was poor, but opening any of the limited
number of windows meant staff were forced to listen to bagpipes blaring on the street below. 'It was always too hot and
sweaty,' said one senior staff member. 'There were a lot of
men in there and the main office constantly smelt.' Another
Labour source complained: 'It was very male-dominated.
Most of the women got squeezed out.'

However this crowded and dingy HQ was a hive of activity. Among boxes of leaflets, staff were tapping away on
laptops, teenage volunteers would rush in and out, and there
was a continual, palpable tension: 'There was screaming and

slamming doors, and lots of crying in the toilets,' said one Labour source. 'The toilets were horrible.'

'We shouldn't really be doing this,' Better Together's director of operations Kate Watson admitted to a colleague as Jim Murphy went out on the road on the '100 towns in 100 days' tour, launched on 10 June 2014. From the start, there was scepticism: 'It was all about Jim and his ego,' according to a person involved.

The plan was for Labour's shadow International Development Secretary to travel from 'Barrhead to Barra', holding public meetings on street corners with two Irn-Bru crates as his stage. It certainly demonstrated chutzpah: how many other politicians could do something so tough, so old-fashioned, so alien, as to walk the streets without bag-carriers and security, and talk to real people? Impressive though the concept was, and talented though it proved Murphy to be, the long series of events was a drain on staff resources.

Internally, campaigners joked it was 'Jim's leadership tour'. Murphy had privately suggested for months that he was interested in succeeding Johann Lamont as Labour's Scottish leader. This was partly due to his frustrated Westminster ambitions. In October 2013, Murphy had been demoted by Ed Miliband from the shadow Defence brief to International Development, seen as a graveyard in opposition because of the lack of differentiation in policy between the two main parties. The tour afforded Murphy the opportunity to build his profile and meet hundreds of Labour Party members.

At the beginning, ahead of each stop on the tour, 300 letters would be sent to local people to help build a crowd. But, soon, the operation became a disjointed organisational nightmare, falling behind schedule, with Murphy no longer on track to hit the 100th town by his deadline – a fortnight before referendum day. 'It had not been timed properly,' said a staff member involved in a leg of the tour in the Highlands, 'so one day we left Wick at the time we were supposed to be at Golspie, over an hour's drive away.' Turning up late meant there was a danger of local politicians and activists being left waiting, getting fed up and leaving. 'Jim got stressed,' explained a campaigner.

The tour also became a dumping ground for staff who 'couldn't be found roles elsewhere', said a member of the team. 'Give me all your misfits,' another joked. 'They were fucking inept and had never campaigned beyond student politics. One would turn up wearing a cravat and pocket handkerchief.'

But the lack of experience did have an impact: 'It was a comedy of errors,' said a person involved. 'They forgot the Irn-Bru crates, they forgot to charge the microphone and speaker system. When they couldn't be bothered to get balloons sorted, they blamed it on a worldwide shortage of helium.' In another incident, some activists were stopped by police for driving at night without lights: 'They shat themselves and rang HQ for help,' explained a campaigner. But this would prove to be a minor problem in comparison with the latter stage of the tour. The worst was yet to come.

CHAPTER 7

NOT TONIGHT, DARLING

ROUND ONE

Alistair Darling's closest confidante Catherine MacLeod phoned Scottish Labour's director of communications Paul Sinclair. 'Alistair wants you involved,' she said. 'And, I hope you don't find this offensive,' she paused, 'but will you do Salmond?' Sinclair chuckled. He was aware of the similarities – a bullish, aggressive nature, for starters – and delighted at the suggestion he would impersonate the First Minister.

In the grid of potentially damaging moments for the No campaign, the live televised debates stuck out. Darling was experienced and respected, but 'charisma-free'. And everyone on the No side knew it. His caution had secured him a place, alongside Jack Straw and Gordon Brown, as one of only three MPs to serve in Labour's Cabinet throughout their thirteen years in office. As Chancellor of the Exchequer, Darling had guided the UK through the worst recession in living memory. But this 'safe pair of hands' was not blessed with dazzling communication skills. What counted as a

strength in macroeconomic management, was a weakness
on TV.

At no point during Darling's informal recruitment as
No campaign chair was consideration given by Labour or
Downing Street as to his television prowess. As the debates
approached, Gordon Brown was briefly considered as an alternative. Internal polling and focus groups showed he had
the rare gift of being able to engage the all-important C2DE
(working-class) former Labour voters – those who might be
persuaded to vote Yes. Brown had also put in a solid performance in the first TV leaders' debates in 2010, during
his final weeks in Downing Street. But that option was discounted: Darling was leading the campaign; he knew it was
down to him. Privately, senior MPs, MSPs and advisers were
hoping for two draws. Even one win seemed unlikely.

Twice voted the most boring man in Britain, Alistair
Darling relished the referendum campaign, but not the media
appearances. He never has. The former Chancellor is often
caricatured as grey and dull. In reality, he is thoughtful, with a
dry wit: 'He has a black "we're all doomed, we're all fucked"
type of humour,' explained one colleague. But Darling is also
private and always cautious. According to fellow politicians,
he sees publicity opportunities as hazardous. 'The biggest
mistake is assuming you're going in for a routine interview,'
Darling advised a younger colleague. 'Always be scared and
apprehensive. People who forget that make mistakes.'

That might be the right approach if every speech you
make is market-sensitive: a mis-step or word out of place
can wipe millions off the stock market. But preparing for
two prime-time debates was very different. Many perceived
that Darling's strategy was just to get through without
making errors. But, in the crucible of referendum politics,

that modest aim would have been disastrous. He needed to be aggressive, passionate and, crucially, persuasive.

In contrast, Alex Salmond has always seen a media opportunity as exactly that: a chance to make a point, ram home a message and bring new people on board. All agreed the First Minister was a consummate showman, but not necessarily an assured debater: rhetoric took precedence over fact. Television naturally favours drama over detail, and, while Darling was always keen to get the argument right and employ key messages, he was also uncomfortable using cheap lines. Wisecracks and zingers were opportunities to deploy wit as a spotlight on the Yes campaign's flaws, but they were not Darling's style.

The former Chancellor was also out of practice. His last televised debate had been during the 2010 general election on Channel 4, alongside his Conservative and Liberal Democrat shadows, George Osborne and Vince Cable. An expert in presentation and broadcasting was needed to transform Darling and to lead a thorough preparation for the debates. Paul Sinclair suggested journalist turned media trainer Scott Chisholm. The two had worked together on the Alternative Vote referendum in 2011: an unsuccessful attempt to change Westminster's first-past-the-post system to a more proportional method. Sinclair had been the campaign's director of communications, and the two were good friends.

The standout line on Chisholm's CV was crafting Nick Clegg's knock-out performance for the 2010 leaders' debates. The Lib Dem leader unexpectedly outfoxed his rivals with a fresh, natural performance: a compelling alternative to the 'two tired old parties'. 'I agree with Nick' became a campaign catchphrase, while 61 per cent of viewers thought Clegg came out on top.

Blair McDougall was not originally keen on Chisholm or many of the others suggested, but Danny Alexander's recommendation to Darling sealed his involvement: 'If you're doing debates, get Chisholm,' he advised. Alexander had seen first-hand the way Clegg had been coached, and knew Chisholm could cope with the challenge.

Tall and broad with a bushy moustache, Scott Chisholm is a force of nature. The former Sky News anchor set the tone for debate prep with his frank and outspoken manner. He was positive and encouraging. 'He knew he had to get Darling pumped,' said one person involved. For the past twenty years, he had earned a six-figure salary training senior multi-national company execs for select committee and media appearances. It was only more recently he had gained a solid reputation with politicians.

Chisholm recognised that it was critical to treat Darling delicately. Everybody in Better Together wanted to be in on the debate prep: 'It was the fun part of the job,' said one source involved. Yet Chisholm was clear: only those whom Darling was completely comfortable with should be in the room. When the training began, the small team was a curious assortment and some had never even met before. In the first prep session, few recognised Ann Coffey, the Labour MP for Stockport. She had served as Darling's parliamentary private secretary (PPS) during his time as Chancellor of the Exchequer. Also present were Catherine MacLeod, Darling's special adviser at the Treasury, a former political editor of *The Herald* and a close friend of his wife Maggie.

Coffey and MacLeod were vital participants. Darling trusted them implicitly; both had supported him through his difficult time as Gordon Brown's Chancellor. Each possessed a knack for keeping him calm. When told he was doing well, he would not believe most people in the room, but his response was always different towards those two. 'They don't bullshit,' said one present. For a very male-dominated No campaign, this was one moment when three women were key – the third being Scottish Labour MSP Kezia Dugdale. Salmond's forceful style did not poll well with female voters, who were already more sceptical about independence.

Eddie Barnes, the Scottish Conservatives' director of strategy and communications, joined to provide a cross-party perspective. Brian Wilson, former Labour MP, *Scotsman* columnist and old friend of Darling, sat in the corner on a laptop, crafting the opening and closing statements. Wilson was a talented wordsmith, and Darling was a fan of his style. Paul Sinclair's niche was in the one-liners, smackdowns and bitchy comments. Gordon Aikman, the campaign's director of research, was drafted in to ensure everything being said was accurate, providing 'killer facts' and assisting with rebuttal. David Whitton – a dependable former MSP – also helped, contributing both advice from his experience at Scottish broadcaster STV, and the well-timed provision of sandwiches and coffee.

The campaign's now empty former headquarters in Glasgow's leafy Blythswood Square provided the venue for these top-secret sessions. At the back of the long narrow office, the set, as it would appear onscreen, was recreated with two lecterns. A large blackboard with a white circle drawn on was placed opposite Darling, so he could practise talking through the camera lens to viewers at home. Chisholm used his iPad as a countdown timer for the opening and closing statements, and Blair McDougall, by this point an experienced media performer, took the place of the moderator.

The three-part debate format would begin with opening statements. They would set the tone for the following ninety minutes and provided a free hit at the opposition, so a lot of time was spent crafting them. Each needed to summarise the campaign's key messages. Darling needed to be succinct, comfortable with the language – and persuasive. Words and phrases were constantly tweaked, added and deleted.

'If someone has a go at you, rise above it,' Darling was told. 'Don't descend into the gutter.' Cross-examination had been a regular part of Darling's life as an advocate in the 1980s. Detail was his strength. But Salmond was unlikely to put forward a conventional performance, and so preparations were made for all eventualities.

Darling needed to become acclimatised to the verbal barrage and inured to the frontal assault. Nothing coming out of Alex Salmond's mouth could shock or spook him. 'There's an optimistic man. He can cheer up a room by leaving it,' Paul Sinclair sneered, playing Salmond brilliantly. It was almost frightening. Having coached Scottish Labour leader Johann Lamont for her weekly bout at First Minister's Questions, Sinclair had studied Salmond's debating style and knew his weaknesses. He also had a visceral dislike of the First Minister.

Sinclair had done his homework on Darling, too, and ripped into him over his expenses as an MP, tracking down the most pathetically small claims. 'Can you explain why you charged the taxpayer for a 75p carrier bag?' 'Why did you claim hundreds of pounds for an IKEA chaise longue?' It continued to get increasingly personal: 'You're talking about economics, but this is the man who flipped his house! Which house did you make more out of?' In between rehearsals, the audience of advisers would arm Sinclair with ever more left-field insults. In response, lines were crafted that were an amalgam of Darling's dry wit and raw tabloid insult.

It was a fun exercise in an otherwise relentless campaign, and Darling was clearly enjoying himself – his caustic humour on show. Privately, he had long been damning of Salmond – a man he seemed genuinely to dislike. Darling was coached to lean into his lectern. He was trained to respond to questions by first looking at the audience member, before gazing directly at the TV camera. 'Make the camera come to you,' he was told. 'By speaking straight down the lens, they'll have no choice.' Darling asked if he should walk out from his lectern to talk straight to voters, but was advised against it: 'Once you move around, they're watching you move, not what you're saying.'

Feedback was blunt but constructive. However, in the final days of preparation, Scott Chisholm changed tack. It was time to get Darling 'in the zone'. Like a good sports psychologist, Chisholm knew that his player now needed to feel increasingly confident. 'Be careful when you're critiquing Alistair,' he told those giving feedback, when Darling was out of the room. 'We don't want to look like he's not making progress. We need to make sure we're measured and delicate.' Many came to the conclusion that Darling, a good debater and a highly intelligent man, was also quite shy.

The rhythm of preparation was important, and sessions were held daily. Darling's opener, cross-examination and quick-fire questions were rehearsed again and again. At weekends, the team was summoned to Darling's Edinburgh home, assembled around the kitchen table with cups of tea and black-pudding rolls. When preparations moved to the living room, Maggie Darling would offer tea and cake. It was a friendly, relaxed, informal environment, and Alistair Darling was most at ease.

On Tuesday 5 August, in the final hours before the STV debate, Paul Sinclair had truly mastered his Salmond impression with all the 'bluff, bluster and bombast'. For those watching, it was astonishing. Sinclair and Salmond had morphed into the same person. And, simultaneously, Darling was becoming noticeably nervous. By early afternoon, preparation was over. Alistair had lunch with his wife Maggie, Kezia Dugdale and Paul Sinclair, before taking a nap.

In the car to Glasgow's Royal Conservatoire, Darling was a little ratty. He sat quietly in the front seat. Driving was the campaign's administrator James McMordie. In the back, accompanying Darling, was a good-cop-bad-cop duo. One colleague described them as the 'nice, young and warm' Kezia Dugdale and the 'old, fat and threatening' Paul Sinclair. Gallows humour was the order of the journey. 'I could always crash the car,' McMordie suggested, interrupting the silence. There was a pause: 'Probably not a good idea,' Darling responded. Stopping at McDonald's – another suggestion – was also swiftly ruled out.

Backstage, Alex Salmond barely acknowledged his opponent. Darling sensed he was either extremely confident or not at all. Salmond was flanked by former SNP MSP Duncan Hamilton. When he bumped into Paul Sinclair backstage, Hamilton seemed confident the First Minister would wipe the floor with Darling. SNP MP Pete Wishart claimed: 'It'll be a slaughter worse than the Bannockburn re-enactment if they put out the angry, agitated Alistair to debate with the First Minister.'

As the clock struck 8 p.m., it was show time. From opposite sides, the two marched centre stage for a handshake, in front of the applauding audience. Salmond, having won the coin toss, gave his opening statement first. But, right from the start, it did not go to plan. His nerves were not noticeable until he moved onto his key pitch, and stumbled: 'The question is not should...' – he said, getting tongue-tied – '...*could* we become an independent country, but *should* we become an independent country?' Moving on to the proliferation of food banks, he argued: 'How is it, in this prosperous country of Scotland, we have thousands of children with families...' – again muddling through – '...families with children in this prosperous country reliant on food banks?' Rehearsed lines were jumbled and his gaze flickered between his notes and the audience.

There was also an early sign he would rely on messages seemingly aimed not at floating voters, but at core nationalist supporters: 'Project Fear are telling us that this country can't run our own affairs,' he said.

Darling, by contrast, performed his opening script smoothly. It was packed with key messages to appeal to Don't Knows: the referendum was the 'biggest decision that we've ever made in Scotland'; we can have 'the best of both worlds'; 'a vote for No Thanks to the *risk* of independence is not a vote for no change'. Any players of Better Together 'key-line bingo' would already have a full house. Darling also nailed his rival's obfuscation over the issue of currency during the cross-examination. He accused Salmond of dodging crucial questions that 'haven't been answered in the last two years' – questions the First Minister 'either can't or won't answer'. Darling continued: 'We cannot make this decision on the basis of guesswork, fingers crossed or' – jabbing his finger at Salmond – '*his* blind faith.'

The former Chancellor was a revelation. And, most

surprisingly of all for the audience, he was actually quite funny. When Salmond used the argument of Scotland not getting the government at Westminster it had voted for, Darling responded, gesturing at the First Minister: 'I didn't vote for him but I'm stuck with him.' It got an early, unexpected laugh.

Then came twelve minutes of cross-examination. Darling began: 'You said you want a currency union if we vote for independence, which seems to me a bit like getting a divorce and keeping the same joint bank account. If you do that, you've got to get an agreement, and the other side is saying no. So it won't happen. What's Plan B?'

Salmond replied: 'Well, we'll be keeping the pound, Alistair, because it's our pound as well as England's pound.'

In his second question, Darling probed again: 'What is your Plan B if you don't get a currency union? This is most important.'

The audience applauded, but Salmond's argument hardly changed: 'This is Scotland's pound. It doesn't belong to George Osborne. It doesn't belong to you.' Salmond then went on the attack, citing a *Newsnight* interview in which he claimed Darling said a currency union was 'logical and desirable'.

Darling batted that off and his questioning continued: 'I want you to do something that will be really difficult. I want you to contemplate, for just one minute, the fact you might be wrong. What is Plan B?' Perfectly puncturing the First Minister's perceived arrogance, this line by Brian Wilson elicited a mixture of cheers and groans from the crowd.

Alistair Darling clearly had the upper hand and Alex Salmond's answer did nothing to alter that: 'I am going to do something even more difficult than contemplating I'm wrong. I'm contemplating you were right last year when you said it was logical and desirable.' Groans from the audience and heckling interrupted Salmond's next line: 'I believe … I believe … I believe…'

Audience members shouted 'Answer the question!' and Darling interjected: 'You're not doing yourself any favours here, you know.' Again the audience showed their support. Darling then deployed a line thought up by Paul Sinclair: 'Any eight-year-old can tell you the flag of a country, the capital of a country and its currency. Now, I assume the flag is the Saltire. I assume our capital will still be Edinburgh. But you can't tell us what currency we will have. What is an eight-year-old going to make of that?'

Yet again, Salmond refused to develop his argument.

Darling moved to a method of deduction to uncover what Plan B might be – going through joining the euro and starting a brand-new currency – and was left with one option: 'dollarisation', the way Panama and Ecuador informally use the US dollar.

Salmond's well-rehearsed arguments, with their rhetorical arcs, ended with silence – no applause. For a man used to cheers and adulation, here there was none. The First Minister did get a hit highlighting Darling's 'record in charge of financial markets' as Chancellor of the Exchequer, but he had struggled to handle Darling's cross-examination.

Darling concluded: 'The answer to your question is that everyone is wrong except you. It beggars belief.'

In response, Alex Salmond took on a line of questioning that even surprised some on his own side. 'Why does the No campaign call itself Project Fear?' Salmond asked.

'It doesn't,' Darling shot back.

Some of the audience seemed unconvinced by Darling's

claim, but the First Minister's follow-ups continued on another unexpected topic: 'The No campaign have said that independence will mean we have to drive on the right-hand side of the road. Is that true, Alistair?'

It was a comment from Andy Burnham, a senior Labour colleague of Darling's. Yet, when pressed, the former Chancellor was mocking: 'He said it as a joke. Do you know what a joke is, Alex?'

Salmond cited a comment from the UK's Foreign Secretary Philip Hammond: 'Independence will make us more susceptible to attacks from outer space.'

Again a withering put-down: 'If we're going to have a bar-room chat and a series of jokes…' Darling said with exasperation and delight.

The European Union was added to this heady mix and the First Minister concluded his arguments with questions such as: 'Can you disavow these statements that have been made?' and 'Will you withdraw that claim from the No campaign website?'

Darling was in his comfort zone, making the most of his vast government experience, and running rings around Salmond. The First Minister, in contrast, with his upper lip sweating, realised he was losing the audience and losing the argument. Salmond's final line of questioning was his strongest, but it was too late to turn the tide of criticism coming his way: 'Could Scotland be a successful independent country?' he asked.

It was such a loaded question for Darling to answer: say 'no' and talk Scotland down, or say 'yes' and suggest your support for independence. So, the former Chancellor did his best to dodge.

'Do you agree?' Salmond repeated again and again, before saying: 'I feel like Jeremy Paxman and Michael Howard here.'

Yet Darling, by this point confident and enjoying himself, retorted: 'Well, you're more Michael Howard than Jeremy Paxman.' Before long, the twelve minutes was over, and Alex Salmond's free hit on his debating nemesis had failed completely.

Questions from the audience – the third and final section of the broadcast – seemed almost anti-climactic. STV's Bernard Ponsonby kept everything under tight control, with no room for over-confident audience members. There were questions on the currency, Scotland subsidising the rest of the UK, and tuition fees. Salmond had been told by STV the whole stage would not be lit. Yet his team were convinced of the 'authenticity' of walking in front of his lectern to address the audience. So he did. Into darkness. A question on pensions prompted a response from Darling more akin to a primer on personal finance than a persuasive vote-winning argument. The body language of audience members had changed: arms crossed, faces in hands, rubbing eyes.

As the evening came to a close, Darling's final one-minute statement was delivered straight to Scots watching at home. As the camera zoomed in, he did not look down to his lectern, he knew it off by heart: 'I am optimistic about Scotland's future ... we can have the best of both worlds.' In turn, Salmond's pitch for 'ambition over fear' received a sustained cheer. But, as that sound faded and the two debaters shook hands with the moderator, the winner had long been decided.

Paul Sinclair was backstage talking on the phone immediately. As Salmond's aide Duncan Hamilton passed him, the delighted Sinclair shouted over: 'I'd sack the coach if I were you.' Hamilton looked like he might explode.

Darling left the building swiftly. But, on the short journey

back to campaign HQ, this time on foot, flanked by buzzing, delighted aides, he said very little. He had done what
he needed to. Cheered into Better Together's Savoy Centre
offices, a party with beer and pizza was already in full
swing. Everyone was surprised by Darling's performance.
Campaign staff were taken aback and jubilant. Some made
the rare move of giving Darling a hug: 'He was like a corpse
with rigor mortis,' said one. The victor was not interested in
praise: all he wanted to do was give others the credit.

'Twelve texts!' Darling declared. He was not a fan of the
SMS, but he *was* a big family man, desperate to speak to
his son, Calum. He seemed suddenly at peace once he knew
his performance had filial approval. Soon, an ICM poll confirmed Scots believed Darling had beaten Salmond 56 per
cent to 44 per cent. A buoyed-up Scott Chisholm called, as
did a congratulatory Ed Miliband.

Driven back to his hotel, Darling invited a few of the
team up for a drink. When they arrived at the door to the
Darlings' room, Maggie opened the door. Knowing how big
a moment it was for him, she was beaming with pride and in
tears. He was in a similar state. They had a 'cuddly moment',
according to one present – it was awkward to be there. The
staff who had been looking after Darling were welcomed
into the cramped room for drinks, and, sitting on the end of
the bed, watched the coverage of the event on news channels. A grand win, celebrated modestly.

On Friday 22 August, during preparations for the second
televised debate, Blair McDougall got a call from a friend
who had just been at BBC Scotland's Pacific Quay base.
Former First Minister Henry McLeish was also there for
an interview, and McDougall's contact claimed to have
overheard him saying off air: 'I'm a No voter now, but I

reserve the right to change that position publicly. So watch this space.'

Panicking that this endorsement would be announced by Salmond live on TV, helping Yes Scotland regain momentum, McDougall and his team tried to work out how to blow McLeish's cover. They would have to either force him to say he was a No voter, or get him out early for Yes.

'Just heard from impeccable source that Henry McLeish endorsing Yes on Monday,' McDougall tweeted. 'Hardly a surprise but he's entitled to his view.' McLeish denied it, but was furious at the brouhaha created and complained to Gordon Brown.

ROUND TWO

In the grand central hall of Kelvingrove Art Gallery and Museum, below the huge pipe organ, a purple backdrop with three silver lecterns had been constructed. Glenn Campbell, the BBC's respected moderator, stood towards the edge of the stage, instead of in between the two debaters – to the objection of both campaigns. 'It's like the referee at the side of the pitch,' one aide complained. Originally built for a showdown on EU membership between Nick Clegg and Nigel Farage four months earlier, the set had been transported up from London. The BBC did not have the cash to construct a new one.

It was Monday 25 August, the second and final televised referendum debate. The next morning, postal ballots would be sent out – the method by which one in six Scots would vote. After Alex Salmond's shaky first performance, the pressure was on the First Minister to up his game. In contrast to their first encounter, Yes supporters were protesting outside the building as Darling arrived. Another difference was the two leaders shaking hands before. With only one door to the stage, the rivals bumped into each other. Darling detected his opponent was in a better mood.

Salmond had won the coin toss and chose to deliver his opening statement first. There were cheers from the audience as he confidently set out how Scots could 'complete the home-rule journey'. In contrast, Darling stumbled with his introduction, which focused on one issue: currency. It was early confirmation of the likely focus of Darling's eight-minute cross-examination. The Better Together leader also attempted to pre-empt a change in the First Minister's tactics: 'A good line isn't always a good answer,' he said.

As the programme progressed, discussions moved to the NHS, with some vitriolic contributions from the audience: 'Don't believe a word that comes out of Alistair Darling's mouth,' an older woman shouted. 'You're a hypocrite, Mr Darling. You and your Labour government started the privatisation of the health service.'

'No, we didn't,' Darling responded softly.

She continued: 'I hope you can feel Aneurin Bevan sitting on your shoulder.'

Salmond was thrown by the hostility towards him in the previous debate, but this time his opponent was getting a taste. Darling recognised some of the audience from the protests outside.

After a faltering start, it got worse for the No team forty-eight minutes in, when Alistair Darling started his cross-examination. 'I want to go back to currency,' he said, as members of the audience heckled and booed. 'Because, on Sunday...' – he continued – '...on Sunday, I read in the newspapers...' Spooked, Darling was struggling to read his pre-written question.

In Better Together's preparations, nobody had ever stopped to consider starting the cross-examination on anything apart from currency. Focus groups between the two debates continued to show it remained the most powerful argument in persuading undecided voters to vote No. After being delighted at their success three weeks before, perhaps a different audience would watch this time? They assumed they would get away with recycling the strategy. But it failed. For colleagues in the campaign HQ who were responsible for these tactics, it was excruciating to watch.

'I've heard of one-trick ponies,' Salmond responded, 'but this must be the most extraordinary thing tonight.' Cheers and applause. The plan had been to ask one question on currency, to 'touch and go'. But once that went pear-shaped, Darling took the snap decision to stay on the topic. If he followed the original plan and changed subjects, it would look like he was running scared. He repeated the successful 'imagine you might be wrong' line from the first debate, but Salmond swiftly retaliated with: 'Even your insults are re-treaded ... this is incredible.' The debate descended fast. For long periods, the two talked over each other. In the gallery, the programme's director had a difficult job choosing which shot to use: it was so unclear who to focus on. An exasperated Darling turned around to the moderator Glenn Campbell who had barely said a word and uttered: 'Hopeless, this is hopeless.'

Proceedings moved on to Salmond's eight-minute cross-examination. The First Minister was not going to make the mistake of being mild-mannered and polite this time. 'I will only step in if it gets too heated,' Campbell announced. This was to be a well-crafted, fast-paced, ruthless takedown, using a debating technique Nicola Sturgeon had perfected in previous – if less high-profile – TV encounters. First, Salmond began with a very specific, almost unanswerable question: 'How many children in Scotland is it estimated will move into poverty by 2020 given the UK government's welfare spending cuts?' Darling dodged with 'too many children', but, two seconds after finishing his question, Salmond was already interrupting: 'How many? How many, Alistair? How many? How many?'

Within twenty seconds, as Darling struggled to form an argument, Salmond had moved on: 'Would it surprise you to know it's 100,000 extra children in Scotland moving into poverty with the welfare reforms? Do you think that's a price worth paying for Westminster government?' It was a simple yes or no, but in either answer lay a trap.

As soon as Darling started criticising Salmond's record in government, the topic changed: 'If we move to the National Health Service. "Devolution means they can't run down and privatise our NHS directly, the way they're doing in England. But what they can do is starve it of resources. They are cutting back on the money provided to the Scottish government." Do you think that's an accurate statement?' As Darling's frustration increased, Salmond repeated the question again and again: 'Is that an accurate statement?' He then continued: 'That is a quote not from the Scottish National Party, or the Scottish government, but from Unison the union … Is it an accurate statement?' As the Better Together leader diverted the conversation, the audience became increasingly frustrated: 'Answer the question!' they shouted.

It was unilluminating television and, although Alistair Darling was rattled and his train of thought disrupted, he responded with gusto and received some applause. 'Why are you waving your hands at me, Alistair?' Salmond asked when Darling look liked he might be making headway.

Yet it was the First Minister's final question that was to prove most bruising. The topic – job-creating powers – was a weakness of Darling's. He had not been fully briefed. 'Name three job-creating powers that the Better Together parties intend to give to the Scottish Parliament,' Salmond asked. Darling's efforts to think fast failed, and his rival soon concluded: 'You've just made a wonderful case for voting Yes in the referendum.'

The ninety-minute broadcast concluded with some more audience contributions, supposedly focused on the post-referendum climate. Most either advocated a Yes vote, or were critical of the No campaign. Perhaps this was indicative of Alistair Darling's poor performance, and the comparatively passionate and vocal nature of Yes supporters. But Better Together chiefs – Darling included – were convinced the audience was skewed to the advantage of those advocating independence. Pollsters ComRes, who had selected all but twenty of the audience members, insist their methodology was rock solid. Those in the other small section were recruited via the BBC Scotland website, and many suggest this group may have been responsible for the problems. Better Together advisers claim that, in a subsequent meeting with BBC Scotland's director Ken Macquarie, the corporation did not defend the balance of their audience.

In any case, it was universally recognised that Salmond had made a career-defining comeback. A *Guardian*/ICM poll of Scots watching claimed Salmond had won 71 per cent to 29 per cent. 'The whole thing was a car crash,' said one source close to Darling.

Publicly, Better Together spun the encounter as being demeaned by a 'shouty, blustery Salmond', yet Darling had hardly been calm. 'Not tonight, Darling' was the *Scottish Sun*'s front page. Even the Labour-friendly *Daily Record* headlined their coverage of the 'mêlée on the telly' as 'Salmond bounces back'.

In the car back to Better Together HQ, Darling was furious: 'The fucking BBC,' he raged. It was almost unheard of him to swear in front of staff. But he felt the audience had swung it for his rival. He was also frustrated with himself for a weak performance, and felt he had not prepared enough. Darling was desperate to speak to Maggie, but her phone had died so he could not get through.

It had been a bad night, Darling was acutely aware he had lost and there was a markedly different tone at campaign HQ. Staff tried to tell him he had done well, but he knew they were not being genuine. He apologised. Darling was not upset or disappointed, he just felt resigned.

Colleagues expected him to leave swiftly to return to his hotel. He would not want company, they thought. He had every right to feel raw. Yet Mrs Darling was insistent that some of the team, including long-term adviser Catherine MacLeod and her partner George Mackie, joined them at the Grand Central Hotel for a drink. Otherwise, Maggie thought, it would demonstrate there really was a problem. Unlike the first debate three weeks earlier, the Darlings had a suite. Trays of drinks and Marks & Spencer sandwiches were shared around. Alistair was not depressed, but relieved the debates were over. His formal role was done. But the real race was only just beginning.

CHAPTER 8

NIGHTMARE ON SAUCHIEHALL STREET

The day after Alistair Darling's defeat in the second referendum debate, Better Together posted a video on their Facebook and Twitter sites – a short political broadcast to be shown on the BBC and STV that evening. Lasting two minutes and forty seconds, it was a monologue, delivered at the kitchen table by a Scottish mum. It was scripted, almost entirely verbatim, from the contributions of female participants in focus groups. 'We were relaying back to people what they were thinking, holding up a mirror to female C2DE voters,' explained someone involved.

'Best time of the day, this,' it began, the unnamed mother sitting down with a cup of tea. 'When they're all out. Nice and quiet. Gives you time to think.'

'The woman who made up her mind' has been viewed over 500,000 times on Better Together's YouTube channel – nearly ten times as many hits as the next most popular video: 'Alistair Darling's ice bucket challenge' – so that might suggest it was a hit. In fact, it was a public relations disaster.

'D'you know? My Paul is worse than the telly these days,' she says, talking to camera. 'He will not leave off about the referendum.' The mum continues: 'He started again, first thing this morning: "Have you made a decision yet?" I was like, "It's too early to be discussing politics. Eat your cereal."' Soon 'eat your cereal' was the joke insult of choice. Parody videos and memes were posted online, and the hashtag #PatronisingBTLady started trending on Twitter.

One Yes supporter online described the video as 'a total cringe bag of sexist patronising tripe. Don't fall for it people!' Another tweeted: 'The dour sexist No camp want to transport us back to the '50s. Over my dead body.' 'Thinking is hard. Vote no,' read one particularly popular meme.

Sarah Waddell, the London-based Glaswegian actor performing the controversial monologue, managed to keep a low profile after the advert aired. Her Twitter account does not include any opinions on the referendum. Elsewhere, her skills are listed as including salsa dancing, karate and cow-milking. The advert has been omitted from Waddell's extensive CV.

'We did not test it,' admitted one senior strategist. A lack of money with the onset of the regulated spending period meant no internal polling was carried out between March and the end of the campaign. Focus groups were still taking place, but this advert was never shown to voters before being aired. It was presumed, because so much of the script was taken from women in the target segments, that there would be no issues.

The male-dominated campaign leadership was a factor. 'It was as patronising as the Nats described, and fed directly into the nationalist narrative,' a female Better Together activist said. Yet one senior campaign figure still stands behind the broadcast: 'It's annoying it became a story because it's a hugely effective piece of political communication. I object to the sneering way people look at it, especially the middle-class commentariat, because that is what people were saying, that's the conversation they were having.'

If that advert had elicited a critical mauling, another – which never saw the light of day – would have been far more controversial. This was scare tactics on steroids: a negative, dark, moody and threatening broadcast. 'Girders were breaking, oil was spurting out. It was awful,' said one campaigner. 'There were kids walking up to the edge of a cliff looking over as the UK was being ripped apart,' said another. 'It was an "in emergency, break glass and let's roll this bad boy out" option.' The advert was made at a cost of £50,000, but was never deployed.

When the campaign team gathered around Rob Shorthouse's computer to get a preview, there was stunned silence. Staff looked at each other with concern. 'Surely we can't do that?' said one. Shorthouse was equally sceptical. Yet it was Maggie Darling who ensured voters never saw it. 'It's like *Nightmare on Sauchiehall Street*,' she told her husband, referring to the major Glasgow thoroughfare on which the campaign headquarters was based. Darling made it clear to her husband, in no uncertain terms, that the advert was a disaster.

On the same day the #PatronisingBTLady advert was released, the final leg of Jim Murphy's '100 towns in 100 days' tour began in Aberdeen. The atmosphere had already turned negative, with the first TV showdown between Alistair Darling and Alex Salmond in early August a turning point. 'It properly kicked off after Alistair won the first debate,' said a Better Together staff member. 'It got nasty after that.'

In Shawlands, Murphy was called a 'fucking parasite', and in Wishaw he was told, 'You're a Quisling.' In Motherwell, a table of Better Together campaign materials was thrown over

with a man shouting 'You're a traitor!' at Murphy. The team
had started using their mobile phones to film each event in
case of violence. They were keen that, if tensions flared, there
would be footage as evidence: to protect the staff and also
as a record of what Murphy was saying, so his words could
not be distorted or taken out of context.

On 27 August 2014, the tour was due to stop in Dundee.
But a far bigger event was happening that day: for the first
time in years, Alistair Darling and Gordon Brown would
appear together on stage at a joint event. Campaign strategists were keen to use the pair's putting aside of their political
differences to promote the positive side of the campaign.

Legendary sports broadcaster Archie Macpherson was
also due to speak. He arrived at the Caird Hall first, with
his wife. Brown entered soon after, followed by his security
detail and media adviser Bruce Waddell. The Macphersons
discussed football with the former Prime Minister, until
Alistair Darling walked in, a few minutes late. It was the
first time the pair had been in the same room for a long time.
Their grievances had been well aired. 'Gordon,' Darling
nodded. 'Alistair,' Brown replied. And that was it. No shaking of hands. No 'How are you doing?' No general chit-chit.
To those witnessing this much-anticipated reunion, it seemed
utterly bizarre. Two men who had been close for decades,
who had lived and worked side by side at the highest levels
of government – their relationship reduced to a nod of
the head.

Later, as the pair stood outside the hall waiting to go in,
there was some – minor – small talk. 'You go in front of me,'
Darling offered. 'No, no. You're in charge,' Brown responded. No warmth in their voices. Although it was a spectacle
seeing these two political foes together again, this carefully

planned Better Together news story was about to be up-staged, and, this time, it was by one of their own supporters.

Aged seventy-nine, Archie Macpherson was a popu-list addition to the line-up. But no one expected him to upstage the two politicians. He started his eight-minute speech, explaining why he wanted to speak out: 'Sitting watching the obfuscation and evasion streaming out of the independence campaign, I couldn't stand it any longer,' he said. Macpherson attacked the 'deception, deceit and fantasy' of Alex Salmond's campaign, before encouraging voters to 'say "no thanks".' There was rapturous applause from activists, and the next day's papers documented his 'electrifying speech'.

Later that day, just around the corner from the Caird Hall, the Murphy tour team was preparing for another street event. And they were worried. 'We thought if Jim was to be hit or assaulted, it would be then,' said a member of the group. Yes activists had surrounded the No campaign's planned meeting point. 'If we were to go to where we'd ad-vertised, there would be trouble.' But although there was yelling on both sides, and Murphy was told, 'Go back to London, go back to your nest of paedophiles,' there was no violence.

The tour team thought they were past the worst. 'The sense was it will be better from here, and the next day in Fife would be easier,' explained a campaigner.

Just before 3 p.m. the following day, the '100 towns' tour team reached Kirkcaldy. It was raining and miserable but they were nearing the end of a hard week. At the last minute, Murphy and his adviser Lynsey Jackson decided to move the meeting location to a different section of the road. But, as they arrived to begin the event, protestors appeared.

'Nationalists started following us down the street. It was the most physically aggressive event we'd seen, with people elbowing us out the way.'

'I'll fucking knock you out,' a protestor told James Glossop, a photographer for *The Times*, who has an English accent. This Yes supporter, a burly man named Stuart Mackenzie, soon left the meeting on a mission to Tesco.

As Murphy tried to speak atop his crates, surrounded by blue Yes signs, No supporters shouted, 'Let him speak!' But their voices were lost in the barrage.

'Then I saw Jim stagger on his Irn-Bru crate,' explained one No campaigner. 'I didn't realise it, but he was dodging an egg.' Mackenzie had returned from the supermarket with a box of half a dozen farm-fresh projectiles. Murphy skilfully avoided the first, but his attacker walked around the crowd, and, at close range, threw an egg at Murphy's back. It cracked over his white shirt and Mackenzie swiftly walked away.

'I'm really sorry this sort of thing has happened,' one local Yes campaigner apologised. There were those on the pro-independence side keen to smooth things over. But the damage had been done.

Murphy returned to the Glasgow office with Lynsey Jackson and convened a discussion with Blair McDougall, David Ross and Frank Roy. 'Fuck! This is great,' said one at the meeting, realising that they could exploit their opponents' actions for their own gain. 'It looks great: Nat bastards chasing us off the street.'

Jim Murphy immediately saw the opportunity to shape the news agenda, but Frank Roy was more preoccupied with the safety of campaign staff. It was swiftly agreed that the tour would be suspended on safety grounds and Murphy would hold a press conference the next day at Better

Together's Blythswood Square office, which, because of a contractual oversight, remained in occasional use long after the team had relocated to the Savoy Centre.

When Blair McDougall searched pro-independence groups on social media, he found a long trail of posts tipping off Yes supporters with the details of Murphy's events across Scotland.

The local branch of the Yes campaign in Kirkcaldy, the scene of the egg-throwing, posted on Facebook: 'Jim Murphy from the No camp is appearing in Fife tomorrow – Leven High St at 1.30, and Kirkcaldy High St at 3.00; let's give a warm YES welcome.' One Yes supporter had commented: 'Anyone able to attend … and make his visit one to remember?'

On Friday 29 August, the suspension of Murphy's tour was announced. 'Jim did his best concerned face for the cameras,' said a Labour source. Murphy told journalists: 'We've been in contact with the police to discuss safety because Yes Scotland have organised mobs to turn up at these meetings, and tried to silence people.' Despite the serious tone, Murphy still joked: 'I don't mind heckles and – d'you know what? – I don't even mind people throwing eggs. That's just a dry-cleaning bill.'

In a YouTube video compilation of Murphy's various encounters released that weekend, he said, 'Yes Scotland turned this tap on – it is really very sinister – and they can turn it off.'

There was no evidence of the central Yes Scotland campaign office attempting to disrupt the tour although activists from some local groups were most definitely co-ordinating protests. Stuart Mackenzie's lawyer later told a court that the egg-thrower was 'not part of any concerted attempt to disrupt meetings by Better Together and if there are concert-ed efforts he wants no part of them'. He was sentenced to eighty hours' unpaid work on a community payback order.

Alex Salmond called Murphy's allegations that Yes Scotland had been involved 'ridiculous', telling Sky News: 'If Mr Murphy comes bawling and shouting on a street corner near you any time soon, keep doing your shopping. Go on with what you're doing. It's just like a guy with an "end is nigh" sign round his neck: he'll go away soon.'

A few days later, on Tuesday 2 September, wearing a freshly laundered white shirt, Jim Murphy resumed his tour in Edinburgh. 'It was always going to be suspended, and would always start again,' admitted one Better Together source. The authorities had agreed it was safe to do so. 'We spoke to the police,' explained one person involved, 'they said, "Ach, you're fine, fuck off."'

A location in the centre of the capital meant a large pack of photographers and TV cameras were there to welcome Murphy, alongside a huge group of No supporters, many, rather incongruously, Conservative Party members. 'I don't know where we'd be without them,' joked a Labour activist. 'Morningside is a new Labour heartland.'

The Sun had sent a journalist in a chicken outfit to join the mêlée, but Murphy deftly embraced this new arrival and posed smiling with him, creating another memorable campaign image. There were just two protestors, one shout-ing, 'People are being deceived,' the other quietly holding a Yes Saltire.

Whether raising the profile of these angry encounters convinced anyone to vote No is unclear. Many in Better Together are doubtful: 'No one changed their minds,' said someone involved. 'But it reinforced views. People who hated Jim hated him even more.'

Later that day, Ruth Davidson was sitting in the campaign's Blythswood Square office with a team of advisers preparing for a debate on STV in which she would be going head to head with Scottish Green Party co-convener Patrick Harvie to discuss 'Scotland's place in the world'. Rob Shorthouse got a phone call. It was *The Sun*'s chief political correspondent Kevin Schofield calling to tell him the numbers from the latest poll in the next morning's paper. After excluding Don't Knows, Yes were on 47 per cent, No on 53 per cent.

Ruth Davidson took one look at Shorthouse's face and was instantly concerned. 'Shit,' he said. As a senior staff member, he was not supposed to spook people, but Shorthouse suddenly caught himself swearing. This shift was bigger and quicker than expected. There was already a febrile atmosphere in the country, and, with the campaign based in the centre of Glasgow, that mood was inescapable.

'Victory in reach for Salmond' was the *Times* headline the next day. The First Minister was now within 'spitting distance' of victory, said *The Sun*. There had been an eight-point swing in just four weeks. And, with another poll due that weekend, it was all about to get worse.

CHAPTER 9

PANIC ATTACK

ELEVEN DAYS TO GO

George Osborne was sitting in his ministerial car on the way to New Broadcasting House for an interview on the BBC's *Andrew Marr Show*. It was Sunday 7 September and Westminster was waking up to the real possibility of the break-up of the United Kingdom. According to a poll published in the *Sunday Times* that morning, the Yes campaign was ahead: 51 to 49 per cent. 'Yes leads in Scots poll shock' read the front page. According to Rupert Murdoch: 'Everything [was] up for grabs'.

But, among the Chancellor's pile of newspapers in the back of the car, another had caught his eye. *The Observer*'s headline was: 'Scots to be offered radical new deal in bid to save the union.' Quoting a senior government minister – some suspected Danny Alexander – it said: 'The people of Scotland are to be offered a historic opportunity to devise a federal future for their country before next year's general election.'

Osborne phoned David Cameron, who was at Balmoral

on his annual visit to the Queen's Highland estate. The Chancellor asked if he had seen the *Observer* article? Should he stand it up or knock it down?

The Prime Minister was clear: you can't knock it down.

In the TV studio, Andrew Marr quizzed Osborne about the article: 'Is this a plan agreed by all the main Westminster parties or not?'

'Yes,' Osborne replied. 'So we've been discussing with the other main political parties in Westminster – with the Labour Party, with the Liberal Democrats. We are working on that plan of action. We will set it out in the next few days.'

But Marr wanted details: 'And, to be clear, we're talking about more tax-raising powers?'

'More tax-raising powers, more...'

'Going as far as fiscal autonomy?' Marr interrupted.

'Well, much greater fiscal autonomy,' Osborne replied, doing his best to freestyle through the interview. There was, as yet, no cross-party agreement on the details of further devolution.

As Osborne left the studio, 330 miles to the north, Scottish Labour's policy expert Ross Christie was asleep at home in Edinburgh. He was suddenly awoken by a text. Christie's eyes widened and irritation transformed into intrigue as he read it: 'The tectonic plates may be starting to move soon on more devolution. I might need your help.' Christie knew he had better get up.

Sixty minutes later, the tone had changed: 'Am now drafting material which I will send in an hour for urgent review,' the text read. Christie was, by this time, on his way to the Scottish Parliament. A dishevelled figure that masks a furious intellect, he was the man responsible for Labour's policy development in Scotland. This unexpected text correspondence was from Jim Gallagher.

Brown had, as usual, been up at dawn at his home in North Queensferry, overlooking the Firth of Forth. He had mastered the complexities of devolution months before, possessed a far deeper understanding of the issues than any of the UK party leaders and, now, in the final ten days of the campaign – with the help of Gallagher and Christie – he could put that knowledge into action. He knew this was his chance. In the coming days, the former Prime Minister was to make the political performance of his career and redefine his legacy.

TEN DAYS TO GO

The next morning, as Torsten Bell stepped off the Caledonian Sleeper, he looked up at Glasgow Central station's famous clock. It was 7.18 a.m. He knew the next ten days would be intense. There was no time to waste.

Ed Miliband had sent Bell, his director of policy and one of his most trusted advisers, to Scotland to bolster the No campaign in its crucial final days. Having worked in the Treasury as an adviser to Alistair Darling, Bell remained close to the former Chancellor. Maggie Darling had even advised on the catering for his wedding. Bell had been Miliband's key link to Scotland for months, visiting Edinburgh or Glasgow every six to eight weeks. Now he was up for a longer stay, with a clear brief: get a grip on the campaign and make things happen.

The newsstands he passed on his journey to the Better Together headquarters made bleak reading for anyone in the No camp. Twenty-four hours after YouGov's poll for the *Sunday Times*, the rest of the print media were catching up.

'Panic attack' was *The Sun*'s headline. 'Ten days to save the union' warned the *Daily Telegraph*. 'Don't let me be last Queen of Scotland' screamed the *Daily Mirror*. But most striking of all was the front page of the *Daily Record* – Scotland's left-leaning tabloid – slating the three UK party leaders as 'three blithe monkeys' covering their ears, eyes and mouths to cries for further devolution. 'Hear no devo, see no devo, speak no devo' read the headline on Scotland's second biggest-selling paper.

An angry front-page editorial argued: 'The three leaders have been too complacent or arrogant in their refusal to present a credible and unified alternative. It is frankly not good enough.'

The paper's editor Murray Foote had a growing sense of frustration with the lack of a clear offer on further powers for Scotland. So, later that day, after the *Record*'s critical front page, he assembled his top team of executives around the long wooden boardroom table in his vast Glasgow office. 'Does anybody believe what they're hearing about further powers?' Foote asked. As he went around the table for responses, every member of his team said no.

Monday 8 September would mark the start of a frantic series of interventions, as the three pro-UK parties battled to save the United Kingdom, and David Cameron fought to save his job. And, with no time to waste, further devolution was thrust centre stage.

Margaret Thatcher's PR adviser Lord Tim Bell once said there are only two election campaigns: 'It's time for change', or 'Don't let the other lot muck it up'. But the Scottish independence referendum – with its sky-high levels of democratic engagement – was different. No pro-UK politician was willing to simply argue: 'Stay with what you've got.' An offer of more devolution was an essential component of the No campaign, yet, up until that point, the three parties had failed to square that circle.

Better Together's polling suggested Scots supported a move to so-called 'devo max' – power over all areas bar defence and foreign affairs. Yet few voters understood what powers Scotland already had, or were able to articulate what further powers they specifically wanted. 'They had absolutely no idea,' said one senior strategist, 'meaning there was no correct answer to the question of what more to offer.'

Focus groups did little to help: support for 'devo max' seemed more emotional than practical for voters. 'Much of the electorate believed decisions should be taken in Scotland in every area possible, up to the point when it becomes incredibly risky,' said one researcher. Yet when a list of powers already devolved was read out, participants were astonished: 'They were silent, looking at each other,' according to one present.

This puzzle was not helped by the divergent constitutional positions of the three pro-UK parties. The Liberal Democrats had a longstanding policy of federalism. There was a schism within the Labour Party, where MPs and MSPs disagreed on powers moving from Westminster to Holyrood. And some in the Conservatives admitted they were 'reluctantly being dragged along' to further devolution.

At Better Together's headquarters, Ed Miliband's adviser Torsten Bell was making his mark. 'He marched in and took charge,' explained one senior figure. 'He rubs people up the wrong way, but has great ability and proved very effective.'

After two and a half years of campaigning, most of the

staff were exhausted. 'In the last weeks, we staggered toward the finish without anyone leading apart from Gordon from afar,' a Better Together source admitted.

Bell's arrival brought a renewed drive to win. 'He's a fucking smart, Scandinavian, baby-faced assassin who comes with the authority of the leader,' said a colleague. 'Unlike anyone else, he is able to sit there and make decisions on behalf of the Labour Party. He has the gravitas and licence to get on with it.'

Labour advisers from the Blair years were also hauled into service, including John McTernan and Alastair Campbell. The latter was in the office studying the campaign's polling data and Douglas Alexander's messaging one day, when he concluded: 'This is a patriotic argument. You want people who love Scotland to vote No. The message should be "Love Scotland, Vote No".' Blair McDougall was relieved: his team had recently come to the same conclusion and ordered thousands of pounds worth of placards with that exact slogan.

Determined to keep control of the news agenda, Better Together worked alongside Gordon Brown to ensure that, over the next three days, they could take maximum control of media coverage. A three-part plan was hatched starting with an intervention that evening from the former Prime Minister.

Loanhead Miners Welfare & Social Club in Midlothian was used to hosting bingo nights, Weight Watchers meetings and over-fifties dance classes. But, for Gordon Brown's serious speech on Scottish devolution, the beer mats had been stashed away and the dance floor populated with chairs.

On Monday evening, in front of a grey-haired audience of Labour supporters, Brown outlined an ambitious timetable for new powers. It was bizarre – a former Prime Minister essentially announcing government legislation. 'A

No vote on 18 September will not be an end point, but the starting gun for action on 19 September, when, straight away, we will kick off a plan to deliver the enhanced devolution that we want,' Brown argued.

Proposals, set out in a command paper, were to be published by the UK government in October, it was announced. After consultation, a White Paper would be published in November, and a new Scotland Bill drafted by January 2015. 'This was breakneck speed, but, most importantly, it was tangible,' said one strategist. 'It was something real that people could point at and hold us to.'

Yes Scotland responded: 'Gordon Brown is in no position to offer anything – he is a back-bench MP, and the Tories are in power at Westminster.' But Downing Street welcomed the intervention from its former occupant: 'We are content with the proposed timetable,' said a spokesman.

NINE DAYS TO GO

'How can you be a Tory, Ruth?' It was Scottish Labour leader Johann Lamont's regular lament to her Conservative counterpart Ruth Davidson, as they struck up the most unlikely of friendships. Lamont, a strong feminist, was 'quite conflicted in that she's Old Labour and Ruth's the enemy', one observer commented, characterising their interaction as an 'auntie–niece relationship'.

Alongside Scottish Liberal Democrat leader Willie Rennie, Lamont and Davidson worked closely together over the campaign, ending up as a surprisingly tight unit. They looked out for each other. In the final weeks, Davidson and Lamont worried that Willie Rennie was getting down about the likely referendum outcome, and disappearing into himself. Both women would send Rennie supportive texts: 'We can do this,' read one.

The three leaders had already held two joint events committing to further devolution. At one stage, an adviser had suggested emphasising their point by carving the pledge in stone. Fortunately, Lamont kiboshed the idea, arguing it would 'look like a gravestone'. Later, Ed Miliband would resurrect the same concept during the general election: it was a PR disaster.

On Tuesday 9 September, this cross-party Holyrood troika held its third media call to promise more powers, supporting Gordon Brown's timetable. The Scottish Parliament and activists holding 'Best of both worlds' placards were the backdrop as Lamont told the assembled press she was 'delighted to endorse the delivery plan'.

However, one senior Conservative believed the event 'became a cleaning-up exercise for Osborne's *Marr* appearance', in which some argue the Chancellor accidentally overcommitted. The SNP's Angus Robertson dubbed it a 'cynical last-minute bribe'.

Over in Glasgow, Gordon Brown was preparing to make another speech, this time on the NHS. After the first TV debate in early August, the Yes campaign had succeeded in persuading many Scots to join their cause with the emotive argument that NHS privatisation in England would impact on the health service in Scotland. The UK government denied this, pointing out that Scotland's health service was already devolved.

Yet, in focus groups, the issue was resonating with undecided voters. 'It gave real power to the "no more Tories ever" argument,' explained one senior figure. 'These people had already decided that Tories would want to privatise the NHS. So not just for Scotland's future, but for the NHS's future, many were persuaded to choose Yes.'

This shrinkage in support was overwhelmingly among very 'culturally Labour' people, meaning Better Together needed a trusted Labour figure to communicate their counter-argument. At one meeting, the shared conclusion was: 'There aren't many problems to which the solution is "Send for Gordon Brown!" But this most definitely is one.'

Brown had already made one intervention on the NHS, but, because it had been at an evening event in North Lanarkshire, it got very limited coverage. David Cameron approached Brown directly with a plea to return to the subject: it was a powerful speech. 'You need to deliver another,' Cameron said.

In front of a room full of Labour supporters, Brown's voiced cracked with emotion as he spoke of his late baby daughter, who had died from a brain haemorrhage in 2002. 'The NHS did everything for my baby Jennifer,' he said, close to tears. The former Prime Minister spoke also of his own experiences as a patient: 'When I lost the sight of my eye and faced the prospect of going blind, my sight was saved by the NHS.' He continued: 'Do you think that I or anybody else who cares about the NHS would stand by and do nothing if we thought the NHS was going to be privatised in Scotland and its funds were going to be cut? Would we stand back and do nothing without a fight? Of course not.'

EIGHT DAYS TO GO

Part three of the devolution strategy took place on Wednesday 10 September, when the three Westminster leaders made a highly unusual move and scrapped Prime Minister's Questions in the House of Commons to travel up and campaign in Scotland. 'There is a lot that divides us – but there's one thing on which we agree passionately: the United Kingdom is better together,' said a joint statement. The last time PMQs was cancelled was in 2009, after the death of David Cameron's son Ivan.

Alex Salmond delighted in telling reporters: 'The No campaign is in complete and utter disarray, and they are making this farce up as they go along.' Many pro-UK politicians and activists had warned against the move: 'It will look panicked. It will devalue whatever you say. And it will reinforce you're coming up from Westminster on a day trip,' one senior Conservative advised to no avail.

Clegg visited the Borders, Miliband travelled to Cumbernauld, and Cameron made a speech at the Scottish Widows headquarters in Edinburgh, saying: 'I would be heartbroken if this family of nations ... was torn apart.' He also emphasised that voters should not treat this as an election: 'If you're fed up with effing Tories', this was not a chance to 'give them a kick', the Prime Minister said. It was a blunt phrase, and one Cameron had written himself.

'This is just a tremor. If there is a Yes vote we will see the earthquake.' Chief Secretary to the Treasury Danny Alexander knew the potency of the YouGov poll; its tangible effect on financial markets could be used to the No campaign's advantage by emphasising their key message of risk. The day after the poll was published, the pound sterling fell to its lowest level in ten months, and billions were wiped off the value of Scottish-based businesses including RBS, Lloyds Banking Group and Standard Life.

In addition, the poll galvanised the pro-UK parties to

campaign tirelessly in the final ten days. It also gave a strong message to No supporters: this is so close; you must get out and vote. Companies previously sceptical of getting embroiled in the referendum debate made strong public statements. On the same day that Prime Minister's Questions was cancelled, oil giants BP and Shell spoke out against a Yes vote, Standard Life warned that independence could see transfer of investments to new companies in England, and Lloyds Banking Group confirmed its head office would move south of the border. Nicola Sturgeon described these announcements as a 'Downing Street-orchestrated campaign'.

Better Together bosses had been briefed by strategist Andrew Cooper early in the campaign that Don't Knows moving to vote Yes would do so before those choosing No. '"Heart" voters would make their minds up early, whereas "head" voters could leave the decision right up until the walk to the polling station,' a campaign chief explained. 'Cooper got it bang on. Scarily so.'

At Better Together's headquarters, Danny Alexander and Labour strategy chief Paul Sinclair hatched a plan: this was to be 'Alex Salmond's Black Wednesday'. Sinclair rang round a long list of journalists to brief them on the snappy sound bite, while Alexander insistently told the team of press officers: 'We have to brand this.'

The YouGov poll was also a catalyst for renewed national media interest: London-based journalists suddenly realised the pressing significance of a possible vote for independence. Yes Scotland understood how this could damage their final campaigning days. 'To the BBC, nationally, a lot of this was new,' explained one Yes campaign source. 'There was wall-to-wall coverage going through the policies we'd persuaded people on months ago.' Those issues, especially the currency, were suddenly being picked up again on the doorstep by pro-independence campaigners. 'It then took twenty minutes to convert a voter on currency, and that's only if you're well briefed.'

Alex Salmond would later admit the poll showing Yes ahead for the first time came a week too early for his campaign.

SEVEN DAYS TO GO

On Thursday 11 September, exactly a week before polling, Ed Miliband led 104 Labour MPs and MEPs from across the UK on a visit to Glasgow in a demonstration of solidarity. Yet it was overshadowed by protests, including a man following the group in a rickshaw blaring out 'The Imperial March' from *Star Wars* and using a megaphone to shout: 'Say hello to your imperial masters ... People of Glasgow, your imperial masters have arrived!'

That afternoon, *Daily Record* editor Murray Foote texted Bruce Waddell, a predecessor at the paper, who was now handling media relations for Gordon Brown: 'Would Gordon be able to get the three party leaders to sign an agreed *Daily Record* pledge for more devolved powers (subject to a consultation process as per Gordon's timetable)? We could then present that as a front-page document.'

Soon there was a firm reply: 'Gordon loves it.'

Brown and Foote spoke on the phone to firm up details. The former Prime Minister was tasked with speaking to Cameron, while Foote would have to convince Ed Miliband. This was a role reversal for the Labour leader, who had spent much time – with little success – trying to persuade the *Record* to publicly support the No campaign; it had been explained to Miliband that, for a paper whose readers now represented Scotland in all its political variety, endorsing No would be 'commercially suicidal'.

That evening, George Galloway was backstage at Glasgow's Hydro arena, a venue more used to hosting pop superstars like Lady Gaga and Beyoncé. In the dressing room, Galloway kept on his trademark hat – a black fedora – as make-up was applied. The Respect MP for Bradford West was keen to show off a picture of his baby son wearing a Celtic onesie.

He was preparing to take part in *Scotland Decides: The Big, Big Debate*, an ambitious one-off BBC programme. The corporation claimed the 'landmark debate' would give 'sixteen- and seventeen-year-olds [who were able to vote for the first time] the opportunity to air their views'. So why was sixty-year-old Galloway chosen to be one of just two pro-UK politicians taking part?

Even though he was much older than the event's audience, Rob Shorthouse and Blair McDougall thought Galloway would be able to 'speak to' working-class Glasgow Catholic men watching on TV – a key demographic the campaign needed to persuade. And they presumed teenagers would like Galloway, too. 'We thought kids would be eating out of the palm of his hand,' said one senior figure.

Earlier that day, at an 'international press conference' in Edinburgh, Alex Salmond had clashed with the BBC's political editor Nick Robinson, later accusing the corporation of 'bias'. Yet heated arguments with the broadcaster were not just taking place on the Yes side. Relations between the BBC and Better Together had deteriorated throughout the campaign.

There had been continual frustrations about balance on the BBC News website, which Better Together's research showed was far more influential than any other newspaper or online outlet. No campaigners also believed the BBC TV debate between Salmond and Darling had been badly handled, with more audience contributions from supporters of independence than supporters of the union.

At one stage, Better Together refused point blank to take part in the Hydro debate. The BBC responded by booking guests themselves: 'They contacted Galloway directly and sorted him a hotel,' complained an angry campaign chief.

Days before the televised debate, a hot-tempered crisis meeting was held between BBC executives and a four-strong team from Better Together. 'We were a fantastic tag team of cunts,' boasted one No representative.

One area of disagreement was the political composition of the 7,500 school kids. 'Have you polled them?' asked a senior No campaigner. 'Well, no, we couldn't,' was the corporation's reply, although those among the audience of 500 young Scots invited to ask questions would be evenly split. This left Better Together unsure if the arena would be full of Yes-supporting teenagers or the opposite. 'We didn't know if it was going to be Bannockburn or Last Night of the Proms,' complained one person involved.

On the night, the four participants were waiting backstage. All knew it would be a tough gig. Deputy First Minister Nicola Sturgeon and Patrick Harvie of the Scottish Greens would argue for independence. Joining Galloway on the No side was leader of the Scottish Conservatives Ruth Davidson, who had been pushing hard to be involved, realising that a political event on this scale would never be repeated. Others, including Labour MSP Kezia Dugdale, had refused to share a platform with Galloway, whom some considered a 'rape apologist' after he said the sexual assault allegations against

WikiLeaks founder Julian Assange (which Assange denies) were, at worst, 'bad sexual etiquette'.

At the centre of the BBC's vision for the event was a focus on school students airing their views. After a long wait in the venue, they certainly did that – but not quite as the broadcaster had intended.

Waiting in the green room, the four watched their Twitter feeds as the hashtag #BigBigDebate started trending. They could sense the rising tension. Schoolchildren were venting their frustrations about the venue's expensive food and poor ventilation. 'If Scotland goes independent will the Hydro get air conditioning?' asked Callum Davidson. 'It's so warm my Toffee Crisp is melting,' wrote an attendee called Megan. 'Tanning under these lights, turn them down!' added Charlotte Gilgallon. 'I would have saved all my Christmas and birthday money if I knew the food was so expensive here!' another complained. Katie Armour joked there was a 'queue like an execution' for the toilet. And there was even an element of romance, with one teenager tweeting: 'Khaira just asked me if I'd shag her at the Hydro.'

When the debate eventually began, the four politicians were spread out in a row on white leather chairs and, because of the positioning of the amplifiers, found it difficult to hear. This meant some started to shout their answers. Within twelve minutes, George Galloway was being booed. 'We thought he would be great,' said a No campaign chief. 'He wasn't.'

The plan had been that Galloway would take the lead, with Davidson standing by with facts and figures. But the strategy soon changed, and the Conservative ended up being far more prominent. It turned out to be an engaging hour of television, but much of the discussion afterwards focused on why on earth Galloway had been chosen to take part.

FIVE DAYS TO GO

On Saturday 13 September, the surprise arrival of Rupert Murdoch's private jet in Aberdeen could mean only one thing. The media tycoon was about to make a final decision on whether the *Scottish Sun* would back Scottish independence.

'We were extraordinarily worried about *The Sun*,' explained a senior Better Together figure. 'Not because of the impact on voters, but because it would take us straight back into crisis mode.' After the onslaught of criticism in March and April, the No campaign worried that the paper's endorsement would be the dominant story for the final week, creating late momentum that would carry Alex Salmond to victory.

Accompanying the 83-year-old billionaire, on what was supposed to be an 'incognito' tour, were his son Lachlan – recently promoted to be co-chairman of News Corporation – and his chief of staff Natalie Ravitz. On hosting duty were Gordon Smart, editor of the *Scottish Sun*, and David Dinsmore, editor of the UK title. In an attempt to not attract too much attention, they were dressed casually: Rupert Murdoch in black trainers and an open-necked blue shirt, Smart and Dinsmore in jeans.

Generations of the Murdoch family – Rupert referred to them as his 'Scottish preacher forefathers' – had lived in the tiny Aberdeenshire fishing village of Rosehearty. His grandfather Patrick John Murdoch, a Presbyterian minister, had sailed to Australia in 1884. Murdoch was proud of his Scottish roots, even naming his £18 million sailing yacht *Rosehearty*.

But sentimentality would play no part in his paper's decision as to which side to take. The *Scottish Sun* was – and remains – the biggest-selling paper in the country, bought by about 5 per cent of Scots. Research from Populus for Better Together concluded that 40 per cent of the No campaign's target voters read the *Scottish Sun* – more than any other title.

David Cameron met regularly with executives from the *Sun* papers, including David Dinsmore – who many concluded was 'very supportive' of the No cause – as well as Gordon Smart. Downing Street sources claim that, after Cameron met the *Scottish Sun* editor, they worried the tabloid was sceptical of remaining in the UK and 'ready to go Yes'.

Better Together's senior staff met Smart far more regularly than Cameron. The editor's background may have been in showbiz reporting, and he had been living and working out of Scotland for the past decade, but Smart absolutely understood his readers. 'He's Scottish, he's passionate, and he never once expressed a personal view,' said one senior figure.

But Smart implied that support was far from guaranteed: 'In my office, there are lots of people who are Yes voters,' he said. Better Together chiefs who sat in meetings with the editor attempted to guess how he would vote, but their assessment of his opinions would change regularly. Towards the end, they were 'reasonably certain he's a No voter', while being very concerned his paper would still come out with the opposite view.

'Relationships with editors are strange to maintain,' explained one senior figure. 'You have a conversation about what's going on, tell them they are important, ask them what they think. But rarely do you directly ask: "Will you do this for us?"'

It was only in July 2014 that Better Together representatives were more direct: 'When will you stop kicking us?' they asked Smart, frustrated at the consistently negative stories appearing in the *Scottish Sun*. 'If you want to back Yes, just do it instead of criticising us all the time.'

Throughout months of discussions, Smart made it clear he was not the only arbiter, and alluded to 'what's going on above me': the views of Rupert Murdoch. The *Scottish Sun* had first come out in support of the SNP in the 1992 general election, although the day Alex Salmond was swept into minority government in the 2007 Holyrood elections, the paper's front page was: 'Vote SNP today and you put Scotland's head in the noose.'

Since then, Salmond had worked hard to foster far closer relations with Murdoch and his companies. In the 2011 Holyrood elections, the *Scottish Sun* backed the SNP, and, the following February, the businessman tweeted his most public support yet for the First Minister: 'Clearly most brilliant politician in UK. Gave Cameron back of his hand this week. Loved by Scots.' While Salmond developed – and, most impressively, maintained – a relationship with the proprietor, having few close links to Murdoch contrastingly hampered the pro-UK parties. David Cameron's relationship with the company is said to have cooled after the Leveson Inquiry. Alistair Darling had not met Murdoch since a Downing Street dinner party for President George W. Bush in 2008, and Ed Miliband's call for the break-up of the media empire in 2011 had ensured he was a *persona non grata*.

On his fact-finding trip, Murdoch and entourage visited Sloans Bar in Glasgow and the Prince of Wales pub in Aberdeen: 'No politicians, just street and pub talks,' he later tweeted. 'Everywhere alive with debate. Democracy truly at work.' Yet senior politicians in the No campaign believe Rupert Murdoch was expecting something very different from what he found on his visit to Aberdeenshire and Glasgow five days before the referendum.

'I think he arrived with a pre-conceived vision of a Celtic low-tax tiger,' said one source. 'Then he saw Trots on the street.' Another thought Murdoch had a 'genuinely emotional connection to Scotland', but recognised 'he had the opportunity to fuck Cameron and fuck Labour at the same time'.

The involvement of the Scottish Greens and the Scottish Socialist Party in the Yes campaign clearly had some impact on Murdoch's decision – he would later tweet: 'Have to worry about some of Salmond's allies. Far-left socialists and extreme greenies. Must change course to prosper if he wins.'

In the end, Murdoch's *Scottish Sun* never backed either side. The paper's front page on 18 September was: 'Yes or No. Today Scotland starts with a blank page.' The UK edition was more decisive: 'Better Together' was the headline, above a story that Prince Harry and his girlfriend Cressida Bonas were dating again.

THREE DAYS TO GO

David Cameron made his final intervention in the campaign on Monday 15 September, three days before the vote. A copy of his speech, delivered at a conference centre in Aberdeen, had been sent in advance to Gordon Brown for feedback. Brown made just two minor suggestions.

First, he advised Cameron to clearly make the point that a No vote did not mean no change, and to hammer home the message that Scots could have change without the risk of independence. Second, Brown advised his successor to reinforce the point that Scotland is helping to shape and change the UK, and a No vote is a patriotically Scottish thing to do.

Neither politician could have expected, even a few months earlier, that, after Brown's painful defeat in 2010, they would build a strong, productive working relationship. The pair spoke on the telephone at least twice, and continued contact through their respective advisers. 'They are opponents but members of the club of prime ministers,' explained one source close to the action. 'What came through in their conversations was that, with the Isis hostage situation and Boko Haram, Gordon could understand the pressure the Prime Minister was facing: there were lots of big issues on the agenda.'

The original plan was for the *Daily Record*'s 'The Vow' front page – a cross-party commitment to further devolution – to be designed on Sunday 14 September for the Monday paper. However, on the Saturday, David Haines, an aid worker from Perth who had been kidnapped by Islamic State, was beheaded. 'The Vow' was, of course, delayed.

On Monday night, a day later than planned, Foote and his team put the finishing touches to their paper: the front page mocked up like a vellum scroll with the headline 'The Vow' in thick black capital letters. At the bottom were the signatures of David Cameron, Ed Miliband and Nick Clegg. It read:

> The people of Scotland want to know that all three main parties will deliver change for Scotland.
>
> WE ARE AGREED THAT:
> The Scottish Parliament is permanent, and extensive new powers for the Parliament will be delivered by the process

and to the timetable agreed and announced by our three parties, starting on 19 September.

And it is our hope that the people of Scotland will be engaged directly as each party works to improve the way we are governed in the UK in the years ahead.

We agree that the UK exists to ensure opportunity and security for all by sharing our resources equitably across all four nations to secure the defence, prosperity and welfare of every citizen.

And because of the continuation of the Barnett allocation for resources, and the powers of the Scottish Parliament to raise revenue, we can state categorically that the final say on how much is spent on the NHS will be a matter for the Scottish Parliament.

We believe that the arguments that so powerfully make the case for staying together in the UK should underpin our future as a country. We will honour those principles and values not only before the referendum but after.

People want to see change. A No vote will deliver faster, safer and better change than separation.

The paper would hit the newsstands and land on doormats just two days before polling. As the *Record* team left the newsroom at 10 p.m., each knew their day's work would cause a stir. But it was only when turning on Sky News at home that the scale of this became clear. Sky was leading with the story. During the paper review, the front page was displayed on a massive screen behind the presenter, and, the next morning, national TV and radio bulletins were covering the three parties' commitment. It was to be by far the most memorable and important front page of the whole two-and-a-half-year campaign.

TWO DAYS TO GO

Ed Miliband had been told that non-Scottish Westminster politicians coming up to campaign in the referendum was toxic. Yet his team recognised a need to be seen as part of such a big story. The 2015 general election was just eight months away. 'He wanted to be associated with victory,' said a Labour figure. 'But that wasn't going to happen. No one's going to say, "Thanks, Ed, for saving the union!" It was a complete sideshow.'

Tuesday 16 September was Miliband's last chance for publicity, yet another Labour Women's campaign event was already arranged. On the day, a junior party organiser decided that, to meet 'real people', Miliband should visit Edinburgh's St James Shopping Centre – a cramped arcade, soon to be demolished. There had been no recce, no plan of the leader's route, no idea of emergency exits.

The event was mid-afternoon, meaning both TV and newspaper deadlines were fast approaching and everyone was desperate for a story. Its start was delayed, with TV cameras, photographers and journalists waiting outside the centre, alongside Yes and No supporters. That was until a press officer remarked, 'Oh, he's just inside,' starting a rampage of media and activists alike. Miliband was soon enveloped by a cacophony of sound: 'You're a liar, Ed!' shouted protestors with Yes placards. Shoppers were knocked out of the way, and one cameraman had some of his kit smashed in the scrum.

Paul Gilbride in the *Daily Express* wrote: 'He was trapped outside a hairdresser's called Supercuts and Yes supporters chanted, "Vote No for super cuts."' Quentin Letts of the *Daily Mail* said in his column: 'While having an elbow jammed up my left nostril and a stranger step on my ankle, I copped a clear view of Ed's eyes – two liquorice gobstoppers, rotating slowly in different directions.'

The Labour leader met only a handful of shoppers before the event was abandoned and he was forced to escape via a back entrance. Johann Lamont went 'ballistic', according to someone close to the action. 'It was horrible and dangerous,' she told aides. But Miliband was pleased with the event. 'He quite liked the idea of a mob,' revealed one Better Together source. But not all aides were supportive: 'As a rule of life, I'm generally opposed to riots,' said one.

The staff member behind the event was certainly not proud: 'She burst into tears and walked out of the office,' explained a senior Labour figure.

ONE DAY TO GO

What would Alex Salmond do the morning after the referendum if he lost? Both the No campaign team and Downing Street were concerned about the First Minister's next move if Scots voted No. One prediction was that, even after defeat, Salmond would 'get out of a helicopter echoing his 2011 Holyrood election win, and snatch victory out of the jaws of defeat by announcing his own constitutional convention'.

To prevent this, the pro-UK parties needed to firm up the process for agreeing details of further devolution following a No victory. One name floated to lead this was Kenneth Calman, who had headed up a commission on devolution for the Scottish Parliament. But senior campaign figures were keener on another respected figure: Lord Smith of Kelvin.

A week ahead of the vote, David Cameron spoke to Robert Smith to ask if he would take on the role in the event of a No vote. Smith made clear that it was important that he could command the support and confidence of all parties, including the SNP, who Downing Street wanted to ensure felt able to take part.

Smith, seen by many as Scotland's premier industrialist, was above party politics, not aligned to either side in the referendum, and, most importantly, he had the confidence of the SNP, due to his role chairing the organising committee of the 2014 Commonwealth Games in Glasgow. The cross-bench peer had authority, credibility and vast experience of negotiations. Unlike the earlier long-running Calman Commission, Smith's responsibility would be to knock heads together and achieve an outcome in a constrained time period.

Yet Alex Salmond was not planning for defeat. Far from it. His pollsters were advising him that he would be victorious. Salmond told his closest confidants: 'We're going to win – and by more than anyone thinks.'

The First Minister knew a Yes vote would impact on the financial markets and knew he would have to move fast on one issue above all: currency. On 16 and 17 September, Salmond recruited a series of top-level names in the City, business and even from the Bank of England to form a 'Scottish Monetary Committee'.

He even planned the timing. In conversations with his new recruits, the First Minister explained that, on Friday 19 September, after David Cameron's concession speech and his own victory address – both early in the morning – there would be an announcement at midday. It would set out the role of the new committee in resolving the currency for an independent Scotland.

Maryhill's Community Central Hall in Glasgow was built in 1924 by the Methodist Church. The building's large Reid Hall, with art nouveau interior, was to be the setting for Brown to make his final sermon to Scots. It was Wednesday 17 September – the final day of campaigning, the last chance to convince undecided voters. Better Together hoped the former Prime Minister's words would be in the minds of those walking to polling stations the next day.

As TV cameras set up their live feeds in the main hall, in a backstage meeting room scattered with grey plastic chairs, Better Together's popular head of events Kitty Raven was reading out the order of speakers to a large group. Few were sitting down. This was not a time to relax.

The three Scottish pro-UK parties' leaders were listening closely, as were a group of 'ordinary voters' primed to speak movingly about their support for staying in the UK. On one side of the room, paying little attention to the briefing, Gordon Brown was sitting at a table – a plate of biscuits and styrofoam cups next to him – shuffling his notes for his much-anticipated speech. His trusted aide Bruce Waddell was close at hand. On the opposite side of the room, Alistair Darling was moving around nervously with his own sheaf of paper. Torsten Bell was scratching his chin; Eddie Izzard was cracking jokes.

In front of a packed audience, the event began with bagpipes, comedy and, most importantly, energy. The room was buzzing; 'Love Scotland, Vote No' placards were being waved. At last, Better Together was starting to emulate the carnival, partying atmosphere of Yes Scotland's recent rallies.

Brown's entrance was choreographed so he would come on later in the proceedings – he would not share a platform on an equal pegging with the leader of the Scottish Conservatives.

As speeches were in the main hall, the former Prime Minister waited in a dark corridor at the back of the building, leaning towards the light shining through a frosted-glass window, his two-man security detail standing close by. He was re-reading the text of his speech, adding scrawled notes with his trademark black felt-tip pen. Brown had been honing this argument for months. Today, it needed to be perfect.

On cue, Brown walked out to a wall of cheers and a standing ovation as he picked his way through the crowd. He hushed them and began to speak – without notes, pacing up and down the stage, in complete command of his audience. 'At last, the world is hearing the voices of the real people of Scotland.' There were more cheers and placard-waving, but, keen to maintain the pace of his oratory, Brown cut the clapping off, like a conductor with a swipe of a hand. 'The silent majority will be silent no more,' he boomed.

'Scotland belongs to all of us. And let us tell the nationalists this is not their flag, their country, their culture, their streets. This is everyone's flag, everyone's country, everyone's culture, everyone's streets.' Brown was on form: 'If you're like me and a million more people, who are convinced that the case for cooperation is greater than any case put for separation, then I say to you: hold your heads high. Show dignity and pride. Be confident.'

Over thirteen minutes, the former Prime Minister delivered one of the most passionate, barnstorming speeches of his career. He ended with a rallying cry: 'Have confidence and say to our friends: for reasons of solidarity, sharing, justice, pride in Scotland, the only answer for Scotland's sake and for Scotland's future is vote no.'

Even media outlets once hostile to Brown were full of praise. the *Mail*'s Alan Roden declared it 'the defining speech of the historic referendum battle'; Lindsay McIntosh of *The Times* called it 'a tub-thumping, angrily passionate address'; and Sky's Faisal Islam said the performance 'could be remembered as one of the greats'. Isabel Hardman from *The Spectator* tweeted with surprise: 'There are people on the streets of Glasgow talking about Gordon Brown's speech.'

For Better Together's exhausted staff, this would be their final campaign rally. It had been a huge success, but with the race still tight, and a record turnout expected, some had a niggling anxiety. 'Why didn't we do this sort of thing earlier?' Rob Shorthouse whispered to a colleague.

Later that day, in Westminster, David Cameron was walking up to his Downing Street flat when he bumped into an adviser. 'What's the result going to be?' the Prime Minister asked. His aide reassured him that the No campaign were on course for victory. 'You better fucking be right,' Cameron replied.

CHAPTER 10

SCOTLAND DECIDES

On the morning of 18 September 2014, Douglas Alexander's phone buzzed. It was a text from Jack Straw, former UK Foreign Secretary under Tony Blair. 'It must feel like all nine of my general elections rolled into one,' the message read. The fraught final fortnight of campaigning had, for once, made Scotland the focus of the world. Yet referendum day was itself a deeply personal moment for millions of Scottish voters. It was the conclusion of two and half years of debate; a national conversation that had split families, workplaces and communities. Better Together's research showed, for many, it had been repetitive, confusing and frustrating. Those who thought 18 September would finally resolve this predicament would soon be disabused.

As polling began, Yes Scotland strategists realised that turnout was going to be huge. 'Abandon get out the vote,' activists were told. Instead of knocking on doors, supporters of independence were advised to be visible and high-profile, creating a carnival atmosphere.

The day's only stir was caused by Andy Murray tweeting a last-minute endorsement for the Yes campaign at 1.08 a.m.: 'Huge day for Scotland today! no campaign negativity last

few days totally swayed my view on it. excited to see the outcome. lets [*sic*] do this!'

The timing of the tennis champion's tweet – after newspapers had gone to print and when TV and radio stations
were under election day restrictions – meant it got limited
coverage, largely confined to news websites and social media.
Murray later admitted the manner he pledged his support
was not one he would repeat: 'I don't regret giving an opinion
… the way I did it, yeah, wasn't something I would do again.'

As the clock struck 10 p.m. and polling stations across
the country closed, the mood among the No campaign
was cautious, even downbeat. Blair McDougall told one
close colleague: 'I feel utterly impotent.' Senior staff had
been under strict orders to sleep in that day so they could
be on the ball throughout the night. But it had been all hands
on deck for the rest of the team, with everyone on the streets
to get out the vote.

The last ten days of this marathon political battle had
been punishing. As with all political campaigns, many of
those involved had paid a high personal price: they would
now need to repair much-neglected relationships and marriages, reacquaint themselves with their children, and, press-
ingly, start looking for new jobs.

Scotland's democratic re-engagement, record levels of
voter registration and – as was later to become clear – a historic turnout were triumphs. But few in the No camp believed
they could claim much credit for this. While they had created
a well-targeted series of political messages, Yes Scotland had
built not just a base of activists, but a new movement.

The pro-independence campaign chose Dynamic Earth for
their results-night bash. The futuristic visitor attraction overlooked the Scottish Parliament and was round the corner from

SNP headquarters. The venue was a nod towards the tectonic shift they were hoping to make in the evolution of Scotland.

In contrast, Better Together, aiming for functionality, had rented out two floors of Glasgow's four-star Marriott Hotel, a brown tower block in the centre of the city, overlooking the busy M8 flyover. It was a five-minute drive from Pacific Quay, where both BBC and STV were anchoring their overnight programmes, allowing politicians to flit between the studios and the campaign base. Bedrooms allowed key politicians and advisers to rest during the long wait for the final result. £27,000 had been thrown at the event, catering for an over-ambitious figure of 800 attendees, with a cornucopia of curry, and so much beer and wine (sixty-four cases of white, fifty of red) that, afterwards, any staff member with a garage was accommodating acres of free alcohol.

Downing Street, as with any election night, was tense. But this was not just another election. All of David Cameron's advisers knew he would have to resign if Scots voted Yes. Their own secret polling from Ipsos MORI – by now being delivered daily – suggested that this eventuality was unlikely, but not impossible. The final fortnight of campaigning had been so dramatic, any trace of confidence had evaporated. Unlike a general election, where senior staff might base themselves in a war room in party HQ or accompany the Prime Minister to his constituency count, this time, they all just had to sit at No. 10 and wait.

Ramsay Jones had been dispatched to Edinburgh to attend to the needs of the press pack. David Mundell was at his local count in Dumfries – a two-hour drive in his ministerial car from the Scotland Office's Edinburgh HQ in the city's New Town. Philip Rycroft, the senior civil servant to Nick Clegg's office, who had also led on the referendum across government, and Alun Evans, director of the Scotland Office, were standing by in Edinburgh, just in case.

David Cameron and George Osborne sat in the Downing Street press office, part of No. 12 and next to director of communications Craig Oliver's base. The Prime Minister and Chancellor ate a Chinese takeaway in front of banks of television screens, alongside Oliver, Cameron's chief of staff Ed Llewellyn, and Llewellyn's two deputies Catherine Fall and Oliver Dowden. Andrew Dunlop would join them later in the evening.

At 10.30 p.m., YouGov released their prediction: 54 per cent No; 46 per cent Yes. Incorrectly described by some broadcasters as an exit poll – when voters are questioned as they leave polling stations – instead, this was an online survey. It included 1,828 people who had already voted, plus 800 postal voters. All had also been asked earlier that week how they would vote, allowing the pollsters to discover a small but significant last-minute, on-the-day shift from Yes to No.

'At the obvious risk of looking like a complete prat in about eight hours' time,' YouGov's Peter Kellner explained to the news channels, 'I would say it's a 99 per cent certainty it's a No victory.'

At Downing Street, the rising excitement dissipated soon after Kellner's prediction. The Prime Minister decided little was happening and retired to bed. 'If anything happens, we'll text you,' Craig Oliver told him.

On arriving at the Marriott Hotel, Alistair Darling retired immediately to his suite, instructing staff to leave him and his wife Maggie alone to rest. Originally planning to stay up for the first result and then go to bed, Darling ended up in his pyjamas, glued to the television coverage and not sleeping a wink.

On the opposite side of the long corridor, conference rooms had been transformed into nerve centres for both the communications and grass-roots teams, as well as a boardroom for the senior strategists. The press officers – from both Better Together and the pro-UK parties – had very little to do until the result was clear. 'Just the usual election night bollocks,' one source explained. 'The old "confident but not complacent" bullshit.' The atmosphere of quiet nervousness was punctuated with black humour, exploring personal contingencies if Scotland voted to become an independent country. 'Who will defect to the Yes campaign first?' 'Who wants to be Scotland's ambassador to Bermuda?' 'I fancy the Virgin Islands.'

Along the corridor, the tone in the grass-roots office was far more serious. Kate Watson, Better Together's director of operations, was in charge of this hive of activity, alongside MP Frank Roy and his son Brian, Scottish Labour's campaigns chief. The team was receiving and crunching sampling data from counts across the country, and cross-referencing this to turnout figures gained over the course of the day, in an attempt to calculate the national result – and hopefully the margin of victory. The three parties' most talented statisticians – including Patrick Heneghan, Labour's grandly named executive director for elections – had been sent up from their London headquarters to help.

Although comforted by YouGov's 54 to 46 prediction, the No team's far richer sources of information did not paint such a clear picture. Soon after polls closed, they predicted that turnout would be 83.5 per cent. 'This is fine,' Frank Roy told Blair McDougall and Rob Shorthouse. 'We're going to win.'

But, after 11 p.m., the hum of focused activity turned into panic. With more sampling results coming in from counts in Glasgow and North Lanarkshire – which both eventually returned a majority for Yes – their assessment changed. Within half an hour, the message from the grass-roots team was now: 'It's not going well. It's gone bad, very bad.'

'People were walking around shaken, terror on their faces,' according to one person present. Early sampling figures from Dundee compounded the problem, giving what turned out to be a slightly skewed picture. As it became clear that Glasgow would be lost to the pro-independence campaign, Kate Watson broke down in tears.

Blair McDougall tried to escape this hubbub to rest in his hotel room, but the mood was so frenetic that, five minutes after he nodded off, there was a knock at the door: 'Everyone's looking for you,' he was told.

'Why?'

'Just wondering where you are.'

Once this had happened three times, he realised there was no prospect of getting any sleep.

At 1.30 a.m., the first result came through from Clackmannanshire. Although the smallest council by population in mainland Scotland, it was also seen as a bellwether of Scottish opinion, and a must-win for the Yes campaign. Pro-independence activists held their heads in their hands as the returning officer read out the numbers: No had secured 54 per cent of votes. In the Glasgow Marriott, there was a collective and audible sigh of relief.

Meanwhile, at the Aberdeen Exhibition Centre – where Alex Salmond's local Aberdeenshire count was taking place – word spread that, with a No vote increasingly likely, the First Minister would now not be turning up. Photographers from international agencies decided to head straight down to Edinburgh to capture the Yes Scotland results-night event.

With both the city and shire counts devoid of any political celebrities, the local snappers were left looking for a story. And that story was Salmond.

Derek Ironside and Ross Johnston, the only two photographers at local agency Newsline Media, separately drove round key Aberdeenshire locations searching for the silver Skoda Octavia in which the First Minister was regularly chauffeured. Ironside travelled up to Eat on the Green, one of Salmond's favourite restaurants near Ellen, halfway between his Strichen home and Aberdeen. A Skoda was in the car park, but the photographer could not be sure it was him.

Later on, while scoping out Aberdeen Airport, eagle-eyed Ironside spotted lights on inside the local flying club. The building, on the opposite side of the runway to the main terminal, was usually pitch black at that time of night; any activity was distinctly strange. The same entrance was also used to process VIPs flying by private jet.

Suspicions raised, he phoned his colleague Ross Johnston: 'Come down to the airport. It looks like Salmond might be flying to Edinburgh.' While Ironside attempted to cover some of the airport's several entrances, Johnston headed straight to the flying club. On arrival, there was silence. Nothing seemed to be happening.

'Holy shit, that's him.' Johnston was just driving out of the club's car park when he got a shock and braked. Two cars, including the silver Octavia, were driving along the road. Luckily for the photographer, both missed the initial turning, giving him enough time to jump out, grab his camera and stick on a lens as Salmond's driver found a parking space.

The First Minister's assistants, who had not been expecting any media, spotted him: 'We want you to go. Mr

Salmond won't be posing for any pictures.' But the photographer stood his ground: 'I'm not going anywhere.'

Next, the airport police arrived, having spotted Johnston's car parked in front of the fire service building at a jaunty angle, with both the driver's door and the boot open. His heart sank, assuming he would be forced to move his car and lose his exclusive, but, after explaining the situation, the officer let him get on with his job.

The standoff continued, with Salmond and his wife Moira now sitting in the back of their Skoda in the car park. It was 2.45 a.m., hardly the setting in which the First Minister had hoped to find himself on this most historic of nights. Johnston knew Salmond would either have to walk past him to get onto the airfield, or drive past to go through one of the gates to his jet.

All of a sudden, there was movement. The Skoda quickly moved to drive round to one of the gates. The photographer took a deep breath, and prepared himself for his one chance. In twenty years on the job, he had only taken a handful of shots through car windows, and most had been unusable.

As the car sped past at 2.48 a.m., there was only time for one single flash – one photo. Without checking out his shot, he immediately jumped in his car to join his colleague round the corner and both spent the next few minutes using their long lenses to take pictures of the First Minister climbing onto his jet.

After the plane headed to the runway, both men returned to their cars, Johnston still unsure quite what, if anything, he had captured. He found just three frames: two black, and one in focus. And the shot in focus was perfect: Salmond was sitting in the right-hand passenger seat, looking straight ahead with a tired, dejected gaze.

Within minutes of dispatching the image, their phones started to ring. The BBC and Sky News were keen to run the picture; soon, it went viral online. And in this dark, silent corner of the airport, on the outskirts of Aberdeen, in the middle of the night, the two men celebrated. Teamwork, local knowledge and intuition had helped them capture *the* defining image of the referendum – an iconic photo that would race around the world.

It also offered a rare insight into the real Alex Salmond. For a politician quite so assured with the media, this was a rare lapse: the most human of moments. Even though the First Minister knew a camera was waiting to snap him, he could not – like hundreds of thousands of other Yes supporters across Scotland – hide his sorrow.

David Cameron reappeared in the Downing Street press office just before 4 a.m. as the Dundee result was announced – ironically, one of the few moments overnight when it appeared the gap between Yes and No was closing. By now, at the impromptu pyjama party, crisps and biscuits had replaced the empty takeaway boxes.

After a run of solid results for the No campaign, it became clear Salmond's side would lose. George Osborne turned to Andrew Dunlop: 'Will he resign?'

'There's a good chance,' the Chancellor was told.

As the finish line approached and victory seemed certain, the Prime Minister popped up to his flat to wake his two eldest children, Nancy and Arthur. Their parents had explained the referendum was an important moment for the UK. And Cameron – approaching the end of his first, and possibly only, term in No. 10 – wanted them to join him at this historic moment. When the final confirmation came, the two children were on their father's lap, surrounded by his closest aides. There was cheering and fist-pumping, but no hugs between colleagues. 'We are too restrained for that,' conceded one present.

In Glasgow, Alistair Darling had finally left his suite to join Blair McDougall and Rob Shorthouse around the boardroom table. It was time to work on a victory speech. Various friends and advisers had contributed drafts, including academic Jim Gallagher – 'too long' was Darling's curt response – and Michael Marra, a former aide to ex-Scottish Labour leader Iain Gray. Former Labour MP and *Scotsman* columnist Brian Wilson – Darling's favourite wordsmith – knew the former Chancellor's voice better than anyone, and also contributed, but it was Alastair Campbell – who had known Darling for decades – whose draft proved most useful. Campbell had visited the campaign's headquarters on a number of occasions in the final weeks. He was regularly in Scotland to visit family members, through whom he had built up a clear understanding of the arguments at play, and he knew better than anyone how they should be communicated. But, although Darling had received drafts, he was still in need of the finished version.

In contrast, the Prime Minister's team had been working for over a week on not just one, but two speeches for the referendum result. There was a detailed version if Scots were to vote No, and a sketch of what Cameron would say if they voted Yes. The latter's top line was due to be: 'Scotland has spoken. We have lost. And we respect the result.'

The Prime Minister's chief speechwriter Clare Foges – nicknamed his larynx for her intuitive understanding of David Cameron's speaking style – was in charge. She had begun the process with a brief discussion with Cameron, before sketching out a draft and consulting others to improve it in the run-up to polling day.

At 5.30 a.m., David Cameron called Darling with his congratulations. The Prime Minister explained his speech at dawn would not just focus on plans for further devolution to Scotland, but also announce new legislation to ensure Scottish MPs would be prevented from voting on matters that only affect England. Darling's response was blunt: 'I fully understand you're a Conservative and have your own interests,' he told Cameron forcefully, 'but if you conflate more power and English votes today, you'll let Salmond in by the back door.'

This was, the Better Together chairman believed, a foolish and divisive step. There should be at least twenty-four hours for the victory to sink in instead of allowing the SNP to form 'further grievances about the "Westminster establishment".'

'I hear what you say,' was Cameron's response. But Darling had been in politics long enough to know exactly what this meant: 'I've listened, but I'm not changing my mind.'

Once off the phone, Darling turned to his wife Maggie: 'He's going to fuck it up.'

By the time Alex Salmond's car had sped through the drizzle from Edinburgh Airport into the city, the First Minister had seen *the* photo. This time, as he approached Dynamic Earth and photographers snapped him through the car windows, he made sure he was smiling.

Soon after Salmond entered the building through the underground car park, results were announced from Gordon Brown's Fife heartland. The result – No 55 per cent; Yes 45 per cent – replicated the national picture, but, most importantly, it meant it was arithmetically impossible for Yes Scotland to win. A serious road crash on the A9 in the very north of Scotland had delayed counting in the Highlands, meaning the final national result would be late. But this was no reason for the First Minister to put off the inevitable.

In the main hall at Dynamic Earth, the Yes Scotland rally was understandably subdued, with once excited activists now in despair, having sat through hours of painful results. Victories in Glasgow, Dundee and West Dunbartonshire had been celebrated. But, like their pro-UK counterparts, these campaigners were exhausted, many in tears. At one end of the room was a gigantic video screen with a Saltire displayed across it; in front, a lectern awaited the First Minister.

At 6.15 a.m., Salmond did his best to bound onto the stage. He was greeted by a 45-second standing ovation before he could begin: 'Can I say thank you for that reception, but, above all, for Scotland, for 1.6 million votes for Scottish independence.' He asked his supporters to respect the democratic process. 'But,' he said, 'I think all of us in this campaign will say that that 55 per cent [of course he meant 45 per cent], that 1.6 million votes, is a substantial vote for Scottish independence and the future of this country.'

The message 'One Scotland' had been plastered across the hall, part of new branding originally intended as a message of unity as the country began its negotiations towards independence. Instead, it ended up suggesting that both Yes and No voters should resolve their differences and work together in a still united kingdom.

But, for Alex Salmond, even such a clear defeat was not enough to dilute his rhetoric against the No campaign. His speech was more defiant than magnanimous, largely aimed at his supporters rather than the whole Scottish electorate. 'Over the last few weeks, we have seen a scare and a fear of enormous proportions,' he said. 'Not the scaremongering directed at the Scottish people, but the scare and the fear at the heart of the Westminster establishment as they realised the mass movement of people that was going forward in Scotland.'

'Today of all days, as we bring Scotland together, let us not dwell on the distance we have fallen short, let us dwell on the distance we have travelled.' It was a rousing performance, but at no point did Salmond take responsibility for the defeat by apologising to his activists.

Alistair Carmichael, the Secretary of State for Scotland, had spent much of the night watching results from the Scotland Office in Edinburgh's New Town. His team members were aware the Prime Minister was due to give a speech at 7 a.m., but they were only notified of its contents less than thirty minutes beforehand. Carmichael's special adviser Euan Roddin received an email on his BlackBerry from one of Deputy Prime Minister Nick Clegg's closest advisers. It was a forwarded copy of the speech David Cameron was about to deliver outside Downing Street. Reading its contents and realising the prominence of plans for English devolution, Roddin's face dropped. 'Am I being sent this for comment or information?' he emailed back.

'Information,' came the reply.

From as early as 2.30 a.m., Michael Gove had been hinting in interviews on Sky News and the BBC that the Prime Minister's focus would switch to constitutional change for England. Yet, preoccupied with the actual results and writing speeches, few in the No campaign had picked up on this.

Downing Street sources insist that, in such situations, it is not unusual for only the PM's closest aides to be involved in a statement. But the secrecy with which this announcement was treated was seen by some of the Conservatives' coalition colleagues as a slight on both them and on Scotland. One Liberal Democrat commented: 'He wanted to lance the boil of Scottish independence. Instead, he's going to infest it.'

Desperate to try to define the victory ahead of David

Cameron's impending speech, in Glasgow there was a rush to ensure Darling spoke before the Prime Minister. Another motivation for getting the victory statement out of the way was the swiftly degenerating state of the hotel's ballroom: it resembled the end of a seriously happy wedding. Many of those invited had been drinking free alcohol for eight hours. Some were now out of a job. 'There were a lot of shit-faced people in a hot room with no natural light and no fresh air,' said one looking on. Drunk people were dancing in one corner, accidentally appearing at the back of shot on TV.

Key strategists discussed whether Darling should be flanked by the Scottish party leaders in a final demonstration of unity, shared endeavour and cooperative celebration. Yes, they decided, but Scottish Labour leader Johann Lamont was nowhere to be seen: she was stuck doing an interview on breakfast TV. They held on for her until it was impossible to wait any longer.

At 6.40 a.m., Alistair Darling walked through the crowd like a hero. He climbed onto the stage, which had been decorated with 'Love Scotland, Vote No' banners. Dressed in a perfectly pressed shirt and crisp suit and tie, he looked out of place among the sea of sweaty supporters.

'The people of Scotland have spoken,' Darling said, immediately prompting a cacophony of cheers and a torrent of flashbulbs. 'We have chosen unity over division and positive change rather than needless separation.' Due to the constant interruptions from an ecstatic crowd, who were jumping up and down waving flags, the speech lasted longer than planned. Darling thanked his team, attempted to empathise with the pain of the defeated Yes campaign, called for unity across Scotland, tried to move the national political debate on from the constitution, and promised to fulfil the commitments for further devolution.

Yet overlooked by many were three sentences that hinted at the barrage of criticism Better Together had faced for its perceived negativity: 'This has not been an easy campaign,' Darling conceded. 'Campaigning against Yes for change, it is sometimes more difficult to argue for No. We were obliged to point out that some of the arguments for separation were going to cause damage to our country.'

He continued: 'We have made a decision for progress and change, for Scotland within the United Kingdom.' Then, looking up at the crowd with a very genuine smile, he concluded: 'Come on, Scotland. Let's get on with it together.'

As the crowd went wild, and TV cameras surged towards Alistair Darling, he became the unlikely – and perhaps unwilling – recipient of a ticker-tape shower, as confetti cannons exploded above to the sound of Primal Scream's 'Come Together'.

However, this attempt to reframe the debate and dominate the next day's media coverage would soon fail. Not out of any error, but through circumstance. Alistair Darling was the leader of a now defunct campaign. He spoke on behalf of three parties that would rapidly set off in very separate directions.

As soon as Darling finished his speech, senior Scottish MPs hit the airwaves, continuing apace with their punishing schedules of TV and radio appearances. It was vital they tried to shape the referendum victory in the fifteen minutes before the Prime Minister was due to speak.

As 7 a.m. approached, Margaret Curran, Labour's shadow Scottish Secretary, was standing in front of a camera, wearing an earpiece, in the main room at the Marriott. She was waiting for her slot on ITV's *Good Morning Britain*. At the same moment, Douglas Alexander was on BBC Radio 4's *Today* programme.

A voice in Curran's ear suddenly explained her slot would be delayed: 'Cameron is about to speak. We'll be coming to you in five minutes.' *Today* presenter Jim Naughtie broke away from a discussion with Douglas Alexander and UKIP leader Nigel Farage to cross to Downing Street and hear the Prime Minister's words.

Watching the two large projector screens in the room behind her, Curran could see David Cameron make his speech. Douglas Alexander sat in the BBC radio studio listening through headphones.

David Cameron walked out through the door of No. 10 to his wooden prime ministerial lectern. It was rare for Downing Street to be packed with international TV crews and photographers so early in the morning. They had gathered in darkness, with dawn breaking just twenty minutes before this moment, timed to ensure the Prime Minister was not speaking under floodlights.

'The people of Scotland have spoken,' he said. 'It is a clear result. They have kept our country of four nations together.' Cameron stressed the finality – at least, in his mind – of the result: 'Now the debate has been settled for a generation, or, as Alex Salmond has said, perhaps for a lifetime. So there can be no disputes, no re-runs.' Evoking memories of the late John Smith, a Scot and former Labour leader, he continued: 'We have heard the settled will of the Scottish people.' To continue the devolution journey, he announced that Lord Smith of Kelvin would oversee the process for deciding on further powers. These would be agreed by November 2014, and draft legislation published by January 2015.

Then, four and a half minutes in, David Cameron changed tack: 'I have long believed that a crucial part missing from this national discussion is England,' he argued, prompting the ears of journalists and politicians to prick up. 'We have heard the voice of Scotland – and now the millions of voices of England must also be heard. The question of English votes for English laws – the so-called West Lothian question – requires a decisive answer.'

As he started to explain his government's move on English votes for English laws, in Glasgow, Margaret Curran leaned over to her adviser Martin McCluskey to whisper: 'What's our line on this?' No one had anticipated the sudden focus on England. There had been abstract conversations within Ed Miliband's shadow Cabinet, but no position had ever been taken. Listening to this announcement in BBC Scotland's Pacific Quay, Douglas Alexander was shocked, but not surprised.

Cameron continued his speech with the assertion that English votes for English laws – subsequently known as EVEL – must 'take place in tandem with, and at the same pace as, the settlement for Scotland', provoking further consternation among those listening north of the border.

'I knew immediately it was an act of catastrophic misjudgement,' said one senior Labour figure who had been central to the campaign. The Prime Minister – his critics argued – had the opportunity to fly north to Scotland and make a reflective speech, not dissimilar to that he gave after the Bloody Sunday inquiry in 2010. 'He could have been statesmanlike: humble, generous and grateful. Instead, he was narrow, divisive and partisan.'

Many in Labour, with its forty Scottish MPs able to vote on matters affecting only England, immediately realised quite how damaging such reforms could be for its own prospects of returning to power and governing effectively at Westminster. There was, in addition, a wider awareness that Cameron could – with no time for the victory to sink in and be consolidated – be giving the SNP the opening they craved to snatch victory from the jaws of defeat.

Labour and the Liberal Democrats were enraged. Some senior Conservatives tried to spin the announcement as 'unexceptional – it had, after all, been party policy since 2001'. But, privately, most conceded that 'it could have waited a day, or even the weekend'.

The vitriol directed at Cameron for this decision still bubbles among senior Scottish politicians: 'It was a decision made out of fear not strength,' said one. 'He feared critical Conservative backbenchers in the Sunday newspapers, and so put party management ahead of the interests of his country. History will judge him very harshly.'

As soon as the Prime Minister returned through the black door of No. 10, Better Together turned, as surely as Cinderella's carriage, into a pumpkin. In a flash, the three parties, united for two and a half years, split asunder, their grievances with each other returning almost instantaneously. The campaign's employees were suddenly out of a job; their workload disappeared; the team disbanded.

The final result: 1,617,989 people had voted Yes in support of Scottish independence; 2,001,926 had voted No against it. Better Together won with 55 per cent of the vote.

As Labour politicians left the Marriott and travelled through the rain to Glasgow's Emirates Arena for a celebration with Ed Miliband, other activists sat down for a greasy cooked breakfast in the hotel, and many just collapsed into bed.

The morning rush hour was just beginning in Glasgow.

Another working day – in what would remain the UK's third-largest city – was just beginning. It all seemed bizarrely anti-climactic. Many in the No campaign were not so much feeling delight as a deep sense of relief.

Scotland would now return to normal. Or so they thought.

ELECTION

PART 2

ELECTION

CHAPTER 11

LAMONT'S LAMENT

One senior staffer was spotted grappling with a massive flat-screen TV, desperately trying to squeeze it into the back of a taxi. It was early afternoon on Friday 19 September, just hours after Scotland had voted No, and, as the international media circus moved on, the Better Together campaign was being dismantled – literally.

'It was like after Hurricane Katrina – looting!' remarked one experienced figure looking on aghast. Believing the campaign would run a surplus, staff had been told they could keep their work computers, but some took that to mean everything was up for grabs. 'It was a complete free-for-all,' observed one staff member. 'It was indicative of the lack of responsibility.' And – although no one realised it at the time – Better Together's finances were far from healthy.

SNP politicians knew change was brewing in their party: it was suddenly impossible to contact key advisers and strategists. 'For the first time I couldn't get hold of anyone,' explained one minister. 'I knew something was up. They were all circling around Alec.'

As the afternoon of the 19th wore on, beneath the elaborate plasterwork and glimmering glass chandelier of Bute

House's drawing room, a handpicked group of exhausted journalists awaited Alex Salmond's arrival. Channel 4's Jon Snow sat alongside ITV's Martin Geissler, with Brian Taylor from the BBC behind. Representatives from the *Daily Record*, *The Times* and *The Scotsman* were among just twenty-two members of the media present. However, not everyone was welcome: '*Mail*, *Telegraph* & *Express* excluded from Alex Salmond's press conference,' tweeted a furious Alan Roden, political editor of the *Scottish Daily Mail*. *The Guardian* also turned down an invite after the Scottish government attempted to choose which journalist would attend.

Not everyone who *had* been invited bothered to turn up. The event had been pushed back until 4 p.m. and most journalists had been up all through the night working on live TV coverage of the counts or preparing late editions of the morning papers. Furthermore, reporter after reporter had been categorically told, by the First Minister's special advisers, that Salmond would not be resigning.

And why would he? He was Scotland's longest-serving First Minister, commanding a majority in the Scottish Parliament, there were almost two years left before he faced the electorate, and support for independence had hit a record 45 per cent.

However, when he entered the room, the assembled press knew they had been spun. Salmond was going. The energy, the bravado and the cheekiness were gone. Instead a drained, weary, serious First Minister started a short speech: 'I am immensely proud of the campaign that Yes Scotland fought,' he remarked, before hailing the record turnout, and pledging to 'hold Westminster's feet to the fire' on 'The Vow'.

As he changed gear to the – by now inevitable – resignation announcement, the room was transfixed. Salmond's tone uncharacteristically quiet, his eyes wet. Civil service press officers lining the room showed no emotion but, at the back behind a small row of TV cameras, Salmond's chief of staff Geoff Aberdein had tears rolling down his cheeks.

'For me as leader my time is nearly over, but for Scotland the campaign continues and', looking up to the cameras, he concluded, 'the dream shall never die.' His final line was lifted from Ted Kennedy's 1980 Democratic National Convention concession speech, the work of master speechwriter Bob Shrum. But, thirty-four years later, the provenance was secondary: it aptly summed up the downhearted but defiant spirit of many of his supporters.

Unlike his three predecessors – who had, respectively, died, resigned and lost an election – Alex Salmond was choreographing his own departure. Two months earlier, on 18 July 2014, the First Minister had confided in his deputy and likely successor, Nicola Sturgeon, that he would take responsibility and be 'minded to resign' in the event of a defeat. It would prove a masterstroke, at once drawing a line under the loss, and allowing his party a swift renewal under a new leader.

The next morning, at Scottish Labour's Glasgow headquarters, Jackie Baillie, a senior Labour MSP, broke down in tears in front of her colleagues. 'I'm sorry,' she said. Baillie, who had been heavily involved in the Better Together campaign, was upset that the local authority area of West Dunbartonshire – much of her constituency – had voted in favour of independence. 'She could see the political consequences,' explained one colleague watching on, 'the melting of Labour support and the crystallising of the Yes vote into the SNP.'

Assembled politicians were 'shell-shocked about how the result was so close', remarked another source. 'If you understand anything of history, and of Quebec, it's not that easy.' In Canada, just a year after defeat in the 1980 referendum, the Parti Québécois (PQ) secured 49.26 per cent of the vote in a Quebec general election, their highest ever share and enough to form a majority government.

The aftermath of the 1995 referendum was more complicated: PQ leader Jacques Parizeau's controversial off-the-cuff concession speech included blame apportioned to 'money and ethnic votes'. Five days after the referendum, a schizophrenic Yes supporter unsuccessfully attempted to assassinate Prime Minister Jean Chrétien with a knife. Yet, at the next Québec election in 1998, the PQ were successful enough to form a government, this time with 42.87 per cent of the vote.

Two days after Scotland's referendum, the SNP issued a press release boasting that membership had risen to over 30,000 members, a boost of nearly 5,000. Faced with the possibility that defeat could be the catalyst for nationalist growth, however, Johann Lamont gave little sign she recognised the need to move forward and persuade left-leaning Yes voters to back Labour again.

Unrest had been building about Lamont's leadership, with a secret plot to remove her slowly developing over the previous eighteen months. And the leader's low profile during the referendum itself has led some of her colleagues to despair. 'She was invisible,' complained one Labour politician. 'She wasn't sidelined, she chose not to be part of it. Her passion is combating poverty and inequality. She couldn't give a shit about constitutional politics.'

In addition to her own scepticism, Better Together had been loath to use Lamont for media appearances, because their research showed she was an ineffective communicator. In early 2013, various pro-UK politicians, including Lamont, Alistair

Darling, Scottish Conservatives' leader Ruth Davidson and Labour MSP Kezia Dugdale, had been recorded on camera reading aloud a short series of No campaign messages.

The politicians had been told the videos would be used to test campaign messages but, in fact, they were a covert attempt to test the message carriers. Each video was played to a series of focus groups, and the closely guarded results were bleak for Lamont loyalists. Voters liked Dugdale the most, with Davidson in close second, Darling was 'middling', while Lamont was at the bottom: 'The reaction was very negative,' revealed someone closely involved.

Few believed Johann Lamont enjoyed being leader. 'Over the summer, there was an underlying assumption Johann was finished,' explained a close colleague. 'She took on the leadership out of duty,' argued another senior Labour figure, 'and clearly, outside of some reasonably sparky performances in FMQs [First Minister's Questions], she had no idea how to lead. The job was a burden and she hated it.' Lamont received plaudits for her weekly parliamentary jousts with Salmond, which she privately referred to as 'poking a stick at the most arrogant man in Scottish politics'. But, elsewhere, her success was limited. An experienced party source likened Lamont's attitude to that of 'an exhausted school teacher in a tough working-class comprehensive in east London saying to themselves: "Fuck me, I don't have to do this every day, do I? Oh shit, I do."'

Soon after the referendum, Lamont was walking down Edinburgh's Royal Mile with her press officer Craig Davidson. A respectfully dressed middle-aged man walking past shouted, 'You make me sick,' then turned round adding: 'You're a traitor!' How had it become normal to be abusive to older women? Lamont was finding the leadership a wearing experience.

And her team did little to combat this perception. Paul Sinclair, her chief aide, had approached Torsten Bell, Ed Miliband's policy director, to broach the possibility of Lamont being nominated for a peerage: 'Baroness Lamont of Pollok' had a certain ring to it. Bell advised that such a discussion should be had directly with Miliband.

Sinclair was also coming to the end of his contract. He had agreed to steer Lamont through the referendum and, without her most ferocious guardian, few understood how she would be able to survive.

So who would want to take on the poisoned chalice of the Scottish Labour leadership? One name that arose time and again was the MP for East Renfrewshire and shadow International Development Secretary, Jim Murphy. Lamont had harboured suspicions for the past year that Murphy coveted her role. That was politics. His '100 towns' tour speaking atop two Irn-Bru crates across the country was a very public challenge. But Murphy was clear he was not going to oust her directly: he did not want to be a Heseltine.

'I didn't believe Jim Murphy wanted to be leader,' remarked one senior politician, believing that the MP would prefer to let Lamont preside over the inevitably difficult general election race, before swooping in to save the party.

Yet, at the first post-referendum shadow Cabinet meeting in Glasgow, there was no sign of any attempt to start tackling the party's many problems. One politician present complained: 'I was stunned. It was business as usual.'

As soon as the meeting was over, Lamont travelled down to Manchester for Labour's annual conference. Alistair Darling had also been dragged down to accept the party's praise and plaudits for running the Better Together campaign.

After the referendum, Lamont's team had been pushing

for her to have a more prominent role than the usual 'total sideshow' of 'ten minutes on a Sunday morning'. Could this be the year when the Scottish Labour leader would get more of a say and more media attention? But 'Ed Miliband's office didn't want that', explained one source close to the action. 'Their argument was to hand out Union Jacks to wave at the end of her speech.' This provoked a furious reaction from Scottish Labour: 'Are you mad? Don't you understand what's just happened in Scotland?'

At the conference centre in Manchester, the atmosphere was 'friendly but subdued. No one was euphoric,' according to a senior politician. 'The UK had just gone through a monumentally large political event,' complained someone involved. 'It had been a big existential crisis, that sucked all the energy into it.' This left Labour's annual conference looking slightly irrelevant: 'It was macro high politics followed by the village fair.' The juxtaposition was particularly acute for the Labour Party as theirs was the first conference and they had been the leading unionist force in the referendum.

Lamont had written her speech at the last minute. With Miliband, Darling and other party figures in attendance, as well as a half-full audience at Manchester's Central Hall, Lamont showed energy but no sign of leaving: 'I look forward to working with Ed in No. 10 to lead Scottish Labour to victory in 2016.' The implication was that she would continue, a surprise to many.

Junior members of Team Murphy had been openly briefing at the conference that he would soon take over. Paul Sinclair swiftly got wind of this dissent and crushed it. But he would only be able to plug the dyke temporarily.

Miliband's team claim to have been 'sympathetic and supporting' of Lamont, although there was a 'sense that she was struggling'. But so was their leader, who had his own troubles to deal with. In his set-piece 66-minute conference speech, delivered without notes, Miliband forgot a whole section about tackling the country's £75 billion deficit.

While Labour continued its decline, Nicola Sturgeon was on the opposite trajectory. Just five days after Alex Salmond's resignation, she announced her intention to stand to succeed him. On the same day, SNP membership reached 57,000. Now ahead of the Liberal Democrats, this made it the third-largest party by membership in the whole of the UK.

Opinion polls also suggested a sharp rise in SNP support for the upcoming general election, as Scottish Labour's figures slumped. 'The referendum was the biggest decision most Scots had ever made in their lifetime,' argued a senior Labour MP. 'Sentiments and emotions and affinities so deep do not dissipate in weeks and months. Of course there was going to be an afterlife.'

At the same time, the five Scottish parties (SNP, Labour, Conservatives, Liberal Democrats and Greens) nominated two representatives each to join the Smith Commission – a result of 'The Vow' – set up to recommend the devolution of further powers from Westminster to Holyrood. Former leaders seemed particularly popular choices, with the SNP putting forward John Swinney, Labour selecting Iain Gray, and the Conservatives nominating Annabel Goldie.

After Labour conference, as rumour swirled around about his ambitions, Jim Murphy received an unexpected phone call. It was Johann Lamont and she had a direct question: do you want my job? If you want it, have it – was her approach – if you think this is an easy gig, you are sorely mistaken.

Murphy assured her he was not interested and promised to make that clear. It was a case of credible deniability. But it created a difficult situation: if he did not want the job, she needed to get on with doing it herself.

Surprising many, on 26 September, Lamont announced that she was going nowhere. She told reporters at Holyrood: 'The next phase is to 2016, and yes I want to be First Minister, because I believe I have the life experience and I've got a commitment to change.'

The rest of her party found it a puzzling and unexpected intervention. 'She was trying to assert herself very late; it looked bizarre and weak,' remarked one colleague. 'She drifted into it. You need to be seen to act quickly. Either crush rebellion fast or go.' This did neither.

The whispers about Lamont's leadership had been building, most significantly among MPs, many of whom feared losing their jobs in the upcoming general election. The Scottish Parliamentary Labour Party (SPLP) only met for the first time one month after the referendum, at which point frustrations had reached fever pitch. One MP described the split in opinion on Johann among colleagues as: 'She's useless and will survive, or she's useless and will go.' For many at Westminster, it was hard to respect an MSP, rather than an MP, as leader of the Scottish Party. While Lamont was seen by many at Westminster as a sincere and principled politician, some also believed she 'only became leader because everyone with charisma and presence lost their seats' in the 2011 Holyrood elections.

Chief among her critics in the House of Commons was Lamont's one-time university pal Margaret Curran. The pair's decades-old relationship had started to fall apart at Easter 2014, and collapsed completely over the referendum, when Curran walked out of Scottish Labour meetings in despair at what she saw as its ineffectual campaign.

Some saw Curran's frustration with Lamont as motivated by self-interest: 'Margaret had fallen in love with power and was desperate to hold onto it,' claimed one Labour source. 'She had her corner office in Portcullis House with views of Westminster Bridge and the London Eye. It was showbiz, the big time, and night and day from being an MSP with an office on the ground floor of Holyrood. If they could just get through the general election, Ed would be Prime Minister and she could be Secretary of State for Scotland.'

Others saw Lamont as a scapegoat for far wider problems within the party. In any case, getting rid of a Labour leader is intentionally very difficult. Resignation is the only easy option. Over the coming days, pressure mounted on Lamont. David Hamilton, MP for Midlothian, told her his colleagues were so anxious about their electoral prospects that they thought she needed to go.

Just weeks after the referendum, Better Together's board was convened at Scottish Labour's offices near Holyrood for what proved to be a truly farcical meeting. The first item on the agenda was staff bonuses. Everyone involved in the campaign had (informally) been promised a financial reward if No won, although some were uneasy with the concept.

Director of operations Kate Watson had been told to arrive thirty minutes after the meeting began, to avoid any awkward discussions about the remuneration of her Better Together colleagues. She had been sitting up the road in Starbucks running through the organisation's accounts. 'She's not exactly an optimist,' remarked one colleague, but the news she was to impart quickly changed the nature of the meeting. 'I've actually just been doing the sums, and we only have £30,000 in the bank.'

Over the coming weeks, Better Together's financial

situation was only to worsen, as further problems were uncovered. 'Money was spent like water,' complained one senior figure. The campaign had benefited from a series of large donations at the beginning of the summer – including £1 million from *Harry Potter* author J. K. Rowling. But because spending was capped and tightly regulated during the final months of the campaign, it had to be spent fast.

Staff costs were not included in the limits set by the Electoral Commission, meaning more activists could be recruited. Funds were also spent on a series of pay rises for staff already in post. 'Salaries were stuck up to a ridiculous level,' complained someone involved. 'One employee on £40,000 had their salary increased to £60,000.' Only one staff member refused a raise: Kate Watson.

There had also been what an adviser described as a 'fuck-up with contracts'. A number of senior staff had been employed before the date of the referendum was known, so their contracts ran right through to the end of 2014. After the date of the vote was announced in March 2013, there were no renegotiations, leaving Better Together with three and a half months of hefty bills for well-paid staff doing little.

Adding to the frustrations, two staff members argued that they were entitled to thirty days' holiday pay on full salary. The campaign was forced to pay, even though, as one frustrated board member put it, the pair 'had been watching DVDs in their pants for the last three months'.

In addition to this, the cost of national insurance contributions had not been factored into budgets. Better Together had no dedicated in-house bookkeeper and, when there was money to employ one, Watson refused. Instead, £50,000 had been spent on an advert that was never shown and £27,000 on the overnight results party – a 'horrific' level of expenditure, according to one senior figure. The 'looting' of the campaign's Savoy Centre offices also left the organisation with few assets. Invoices continued to arrive for leaflets that had been printed or events held. In many cases, rates had not been properly negotiated, meaning Better Together was charged much more than expected.

The total shortfall quickly soared to £200,000. The campaign's decision on 12 August to issue a press release requesting no more donations – intended as proof of momentum rather than a prudent financial decision – now looked remarkably short-sighted.

It left Alistair Darling and his board in the excruciating position of, even after winning the referendum, having to ask donors to bail them out, or be faced with declaring the organisation bankrupt. 'Alistair hated asking for money at the best of times,' remarked one senior staff member. 'Every campaign overspends,' explained another involved, 'but this was desperate. Better Together was cursed with crises.' Over the following months, donations were amassed – mainly from businessmen who had previously given generously to the campaign. The largest was £100,000. The shortfall was eventually plugged, but many senior politicians involved were furious: 'The multiple levels of fuckwittery were breathtaking.'

Better Together was not alone in being short of cash. Between September and November 2014, the SNP bailed out Yes Scotland to the tune of £825,000.

On the morning of Friday 17 October, Johann Lamont was standing outside Argos on Argyll Street in Glasgow with her husband Archie Graham, the deputy leader of Glasgow City Council. She received a message that Tim Livesey, Ed Miliband's chief of staff, wanted to talk. Whatever he wanted to discuss, it must clearly be important. When Lamont took the call, she got a shock.

Livesey told her that the central party in London was sacking Scottish Labour's General Secretary Ian Price. Lamont went ballistic: 'If you think the fucking problem with Scottish politics is who our General Secretary is, you have a lot to understand.'

Price, Livesey explained, was taking part in a 'protected conversation' with party bosses in London: a mechanism for trying to come to a settlement for him to leave the organisation without protracted legal wrangling. Lamont was shocked: 'You're telling me you're taking him down to London because *he's* the problem?'

Price had only been in the role for eighteen months. The previous General Secretary Colin Smyth had left soon after a shake-up of the Scottish Labour's structures. But over the referendum, with veteran campaigners being sent up from England to get the party's campaign operation into shape, Price had lost the confidence of the staff.

Among them were Price's most senior colleagues Annmarie Whyte (Scottish Labour's head of corporate affairs and events) and Brian Roy (head of campaigns – and son of Motherwell MP Frank Roy). 'Both couldn't get on with Ian Price,' explained a senior figure. 'He was trying to modernise an organisation that wasn't prepared to modernise, so it shut down on him.'

Whyte was seen as particularly formidable: 'She's fierce, incredibly well organised, very reliable, and incapable of changing how she operates,' said a senior source. One Labour adviser even has his ringtone set to the *Star Wars* 'Imperial March' for whenever Whyte calls. 'She scares the living death out of people,' revealed another colleague: 'You only pick up a call if you know the answer.'

Standing on a bustling street corner in Glasgow, Lamont ended the phone conversation with Livesey. She quickly came to the conclusion that she was in an untenable position. Either she would have to lie and say Price was not up to the job and needed to leave, or it would look like she was feeble: the Westminster party was able to sack one of her most senior staff members over her head and she would not complain.

But the pressure would only increase. A few days later, Lamont received a call from the Scottish Labour Party's chair, Jamie Glackin. 'Ed Miliband and Margaret Curran want you to go,' he said. Lamont also got wind there were to be further stories in the papers with anonymous sources, challenging her position. One Scottish constituency Labour Party would even be passing a motion of no confidence in her.

Sitting in her car one evening waiting for her son – a talented swimmer – outside Glasgow's Tollcross International Swimming Centre, Lamont realised the pressure was too much. She called her top adviser Paul Sinclair. 'I'm frightened,' she said. 'You have nothing to be frightened about,' Sinclair assured her. Lamont's husband Archie had always advised: 'Don't be bullied out.'

Paul Sinclair had an agreement with the *Daily Record*'s editor Murray Foote that if Johann Lamont were to resign, the Labour-sympathising paper would get to tell her story. Sinclair had been the paper's political editor, and the two were close friends.

The controversial details of Lamont's resignation were not formulated by interview but were a collaborative effort by Sinclair and Foote. Punches would not be pulled. Lamont was loyal to the Labour Party but felt it was in danger of closing ranks and not dealing with the reality of its deep-rooted problems. Failing to address these would make her culpable for its continued dysfunction.

Johann Lamont did not sign off her resignation statement by email or via a phone conversation, but over lunch in a five-star hotel with two bottles of wine. On Friday 24 October, Lamont met up with Sinclair, his deputy Craig Davidson, and Murray Foote for an expensive meal at the Blythswood Square Hotel in Glasgow. Lamont was relieved to have made up her mind, but concerned about the future of her party. She was handed the draft wording for her to sign off for the next day's paper. Reading through it at the table, she asked: 'Should I be going as hard as this?' It was agreed she needed to clear the decks for a new leader who could rule with autonomy. As Lamont left the hotel with Sinclair and Davidson, Foote walked back to his office. All four knew that others were getting wind of an impending announcement.

Sinclair gave the exclusive to the BBC via Nick Robinson, to break on the corporation's 10 p.m. bulletin. Choosing the network newsroom would ensure the impact was felt in Westminster and at a national level. But the BBC Scotland political team in Lamont's home city were not informed: scores were being settled.

Two lines, in particular, would cause Labour jaws to drop. In the *Record* article, Lamont commented that 'just as the SNP must embrace that devolution is the settled will of the Scottish people, the Labour Party must recognise that the Scottish party has to be autonomous and not just a branch office of a party based in London'. The phrase 'branch office' would be particularly damaging for the UK party that had tried hard to avoid accusations they were too involved in the supposedly autonomous Scottish party's business.

Lamont also had a dig at her MP detractors: 'There is a danger of Scottish politics being between two sets of dinosaurs ... the nationalists who can't accept they were rejected by the people, and some colleagues at Westminster who think nothing has changed.'

Lamont and Paul Sinclair had various conversations that afternoon with members of Ed Miliband's team who were hurrying to react to the news in the opposition leader's office at the Palace of Westminster. 'When in doubt, have conference calls,' a source involved explained.

Although those on Team Ed were aware that Lamont's departure was to be detailed in the *Daily Record*, they were completely in the dark as to its critical content: 'We didn't realise about the "branch office" until much later,' said a source in the Westminster HQ. 'It became clear slightly too late.'

In Scotland, there was a series of frantic phone calls between various MSPs and MPs. Some were genuinely upset when they were tipped off about the nature of Johann Lamont's departure.

Even those who were no fans of Ed Miliband thought Lamont treated the leader unfairly. Miliband refused almost all media requests but released a brief statement saying: 'I have respect for Johann, for her grit and determination, for these are hard jobs and she fought a once-in-a-generation referendum campaign, so I have huge respect for her.'

The *Record*'s leader column claimed Lamont 'leaves with dignity and her head held high'. Her own party, with just over six months until a general election, felt very differently: 'I will never forgive her for what she did,' raged one colleague. 'Her resignation could have been constructed by SNP headquarters. It was fashioned to cause maximum damage to the party she claims to love. She couldn't have caused more damage if she tried. And she did.'

Another, referring to her 'branch office' jibe, spluttered: 'It was the most disloyal and disgraceful remark I've ever heard in decades in politics. She dynamited herself out of office, burned down the house and walked out the front door. She gutted the Scottish Labour Party.' One senior figure even argued: 'The Scottish Labour Party would have been better if it *had* been run as a branch office.' Another well-known politician complained that the phrase 'will always be part of Labour folklore. The damage is permanent.'

However, there was support from two of Lamont's predecessors. Former Labour First Minister Jack McConnell told BBC Radio Scotland he had sympathy for her position: 'She clearly blames today publicly Ed Miliband and those around him and that's a very serious accusation that requires answers.' Another former First Minister, Henry McLeish, argued: 'This lack of autonomy is costing the party votes, credibility, relevance and authority. The role of any leader in Scotland has turned into a nightmare as the grip of London grows stronger, not weaker.' Some of Lamont's colleagues were also sceptical of the language used in her resignation: 'I've known her for years,' remarked one friend, 'and that was not Johann talking.'

Those with experience of media management claim Lamont's departure was carefully constructed to distract from her own record of making little impact in the media: 'The only time Johann Lamont led the news was when she resigned,' insisted one. 'The way she went was so spectacular, with so many fireworks and so much oil, nobody ever questioned whether her leadership was any good.'

And with just over six months until the general election, with the SNP gaining an unprecedented level of support, Scottish Labour was damaged, leaderless and on course for a painful defeat.

CHAPTER 12

LABOUR PAINS

'Who is good and who isn't?' Jim Murphy asked. He had booked a suite in the Macdonald Holyrood Hotel, a few minutes' walk from the Scottish Parliament. Over the course of Wednesday 29 October, he had arranged a succession of secret one-to-one meetings with sympathetic MSPs and advisers. This was a scoping exercise to understand how to ace the Scottish Labour leadership campaign, negotiate his way through the general election and rise to power in Scotland. As a long-serving Westminster MP, Murphy had little knowledge of Holyrood or Labour's group of MSPs.

Aside from using this as research, Murphy was cultivating an army of well-placed supporters. Each visitor was given a series of fact-finding tasks. He believed he was far more skilled than any of his recent predecessors. His grasp of retail politics, his assured media performances and his energy, he was sure, could turn around Scottish Labour's fortunes.

And Jim Murphy was focused on one prize. 'He only wanted to do it if he could be First Minister of Scotland,' explained one adviser. 'He wanted the office and convinced himself he could win it sooner than anyone expected.'

The vegetarian, teetotal Glaswegian had been an MP for seventeen years. His attention had always been focused on UK – rather than Scottish – politics, aside from eighteen months as Scottish Secretary, six months campaigning in the referendum, as well as his constituency commitments. Murphy had not courted journalists north of the border or networked with MSPs. This changed, however, after his relationship with Ed Miliband deteriorated badly. And the vacant leader's job in Scotland was tempting.

But Murphy would need a seat at the Scottish Parliament as soon as possible if he was to ever lead the Scottish government. The best possibility for achieving this swiftly was a seat swap: Murphy could stand down from his Westminster constituency at the general election, and put himself forward in a by-election for a safe Labour Holyrood seat at the same time. He just needed a sympathetic MSP. Murphy approached two – Ken Macintosh and John Pentland – with his plan. Both refused. This frustrated Murphy, although he was confident at least one of them would change their mind after he became leader.

Murphy's team estimated that between £80,000 and £90,000 was spent on his leadership campaign, including the employment of at least six members of staff on significant salaries. It was effectively a Better Together reunion, with Blair McDougall advising on policy and writing speeches. Three further members of the No campaign – two press officers and one researcher – also joined Team Murphy.

MSPs Jenny Marra and James Kelly were selected to co-chair his campaign: Marra, part of the 2011 intake and a high-flying newcomer, and Kelly, a former Chief Whip who could bend the ears of older parliamentarians.

Murphy invested in polling from the market research

company Populus, focusing on public perceptions of the Labour Party. The findings made tough reading for him and his team. In a word-association exercise, voters linked the SNP to terms like 'fairness', 'equality' and 'Scotland'. The only phrase Labour beat the nationalists on was 'more of the same', despite not having been in power at Holyrood for seven years.

When Scots were asked who they knew within the party north of the border, Gordon Brown came in first place with Murphy a close second. 'Jim saw himself on that level,' explained one aide.

Murphy's two challengers were the left-wing MSP Neil Findlay and Scottish Labour veteran Sarah Boyack. The latter's allies admitted she was standing 'to be part of the conversation' and to 'boost her future electoral chances' rather than with any hope of victory: 'It was all about raising her profile in an attempt to bump her up the regional list.' And while Findlay surprised Murphy's team by raising tens of thousands of pounds in funding with resultant sophisticated campaign materials, the outcome was always clear. 'It was very dull,' admitted an adviser, 'we all knew Jim would win.'

The *Daily Record* on 30 October carried the announcement that Murphy would run. 'I'm applying for the job of First Minister,' he told the paper's political editor David Clegg. Yet a poll on the tabloid's website suggested 71 per cent of readers thought Murphy would not make a good leader of Scottish Labour.

Later that day, STV published a far more significant poll from Ipsos MORI. It suggested Labour was facing 'political annihilation' at the general election: 52 per cent of voters would support the SNP, giving them fifty-four of Scotland's fifty-nine seats at Westminster. Labour was on 23 per cent and just four seats – a drop of thirty-seven seats from the 2010 election. Murphy's East Renfrewshire constituency was not one of the four that would stay red.

That evening, the Scottish Labour Party was due to hold its annual fundraising gala dinner at Glasgow's Grand Central Hotel, with Ed Miliband attending as the star guest. But MSPs, furious at the fallout from Johann Lamont's recent resignation, requested that the event be cancelled – 'We shouldn't be supping champagne!' complained one politician – and a meeting with Miliband be arranged in Edinburgh instead. The Labour leader had no intention of coming to Edinburgh. Changing plans at the last minute would not look good for a start. So an emergency gathering was arranged in Glasgow behind closed doors before the fundraiser.

It was a tense, angry meeting, with accusations flying around, mostly directed at Miliband. MSPs were more sympathetic than their Westminster counterparts to the plight of their recently departed Scottish leader. 'We were not happy about how Johann had gone, and how she felt pushed,' explained one politician present. Miliband attempted to be candid and soothing, and pointed out: 'The party's problems in Scotland are longstanding. You guys have a big challenge.' But he would not be drawn on the departure of General Secretary Ian Price: 'It's all confidential, it's a staff matter, I can't comment,' Miliband insisted.

As if to compound the party's problems, the meeting took place to the sound of chanting pro-independence campaigners, who had set up outside the hotel protesting about the proliferation of food banks. Canny Jim Murphy dropped off a bag of food on arrival, but the very fact there was hostility towards a leaderless opposition party was disconcerting.

Senior MSP Graeme Pearson – never shy of speaking his mind – pointed out to Miliband: 'We're not in government in Scotland, we're not in government in the UK, but we still have protestors outside!' It was a comment many present later admitted brought home the intimidating scale of the challenge Scottish Labour faced.

As the Labour pains worsened, Nicola Sturgeon's assured rise was continuing apace. It was a coronation rather than a contest, but, for senior figures in the party, that was not a problem. 'She's been preparing for this for such a long time,' explained one, 'and she got the job because she's bloody good.' The party defeated in the referendum suddenly had a renewed sense of momentum. 'It was a case of the King is dead, long live the Queen,' joked one nationalist politician.

Three weeks later, on 19 November 2014, Sturgeon was sitting at the front centre desk in the Scottish Parliament debating chamber, with two close colleagues and friends – John Swinney and Shona Robison – on either side. Two rows behind, her mentor and now predecessor Alex Salmond looked on. She glanced up and smiled at her young niece in the public gallery – middle name Nicola – and her husband, Peter Murrell, the SNP's chief executive. She had been waiting a long time for this moment.

Holyrood's presiding officer Tricia Marwick announced: 'I declare that Nicola Sturgeon is selected as this Parliament's nominee for appointment as First Minister.' The chamber erupted in applause. Sturgeon was forty-four years old. She had been a member of the SNP for twenty-eight years. For over half that time, she had been an MSP, and, for a quarter of that time, she had been Scotland's Deputy First Minister. Now she had made it to the top job just as her party's popularity soared.

Pledging to be 'First Minister for all of Scotland', Sturgeon said she was 'very proud' as a 'working-class girl from Ayrshire given the job of heading up the government of Scotland'. In contrast to Salmond, she promised to work consensually with opposition politicians: 'Where we are on common ground ... they will find in me a willing and listening ally.'

Sturgeon hoped her election would send a 'strong, positive message to girls and young women, indeed to all women, across our land – there should be no limit to your ambition or what you can achieve'. Yet this sentiment was somewhat undermined when the first Scottish government press release emailed out under her premiership contained details of the red knee-length dress she was wearing – from 'independent women's wear fashion label and boutique' Totty Rocks.

'I'm from the business world and we make decisions quickly,' Lord Smith of Kelvin told his assembled team. In the 'sterile, lifeless and not that posh' boardroom of the Green Investment Bank in Edinburgh, where Smith was chairman, ten senior politicians had helped themselves to 'bad coffee' and were settling down for more devolution discussions. Their task was to make recommendations to 'deliver more financial, welfare and taxation powers, strengthening the Scottish Parliament within the United Kingdom'. Sessions typically lasted between two and three hours, and were scheduled to fit in with the Scottish Parliament's timetable.

Away from negotiations, the civil servants responsible for keeping the commission on track had plastered the walls of their temporary offices with copies of the *Daily Record*'s 'Vow'.

When new devolution proposals were fed to them, civil servants would ask: 'Does this fit with the framework of

"The Vow"?' It was surprising how one hastily arranged front page had become so central to the changing constitutional position of the UK.

Those taking part claim that Lord Smith treated everyone slightly differently. Former Conservative leader Annabel Goldie was the star pupil: 'He adored her and laughed at all her lame jokes,' revealed one person involved. Labour's representatives, by contrast, were the bad boys of the class. 'He treated them with utter contempt, as delinquents who were argumentative and obstructive.' Johann Lamont had appointed her predecessor as Scottish Labour leader, Iain Gray, and the fiercely intelligent Gregg McClymont, MP for Cumbernauld and shadow Pensions Minister.

However, after Lamont resigned as leader halfway through the commission process, it was not clear from whom the two politicians should take direction. Ed Miliband and his team ended up playing a regular role, and Gordon Brown was kept briefed on proceedings.

Some in the party privately accused Gray of 'going rogue' under pressure and having 'no red lines'. This was backed up by other parties round the table who claimed: 'There was a feeling that Labour were in chaos throughout.' One Labour source concluded that Gray 'has never had to make a decision of real consequence; he wanted to capitulate in every argument and was not interested in what Labour got out of it'.

Smith's relationship with the Greens was more curious: 'He started off being suspicious but developed a great affection and they ended up great pals,' explained one source. The Liberal Democrats had selected former Scottish Secretary Michael Moore and former Scottish leader Tavish Scott to negotiate on their behalf.

The SNP had nominated Finance Secretary John Swinney and ex-Culture Minister Linda Fabiani. The latter's contributions were said to have raised more than a few eyebrows: 'Linda Fabiani was absolutely fucking bonkers,' said one person taking part. 'Wittering on inanely with incomprehensible nonsense. Everyone was looking at each other. Swinney was visibly embarrassed.' In contrast, Swinney – promoted to Deputy First Minister during negotiations – was widely agreed to have been 'the star performer, really top notch, he played it like a true professional'.

Neither the Greens nor the SNP had any solid plans, because, ultimately, they wanted independence rather than further devolution. An additional challenge, according to some involved, was that none of the ten politicians had detailed knowledge of the complexities of the policy areas to which they were proposing to make such massive changes. 'They didn't have a deep understanding of what the UK government could deliver,' argued one source. 'Unpicking the complexities of areas like universal credit, it became apparent that it would be impossibly difficult to devolve and would cost a fortune.' By contrast, the devolution of Air Passenger Duty was easy for Downing Street to transfer.

Some were surprised by how fast the SNP gave up on advocating devolution of the state pension and oil revenue. 'They didn't even make a fight over it. It was off the agenda immediately,' said someone in the room. However, the nationalists' political enemies still credit them with being 'very pragmatic yet principled'.

The Conservatives were keen to keep the UK as a single trading area, therefore avoiding two rates of capital gains tax, two levels of corporation tax and a double-up of regulatory regimes. Swinney is also said to have recognised the 'difficulties' he would face as Finance Secretary if a random assortment of financial powers were devolved.

The final few days of negotiations were 'chaotic and extremely fraught', according to one source. 'There was a lot of to-ing and fro-ing, welfare being the hardest area to resolve.' Conservative leader Ruth Davidson did not attend commission meetings but was effectively responsible for ensuring the delivery by the UK government of whatever the commission decided to recommend. After private one-to-one meetings in Whitehall with the Prime Minister, Chancellor and Iain Duncan Smith – Secretary of State for Work and Pensions – she was still concerned that Downing Street might attempt to row back and legislate for less than the commission had agreed.

Just two days before the final report was published, Davidson made what one Conservative termed a 'Broken Arrow call' – a nod to the US military term used when soldiers in mortal danger request assistance from every aircraft and cavalry unit. She told Andrew Dunlop in no uncertain terms that the UK government 'will have to suck it up' and deliver exactly what the commission requests.

The final unresolved complexity was the devolution of abortion law. Up until this point, Green Party leader Patrick Harvie had done all the talking. Now his fellow Green commissioner Maggie Chapman spoke up. Both were very keen for the powers to be devolved, and there was substantial cross-party agreement. Only Labour opposed it, and, with the matter apparently almost settled, at 6 p.m. on Wednesday 26 November – the night before the report was published – they again asked for it to be taken off the table. Chapman was 'visibly upset and angry' when this was suggested, according to one witness. And, at this late stage,

Lord Smith made a rare intervention and recommended that the issue of abortion be removed from the commission's report. 'It was the only thing he got changed,' revealed one person in the room.

Early the next morning, Lord Smith of Kelvin strode across the Victorian Grand Gallery of the National Museum of Scotland in Edinburgh, clutching a blue folder bearing the words 'The Smith Commission'. His ten 'commissioners' followed behind through the huge, bright atrium, with its slender columns and curving staircases, towards a large, seated group of journalists and dignitaries. Just thirty-six days after their first meeting, the five parties had agreed on a set of further powers for the Scottish Parliament, including some over tax and welfare payments.

David Cameron said he was 'delighted' with the report, remarking: 'We are keeping our promises and we are keeping our United Kingdom together.'

At First Minister's Questions that afternoon, however, Nicola Sturgeon was far less supportive: 'I think the verdict of the Scottish people will be that it is not enough, it doesn't live up to "The Vow", it doesn't deliver a modern form of home rule.' And while the *Daily Record*'s 'Vow' never mentioned home rule – instead insisting on 'the continuation of the Barnett allocation' – some pro-UK politicians had used the term, as well as promising 'devo max' and 'near federalism'.

It was another impressive performance for Sturgeon, who had managed the transition from deputy to First Minister with grace and aplomb. One senior Conservative remarked: 'She's been around such a long time with Salmond, the transition could have been more Blair to Brown, as opposed to the renewal and change of moving from Thatcher to Major.' Yet

Sturgeon had elegantly managed to adopt a different tone and style from her more polarising predecessor. 'She walked on water,' one sceptic complained, 'and with the post-referendum resentment, with such deep antipathy to Westminster, she was expertly placed to exploit the advantage.'

Nicola Sturgeon embarked upon a six-date 'Tour of Scotland', the highlight of which was a capacity crowd at Glasgow's 12,000-seater Hydro arena, more commonly used for pop concerts. The SNP claimed it was 'the largest indoor political gathering held in Scotland – or, indeed, anywhere in the UK – in recent times'. Party merchandise on sale included 'Nicola Sturgeon: The Tour' T-shirts for just £16, as well as mugs, bags and teddy bears. Meanwhile, her predecessor Alex Salmond announced his intention to run for the Westminster constituency of Gordon.

On Saturday 13 December, two nationalist protestors were waiting for Jim Murphy at Glasgow's Emirates Arena. They heckled him as he arrived for the Scottish Labour leadership declaration. Unfazed, he slipped inside the glass elevator that took him up to a packed hall of supporters.

Upstairs, in a small side room, Scottish Labour's director of corporate affairs, Annmarie Whyte, was briefing the candidates. She confiscated their mobile phones and kicked out every adviser. Then, without a pause, Whyte announced: 'Jim, you've won. You're leader.' He had secured 55.8 per cent of the vote. Murphy smiled and said, 'Thank you.' Few were surprised with the result. 'No one in the room thought Neil Findlay would win,' revealed one source. Lothian's MSP Kezia Dugdale was elected as Murphy's deputy.

Next, candidates were brought out in front of the audience of Labour supporters for the public announcement. Jim Murphy hugged Sarah Boyack and shook Neil

Findlay's hand. In his victory speech, he claimed his leadership would be a 'fresh start' for Scottish Labour. 'I would like to invite all Scots, regardless of politics or referendum, to work together in this great land, with a sense of pride, and build the fairest country on earth.'

Later that day, Murphy told the BBC: 'I'm going to get stuck in and I am determined to hold every seat that we currently have.' But Labour's position in the polls had sharply declined many months before, making that pledge almost impossible to keep. In the week of the referendum, one poll on Westminster voting intention put Labour on 43 per cent with the SNP on just 22. But, just after Murphy's election to the leadership in December, Labour support had collapsed to as low as 24 per cent, with the nationalists soaring to a stonking 48 per cent of the vote. It would equate to Labour retaining just four seats, with the SNP on fifty-four.

Yet Jim Murphy brought a sense of optimism and excitement. 'At last we have one of the big boys,' Labour campaigners exclaimed. But he had less than five months to revive his ailing party. Murphy was a professional, experienced, energetic and charming operator. But after seventeen years as an MP, rising as high as UK Scottish Secretary, he was about to face the fight of his life.

CHAPTER 13

MURPHY'S LAW

'**Y**ou all work for me now.' John McTernan was not interested in making friends. And at Holyrood, he didn't. His recruitment as Jim Murphy's chief of staff was a signal of intent from the new Labour leader. He had been an adviser to Tony Blair, Harriet Harman, former First Minister Henry McLeish and, most recently, Australian Prime Minister Julia Gillard.

McTernan had also been special adviser to Murphy between 2008 and 2010, when he was Scottish Secretary during Gordon Brown's premiership. And while McTernan's formal employment ended when Labour left power, he never stopped being a Murphy adviser, continuing to contribute to articles and speeches.

He returned from Australia in September 2013, a year before the referendum. McTernan's links to Scotland, Murphy and Blair McDougall meant a role at Better Together was mooted, yet it was soon vetoed by senior Labour figures. Even within his own party he was a divisive character. McTernan also sounded out the possibility of succeeding Alistair Darling, who was standing down in the Edinburgh South West constituency, but winning the selection was judged too tricky.

After being encouraged by McTernan to run for leader, Murphy now had to do the encouraging. And he succeeded, persuading his former colleague to return from London and join the fightback. As a big-name signing, his new salary was £84,000 – £17,000 more than MPs, including his boss Jim Murphy, and nearly £30,000 more than MSPs, including deputy leader Kezia Dugdale.

'You either want an easy life or you don't,' McTernan told staff soon after his arrival. 'If it's an easy life you want, you shouldn't be in politics.' But even with his tough talking – 'He thinks he's in *The Thick of It*,' complained one colleague – John McTernan quickly gained respect. 'He offers creative thinking, he really pushes you,' argued one politician. 'He can sometimes be a bit left field, but he challenges you and forces you to think. And, let's be honest, we're not blessed with an abundance of thinkers.'

John McTernan demanded a level of professionalism in presentation and writing from researchers and press officers that most admit was a 'shock to the system', but if the party was to stem the haemorrhage of support, they needed to up their game.

The staff team was bolstered by many involved in Murphy's leadership campaign – most of whom had moved over from Better Together – including No campaign boss Blair McDougall, who was appointed the party's new director of policy. There was also serious investment in new media, with the recruitment of Gregor Poynton, former UK political director of Blue State Digital, the media agency used by Barack Obama in 2008 and 2012. A stylist was even brought in and recommended another change: to the colour of Murphy's hair. The Labour leader agreed to stop using dye and embrace the grey.

McTernan also appointed – a decision soon regretted – veteran press adviser Susan Dalgety, to be the party's director of communications. She boasted a successful stint working for Jack McConnell when he was First Minister, but had also once compared the SNP to the Omagh bombers, and described nationalists as 'an assortment of oddballs, extremists and out-and-out racists'.

Dalgety clashed constantly with John McTernan and was regularly in tears. Colleagues were also unconvinced by her attempts to sort out the party's press operation. 'She loved her desk, laying it out all nicely with special pens and charts on the wall,' explained a member of the party. 'But she was not involved in the referendum and didn't understand the new psyche of Scottish politics. She was slow, had been out of the game for a while, and had no relationship with the media.'

Soon after taking over, Murphy also promoted the party's head of campaigns, Brian Roy, to be General Secretary. To avoid accusations of cronyism, and because Murphy had concerns about his ability to do the job, Roy was put through a tough interview. However, there were no other candidates. And, in a change to the previous structure, McTernan was placed above him in the organisational hierarchy.

Murphy's new chief of staff had taken over the office of former General Secretary Ian Price at the party's Glasgow HQ. Price's replacement, Brian Roy, would therefore have to work in the open-plan area alongside everyone else. 'It was a small but symbolic thing: McT wanted everybody to know who was boss,' said one Labour source.

While Dalgety's desk radiated neatness and order, McTernan, a Chelsea fan, plastered his office walls with photos of the club's players celebrating goals, with Tony

Blair's head photoshopped onto them. 'John fills his office with thirty to forty books,' explained another colleague. 'Everything: politics, poetry, historical stuff, Scottish fiction. It's an eclectic mix.' Activists would hear music – sometimes Miles Davis or Jack Johnson – emanating from the room.

An ongoing headache for the team was Murphy's route into the Scottish Parliament. He gave a 'cast-iron guarantee' that he would be a candidate in 2016, but admitted: 'I'd like to be there sooner than that.' Efforts to find Murphy a Holyrood seat to run for in a by-election were not going well. MSP Ken Macintosh, who held the equivalent Holyrood constituency to Murphy's, again refused to exchange seats. 'Jim was furious,' explained a colleague. 'It was the most obvious solution, but Ken was having none of it.' The Dumfriesshire constituency of MSP Elaine Murray was also considered, but Labour-commissioned polling in the area suggested Murphy would have little chance of winning.

In January, Crosby Textor, the polling company co-founded by David Cameron's Australian election strategist Lynton Crosby, carried out six constituency opinion polls in Scotland. Three studies took place in seats that, although deemed unwinnable for the Scottish Conservatives, were nevertheless of longer-term interest to the party – two in the north, one in the south. There, the Conservatives were hoping that the referendum might have created a split between SNP supporters who had voted No and those who voted Yes. However, it was not happening. 'They were thumping us in those seats,' admitted a Conservative source.

The other three constituencies polled included the Scottish Conservatives' sole Westminster seat – Dumfriesshire, Clydesdale & Tweeddale – in which David Mundell was just one point ahead of the SNP candidate, as well as the party's two target seats. The Conservatives knew they had little hope of winning in Aberdeenshire West & Kincardine, 'but we needed to dislodge the Lib Dems and be a clear challenger', one campaigner argued. Alex Salmond's candidacy in the neighbouring constituency of Gordon, a Lib Dem seat since 1983, was an added challenge. 'The Salmond effect squeezed all our media coverage,' complained one Conservative politician.

It was a different story again in the Scottish Tories' top target seat of Berwickshire, Roxburgh & Selkirk, held by Lib Dem and former Scottish Secretary Michael Moore. The figures suggested that, even in a region where 67 per cent voted against independence, the SNP were still in contention: neck and neck with the Conservatives on thirty points, with the Liberal Democrats dropping behind on twenty.

Westminster was not, however, the Scottish Conservatives' sole focus. With fifteen MSPs already at Holyrood, every candidate had one eye on the 2016 Scottish Parliament election. Those selected to contest the Westminster equivalent of winnable Holyrood seats were 'locked in' to a deal for two elections. 'We're spending money raising your profile,' they were told, 'so you need to be sure you are prepared to stand in 2016 too.'

The Liberal Democrats had a similarly focused strategy. Since their collapse in support at the 2011 Holyrood elections, torpedoed by the toxicity of the UK coalition government and the strength of the SNP, they had one priority: clinging on to their eleven existing Westminster seats. During the referendum, all the party's resources were focused on local campaigns in these constituencies, with customised No literature. Each MP did a 'Road to Referendum' tour, with some visiting up to thirty town and village halls over the summer of 2014. 'It was all about having a visible presence and getting ready for the general election,' explained one adviser. 'The referendum was a fantastic opportunity to get in the position of being seen as the viable anti-Nat candidate. We couldn't just stick with what the UK guys were doing.' The UK election narrative was no longer their focus; full fiscal autonomy for Holyrood and the Scottish NHS would soon become hot topics.

The UK Liberal Democrats 'had originally ruled out Scotland', claimed one senior party figure, as they believed holding on to seats would be incredibly difficult. Yet, in December 2014, Ryan Coetzee, Nick Clegg's South African election supremo, came up to meet the Scottish campaign team and other key figures. Internal research showed there had been a dramatic shift, and ten of the party's eleven seats were now SNP-facing. Their Edinburgh West constituency, which had been a Tory marginal, then a Labour marginal, was now an SNP marginal. 'Our heads were spinning,' explained one senior Lib Dem. Hilary Stephenson – the party's director of elections – was also present, and argued that victory would only be possible by securing tactical votes of those opposed to the SNP. Coetzee even put a bet on Lib Dem MP Alan Reid surviving: 'The odds were shite at the time,' a senior source explained.

Thursday 1 January 2015 marked a new year for Scottish Labour, but it also meant there were just eighteen weeks left for the party to turn around its fortunes. In the final opinion poll of 2014, Scottish Labour was seventeen points behind the SNP. The party was facing wipeout. They needed to gain a point a week, and that required shock therapy.

Murphy's team knew they had to win back working-class voters, and so the fightback began just before Christmas with a campaign to re-introduce alcohol at football games.

Some in the party fought to stop it, but Murphy was 'determined' to press ahead. Domestic abuse organisations called the policy 'absolutely crazy', citing the correlation between drinking at matches and increased reports of domestic violence. Murphy – a teetotaller – reported back to colleagues that after one Celtic match, fans who had heard about the plans asked: 'Jim, are you gonna let us have a bevy at the game?'

'It was not a vote-winner, but it was attention-grabbing,' argued one member of the team. 'For working-class Scots in the central belt, it was interesting.' Another senior Labour figure remarked: 'It was populism on steroids. And embarrassingly transparent.'

Continuing in January, Murphy announced a Labour government would create 1,000 new nursing posts north of the border, funded by a mansion tax largely levied on homes in London and the south-east. London Labour MP Diane Abbott called Murphy 'unscrupulous', while Mayor of London Boris Johnson accused the Scottish Labour leader of being 'fiscally vindictive'. But such disagreements gave Murphy valuable headlines, allowing him to differentiate himself from Labour UK and stand up for Scotland.

Murphy also pledged to stop fracking north of the border if he was elected First Minister. He then vocally opposed plans to build a new women's 'super prison'; within weeks, the SNP had scrapped their plans. And Scottish Labour's call for A&E statistics to be published weekly was later approved by the Scottish government.

'We needed to combat the SNP, who manage to be insurgent and incumbent at the same time,' explained one strategist. 'And we succeeded in putting a question mark above their record on health, education and justice.'

The pace Murphy set was blistering, and, at first, it seemed to be working: 'It was like a whirlwind, policy after policy. I didn't agree with everything but at last Labour had something to say,' argued one relieved campaigner. 'Jim's very media-oriented and talented with it,' added another. 'He's brilliant at communications because he always see things in pictures.'

One adviser cites the Canadian journalist Malcolm Gladwell's 'blink' test as proof of Murphy's skill: 'People make their minds up quickly. Jim looks like a leader so they go: "OK, I'll listen to you."'

Later that month, the Scottish Labour leader surprisingly claimed that, although he was a central part of the Better Together campaign, he was 'not a unionist', citing that his family were Irish Catholic immigrants. 'I grew up in a family of trade unionists, but we're not political unionists,' he argued, attracting ridicule from the SNP. Murphy was also tempted to launch 'Yes for Labour' – a campaign to win back former supporters who had voted Yes in the referendum. This was quickly shelved when research proved that shifting those voters would be near impossible.

While not all of Scottish Labour's media coverage was positive, there was lots of it. 'Labour had become sedated, so we were trying to get it in a fit shape to take on the SNP at their strongest point in history,' explained a senior member of the team. 'Every day we would have a story and try to lead the news, instead of just commenting on it.' Feedback from journalists suggested the plan was working: 'I don't agree with what you are doing,' said one prominent commentator, 'but, my God, you are setting the agenda every day.'

Wrangling the party's MSPs into a tight fighting force was more difficult. 'Jim appointed his shadow Cabinet and was soon disappointed with their performance,' explained one colleague. 'They didn't have the same energy or appetite for the job. He saw them as passive commentators on life.' John McTernan had a similar view, claimed another source: 'He had contempt for most MSPs, and they realised it.'

The following week, the Conservative peer Lord Ashcroft published a UK-wide poll showing the SNP on 5 per cent, with the Conservatives on 29 and Labour just behind on 28. The intervention was just one of many from the pollster and entrepreneur that would come to define key moments in the general election north of the border.

Unlike many that were to follow, this Ashcroft study did not drill down in detail into Scottish opinion. Instead, the most interesting revelation was that, when voters were asked to compare party leaders to animals, they likened David Cameron to a fox, Nick Clegg to 'a chihuahua in David Cameron's handbag', Nigel Farage to a weasel, while Ed Miliband was 'certainly not a predator ... one of those animals that, when you go to the zoo, you're not bothered whether you see it or not'.

Gordon Brown had been an asset during the final stages of the referendum campaign. Murphy's team knew that when he spoke, many Scottish voters listened. Hardly an ally of the Blairite Murphy, Brown nonetheless was brought on board, and, on 2 February, gave a joint press conference alongside Murphy at Edinburgh's Point Hotel. With the city's castle providing the backdrop, the pair pledged to build on 'The Vow' and give Holyrood further power over welfare. Yet, soon after the event, the pair fell out. 'Gordon wanted to say things that Jim didn't want him to say. Jim couldn't understand why Gordon would do an announcement.' Murphy told colleagues, 'I should be saying it,' before deciding, 'I don't want to do any more events with Gordon.'

Frustrations increased when Brown continued to ask for – and often got – party resources to stage speeches. 'I can't stress how fucking irritating and unhelpful Gordon Brown was,' raged one senior figure. 'He would just force his way and demand things.' Focus groups were also suggesting that Brown was firmly 'a figure of the past', and research suggested his involvement could, in fact, be 'damaging'. Yet the former Prime Minister still made numerous appearances.

Two days after the Murphy–Brown event, Lord Ashcroft published another poll, this time with a glut of data on Scottish constituencies. The research suggested that fifteen out of sixteen Labour seats polled would be won by the SNP, with swings of support to the nationalists as large as 27 per cent. Casualties would include Labour's Douglas Alexander and Liberal Democrat Danny Alexander. If even the smallest swing identified – 21 per cent – were replicated, Labour would retain just six seats – down from forty-one in 2010. But, alongside the depressing news for Scottish Labour, the Conservative peer did argue that, with a vigorous campaign, 'there remains room for movement before May'.

A last-minute 'urgent communication' from Liberal Democrat HQ in London had sent panic through the party's Scottish branch. Senior UK staff members were suddenly travelling up for an important meeting. 'They're coming to shut us down,' Lib Dem Scottish leader Willie Rennie told aides, assuming that the latest internal polling had suggested hardly any of the party's eleven seats could be won.

Among those arriving at the party's Clifton Terrace offices in Edinburgh were Victoria Marson, the party's head of strategic seat operations. She explained – much to the Scottish team's surprise – 'There is a route to victory in each and every seat,' but each candidate would need to effectively

exploit the nationalist–unionist dynamic. This meant painting themselves as the only viable pro-UK party that could
beat the SNP.

On 4 March 2014, just three days before Scottish Labour's
annual conference, Lord Ashcroft made a much-anticipated
speech with another raft of data. As with the referendum,
polling was again shaping the election narrative. And, in the
run-up to May, Michael Ashcroft was at the heart of it.

The Conservative peer revelled in the suspense of his
latest batch of constituency opinion polls. He had decided
to spend a tiny proportion of his vast fortune working out
quite how far Scotland's political tectonic plates had shifted.
Yes, there were four polls on English marginal seats, but it
was the research north of the border that whet the appe-
tites of political journalists, who were either waiting for his
presentation at a Conservative Home event or were at their
desks repeatedly hitting the refresh key as deadlines loomed.

Ashcroft went through his research slide by slide, keenly
highlighting key findings, but there were too many to choose
from. Twitter went wild with photos of the slides. His focus-
group research was bad news for Ed Miliband. When asked
to liken the Labour leader to a cartoon character, alcoholic
drink and a celebrity, voters chose Elmer Fudd from *Looney
Tunes*, 'a drink like crème de menthe that nobody would
order', and Mr Bean.

Results in Scotland were not just bad for Labour, but
also for its two former No campaign allies. The Liberal
Democrats – Lord Ashcroft's research suggested – would
lose ten of their eleven seats, and the Conservatives' David
Mundell was neck and neck with his SNP challenger. The
Tories' target seat of Aberdeenshire West & Kincardine was
likely to be comfortably won by Nicola Sturgeon's party. In

Scottish Labour seats, there were significant swings to the
SNP, but Jim Murphy was predicted to win – by just one
point. 'This is bad news for Scottish Labour, but great news
for the Tories,' Murphy told reporters, arguing that every
additional SNP MP would make a Conservative government
more likely.

Jim Murphy was standing on stage at the Edinburgh
International Conference Centre's 1,200-seater Pentland
Suite. The vast auditorium was empty and silent. Murphy
had intended to rehearse his speech for the party's conference the next day. Set-piece events were not his forte: 'He's
made some diabolical speeches,' remarked one colleague,
'he's a terrible speaker.' The speech, however, had not been
written. Director of policy Blair McDougall had missed yet
another deadline.

A bigger headache was, however, facing Murphy that same
evening – Friday 6 March – in the form of Ed Miliband. In
his keynote speech the next day, the Labour leader intended
to make a major policy announcement, ruling out forming
a coalition government with the SNP at Westminster. 'It was
the most fraught, fractious and tense point in the whole
campaign,' claimed one Labour source. A 'nightmare' was
how another colleague described Murphy's predicament.
After months of positive campaigning, arguing that Labour
was open to people regardless of whether they had voted Yes
or No, Murphy's entire message was about to be obliterated.

'Jim hated Ed coming up and being the centre of attention,'
claimed one adviser. 'You could see it in his body language.
When they were shaking hands in front of the cameras, Jim
would ruffle him up like a younger brother. Cardboard Ed
couldn't cope with that sort of sporty embrace.'

Late that night in a hotel room, Murphy and shadow

Scottish Secretary Margaret Curran tried to persuade Miliband and his general election co-ordinator Douglas Alexander to ditch their plan. 'If you say that, it will be what defines this weekend,' Murphy argued. 'If you're going to do it, don't do it now.'

The pressure to act had come from Alexander, and, alongside Murphy's testy relationship with Miliband, Murphy and Alexander had a longstanding mutual antipathy. 'Ed won't listen to anybody in Scotland apart from Douglas,' one Labour source explained. Yet Alexander's strategy was not just an attempt to win back votes from the SNP in Scotland, but primarily directed at the rest of the UK, where the Conservatives had been effective in highlighting perceived dangers of a Labour–SNP 'coalition of chaos'.

With the support of Margaret Curran, Murphy won the heated argument, and Miliband's statement was put on ice. Late-night negotiations were hardly the best preparation for either Miliband or Murphy's conference appearances. The latter eventually got a chance to practise his speech during the conference lunch break the next day. 'It was all massively disorganised,' sighed one on the team.

Nine days after the Scottish conference, at a campaign event in Pudsey, West Yorkshire, Miliband finally ruled out a coalition. 'There will be no SNP minister in any government I lead,' he remarked. Within minutes, both the Conservatives and Liberal Democrats had released statements pointing out that the Labour leader had failed to rule out an informal agreement short of a full coalition.

In the final fortnight of the campaign, Miliband would eventually go further and rule out firstly a so-called confidence and supply arrangement – where the smaller party agrees to back a larger party in government in exchange for policy concessions. Later still, he categorically ruled out a deal of any kind. Many in the party – particularly in Scotland – were critical of Miliband's ever shifting position.

As early as January, both Miliband and Murphy had been repeatedly asked to rule out a deal, and repeatedly dodged the question: 'I'm not about deals,' argued one. 'We are not planning for a coalition,' explained the other. A non-answer, however, was a story.

Early Labour research indicated that the party should 'in no circumstances rule a coalition out'. Doing so would risk alienating two key groups of target voters: (i) Those who had voted Yes, but had not supported the SNP at the 2011 Holyrood election; and (ii) Yes voters who had supported the SNP in 2011, but always backed Labour at Westminster elections. When the idea of ruling out a coalition was put to these people in focus groups, the response according to those watching was 'violently negative, as if it would be a slight against Scotland'. Some participants even asked: 'Why would Labour turn against Scotland?'

Labour's focus groups later suggested voters north of the border had been persuaded by the SNP's arguments and thought that, by supporting the nationalists, they could get 'Labour Plus' and Scotland would 'hold the balance of power'. To Scottish Labour's further frustration: 'Two-thirds of people believed without a shadow of a doubt there would be a hung parliament.'

Labour's evasion of journalists' questions week after week at the start of 2015 meant that Scots began to see the possibility of a coalition with the SNP as a welcome opportunity for enhanced Scottish influence, while voters in England saw it as a threat. The Conservatives' Lynton Crosby realised the toxicity of this argument through his own focus groups as early as November 2014, when participants commented: 'Ed Miliband is a very weak man. If the SNP do really well and he relies on them to govern, they will push him around. Who knows what we would get?' It was a fear Crosby ruthlessly exploited.

By the end of January, the Conservatives had produced a poster with Miliband alongside Alex Salmond and Sinn Féin leader Gerry Adams: 'Your worst nightmare just got even worse,' it read. 'The SNP and Sinn Féin propping up Ed Miliband? Chaos for Britain.' Within days, a sixteen-second video with the same message was released, set to Edvard Grieg's 'In the Hall of the Mountain King'.

Ruth Davidson had no objection to such tactics. Indeed, she had first used the argument at the start of January, claiming: 'Ed Miliband and Nicola Sturgeon are already halfway down the aisle.' Later, she argued that 'a weak Prime Minister Miliband with Alex Salmond pulling the strings in Westminster should scare anyone committed to keeping the UK together, as we can only imagine the concessions the SNP would wring from a Labour Party desperate for the keys to No. 10'. This was to be just the start of a relentless Tory focus on the dangers of a Labour–SNP coalition.

The Conservatives received some criticism for the move, arguing it would encourage Scots to vote SNP and, in consequence, further imperil the union. *The Spectator*'s Alex Massie described the poster as 'impressively stupid', and argued it was 'increasingly evident … that almost no one at CCHQ [Conservative Campaign Headquarters] really cares that much about the union'.

'Sorry to be late, but you won't believe this,' Jim Murphy said, arriving for another meeting at Labour HQ with a smile, 'but I'm dealing with a story about sniffing glue.' At a Glasgow

University debate the night before, Scotland's four party leaders had been asked if they had ever smoked cannabis. Murphy had dodged the question, quipping: 'In the housing scheme where I lived, glue-sniffing was the thing.'

However, issuing a statement denying an adolescent adhesive addiction was the least of Murphy's worries. Friday 13 March would turn out to be much more than just unlucky for Scottish Labour. In a meeting at the party's Bath Street office, the facts were laid bare to the leadership about what voters thought of them. It was 'devastating and sobering', according to one person present.

Originally, this was supposed to be a planning meeting to organise the campaign calendar for the next seven weeks, setting out where and when key manifesto announcements, photo opportunities and set-piece speeches would take place. But a presentation of the party's internal polling and focus groups changed the tone entirely.

James Morris from Labour's pollsters Greenberg Quinlan Rosner made it painfully clear that nothing could be done in time to reverse their massive decline. This shift 'has been happening for ten years', he told them. 'You can't turn it round in seven weeks.' The 2007 and 2011 Holyrood election results – with the SNP building support – were initial signs of tectonic movement, but the referendum had 'unlocked the door' to the notion of the nationalists being a viable recipient of Westminster votes. According to the research, Scots were not 'angry' at Labour's failures, but 'resigned' to them.

Part of Labour's problem was the rising popularity of Nicola Sturgeon, whom Morris likened to German Chancellor Angela Merkel in terms of her brand and the strength of her appeal to voters. Sturgeon's own colleagues claim another similarity: like Merkel, the First Minister is scared of dogs.

Focus groups in Scotland also revealed that highlighting the risk of cuts under the Conservatives was resonating with voters. Labour's zero-hour contract and living wage policies were proving popular. However, Scots disliked borrowing: they were only happy with 'progressive' taxes if they were explained as a 'tough choice'. Many in Labour were surprised that a large proportion of voters blamed London and Westminster for the state of the Scottish NHS – a policy area that has been devolved to Holyrood for over a decade. Yet most Scots believed another referendum on independence was not a priority.

Research also showed that the least antagonistic way of ruling out a coalition between Labour and the SNP was on the grounds of policy differences on Trident or defence. The most antagonistic way was to mention independence. But, in desperation, as the party's poll ratings continued to slide, Jim Murphy would be forced to deploy the threat of a further SNP-generated referendum. 'Given we knew this,' complained one source, 'it's pretty shocking that's exactly where we ended up.'

As the team went through the strengths and weaknesses of discussing various policies, there was no area that would significantly change opinion, except one: immigration. While some flirted with pursuing a high-profile anti-immigration line, it was soon decided that, with activists already deeply demoralised, it would be unfair to force them to knock on doors and advocate a policy so far from the party's core values.

While Labour struggled, Nicola Sturgeon soared, delivering faultless speeches and interviews. She travelled to London for set-piece speeches, and the SNP's communications chief Kevin Pringle pushed hard for network TV coverage. His constant argument to the main broadcasters was: you can't talk about the supposed danger of the SNP and not give us the right to reply.

Sturgeon had also studied research into voters' perceptions of her – and changed. Rough edges had been carefully sanded down, she recognised her weaknesses and worked hard to improve. She built trust with voters, and benefited from the momentum and sense of betrayal among a large proportion of the electorate. And the sudden relevance of the SNP in a general election due to the prospect of a hung parliament was the perfect storm.

And, for once, the endlessly used line 'Vote Labour to keep the Tories out' was not going to work. The SNP neutralised that argument early on by pointing out that Labour had worked with the Conservatives in the referendum campaign just a few months before. Whether it was painting Labour as 'Red Tories' or the accusation Labour had been 'hand in glove' with the Conservatives, it worked.

One rare Sturgeon misstep did, however, come after a speech at the London School of Economics. When asked who she would vote for in England, Sturgeon replied: 'If you live in Wales, I'd advise you to vote for Plaid Cymru. If you live in England, I think there is an argument for voting Green.' It was a curious statement given the Green Party in England and Wales were in contention in a handful of seats, and had attacked support for Scotland's oil and gas industry as 'huge tax breaks for the fossil-fuel dinosaurs' – a £1.3 billion package the SNP had welcomed. Ruth Davidson took full advantage of the remarks: 'When she's in London, she urges people to vote for a party that says that we should stop drilling altogether and give hundreds of thousands of North Sea oil workers the sack.'

She had served a seven-and-a-half-year apprenticeship under Alex Salmond, but now Nicola Sturgeon's former boss was beginning to cause her problems. Two interviews in late March 2015 – one with the left-wing *New Statesman* and other with the right-leaning *Spectator* – distracted from Nicola Sturgeon's leadership. In both, the former First Minister invited his interviewer to join him in sipping pink champagne. In one, he said that a second independence referendum was not a question of 'if', but 'when'. In the other, he compared himself to Nelson Mandela.

At Westminster, MPs were approaching the end of their fixed five-year term. On Thursday 26 March, parliamentary business ended, and, four days later, it would officially be dissolved, with MPs reverting back to being members of the public.

On the last night before parliamentarians returned to their constituencies, gallows humour was commonplace. 'Are you coming to my leaving party?' one Scottish MP joked on the way to the Strangers' Bar. Others were more serious: 'I'm not coming back,' a Glasgow Labour MP confided in an English colleague. 'Don't be stupid,' was the reply, 'look at your majority.' Party insiders still believed twenty of Labour's forty-one seats could be saved, but many MPs were convinced that they were on the way out. 'There was not a single bit of research or evidence that supported anything other than a massive wipeout,' sighed one parliamentarian. 'There's little tougher than feigning optimism in the face of doom.'

As the weeks wore on, opinion polls had become far more regular. But they did not move, certainly not in the right direction, for any of the pro-UK parties in Scotland.

Jim Murphy's frenetic strategy was also starting to take its toll on staff. 'It was like drinking a can of Red Bull,' explained one adviser. 'You start with this buzz, but after that initial period there's a major comedown. We were all over the place, but, by the time we realised, it was far too late.'

CHAPTER 14

SANDBAGGING

'Oh, I sound like a north London twat from an over-privileged background,' Ed Miliband groaned. Honing his television debating skills was a rigorous and exhausting process.

Labour's election campaign was relentlessly focused on 'working people'. Miliband constantly trumpeted his plans for a radical mansion tax, so a sprawling mansion in Kent was an unlikely location for the leader's secret TV training sessions. Labour peer and TV mogul Waheed Alli's country pile near Tenterden had, for years, been offered up to senior party figures – although, this time, they were not using the grand house, but the barn.

Money was no object for Labour in preparation for the two televised leaders' debates. The party was taking these extremely seriously. Full tech support was provided. Two professional cameramen filmed the mock encounters, with instant playback available to review Miliband's performance. An expensive set of lecterns had been transported to the rural location, as had a lighting rig and microphones for each of the 'leaders'.

Stan Greenberg, who helped mastermind Bill Clinton's

1992 presidential campaign, had been brought in to run the sessions. His company Greenberg Quinlan Rosner – who were undertaking polling and focus groups for Labour – had more recently helped Rahm Emanuel become mayor of Chicago, and Bill de Blasio mayor of New York. 'Stan is a fucking superstar pollster. He's the god of polling,' explained one Labour source. Greenberg had attended two focus groups in Scotland and was impressed with the level of political engagement, delightedly telling one participant: 'In forty years of polling, you are the first to mention the debt-to-GDP ratio.'

Alongside 69-year-old Greenberg was Mike Donilon, a fixture of the presidential campaigns of every Democrat nominee since Clinton, who had most recently assisted Barack Obama with messaging for adverts and had prepared Joe Biden for TV debates.

Completing this trio – referred to by Labour insiders as 'The Americans' – was Michael Sheehan, the renowned Democrat media trainer who charged Labour $20,000 a day; £184,609 in total across the campaign. Sheehan went to drama school with Meryl Streep and Sigourney Weaver, taught Hillary Clinton how to use an autocue and has advised Barack and Michelle Obama, Google's Eric Schmidt and Facebook founder Mark Zuckerberg. And now: Ed Miliband.

The sessions were intense, at least eight hours long. Two questions were rehearsed over fifteen minutes, the answers were played back on TV screens, feedback was then given, strategy was discussed, and more research was commissioned to help craft the perfect performance. Footage of Miliband's answers was even clipped and 'dial tested' – where groups of voters were given handheld devices allowing them to register positive or negative reactions second by second. Several times, the team did a full run-through to help Miliband build up the stamina needed for a two-hour programme.

'There was a huge amount of resources,' explained one member of the team, 'we knew it was make or break.' These two UK debates – one with seven leaders, one with five – were extraordinarily valuable opportunities for the Labour leader to get exposure, unmoderated by either the editorial lines of newspapers or the tight time limits of TV news packages. The first programme was the only time Ed Miliband and David Cameron would go head to head.

Much time was spent improving how Miliband was standing, his posture and how he looked while others were speaking. He was instinctively comfortable leaning on one elbow; his American advisers thought this looked relaxed and confident on camera, and so they encouraged him to do it even more.

Miliband was also told to 'actively listen' to other leaders' responses, and realise he would always be on camera – because one would be constantly trained on each leader. He was taught how to take advantage of cutaway shots, how to indicate when ending sentences, and even tricks for keeping the camera on him when attacking an opponent.

Miliband's policy adviser Tom Hamilton played David Cameron; Lord Stewart Wood and Chris Leslie shared the role of Nick Clegg; director of policy Torsten Bell took on the role of UKIP leader Nigel Farage. Miliband's former speechwriter James Morris – now a partner at Greenberg – played Leanne Wood of Plaid Cymru. But the star of the sessions was Ayesha Hazarika, a former stand-up comedian and adviser to Harriet Harman, who perfectly captured Natalie Bennett of the Greens.

Instead of the more common one-on-one format, the three

US campaign veterans had six leaders to focus on, perhaps the most unpredictable of whom were Nigel Farage and Nicola Sturgeon. Miliband was not used to locking horns with the pair as neither was in the House of Commons.

To ensure Miliband was match-ready for the SNP leader, Douglas Alexander gave advice and Blair McDougall was sent down from Scotland to provide feedback. But Scottish Labour's major contribution was Kezia Dugdale, the party's deputy leader, who spent hour after hour behind a lectern impersonating First Minister Nicola Sturgeon.

For the first seven-way debate, the aim was to make Miliband look statesmanlike, and for viewers to conclude that only two of the politicians could be Prime Minister, and that he was as good an option as Cameron. Challenging the SNP was less of a priority. 'If 84 per cent of the audience lies outside Scotland,' explained one prominent adviser, 'in whose interests is it to spend your answer rebutting or responding to Nicola Sturgeon?'

Because of the danger of UKIP influence in some English marginal constituencies, much time was spent working on how to deal with Nigel Farage. Everyone realised Miliband needed a 'moment' – something that viewers would talk about at work the next day. The Labour leader wanted that to be a grapple with Farage.

UKIP provided a strategic puzzle. 'Everyone in the room hated them and what they stood for,' admitted one source. 'Farage was a joke, a risible figure. But Labour's focus groups were saying, "Working-class voters in England are drawn to UKIP and immigration is something they're sincerely concerned about."'

Research also proved Ed Miliband could risk angering his own supporters if he attacked UKIP in the wrong way.

If he criticised Farage for being anti-politics or as much of the elite as David Cameron, it went down 'very badly' with Labour voters. Attacking Farage on immigration also risked losing support.

Keeping Miliband's mood up was important. Advisers could see him growing in confidence, so feedback was delivered with care. 'He was treated with kid gloves and never told his answers were shit, even if they were,' explained one colleague, 'because we all cared for him, enjoyed being around him: he has a great self-deprecating sense of humour.'

And, as the first debate approached, Stan Greenberg always brought Miliband back to his one-sentence Labour strategy: 'A government that works for working people.'

At 8 p.m. on Thursday 2 April, all seven leaders stood behind their lecterns on a turquoise set in front of a live audience at ITV's Salford studios as Julie Etchingham started proceedings. During the two-hour debate, Ed Miliband performed confidently, telling Nick Clegg he had 'betrayed the young people of our country' with his tuition fees U-turn, attacking David Cameron for spending plans that were 'dangerous for our National Health Service'.

Unlike Leanne Wood, who declared she was talking to people 'back home in Wales', Sturgeon fused her pledges to 'stand up for Scotland's best interests' and 'make Scotland's voice heard' alongside a wider commitment to 'friendship' with other parts of the UK.

Sturgeon also benefited from the repeated assertions that a hung parliament was likely, and therefore the SNP could hold the balance of power. 'No one standing here is going to win this election outright,' Nick Clegg remarked, 'so you are going to have to choose, like you did last time, who is going to work with who.'

When Cameron and Clegg were arguing, Sturgeon chipped in: 'It's really ironic – isn't it? – hearing Nick Clegg and David Cameron arguing when they've been working hand in glove, imposing austerity on the people of this country for the last five years.'

However, the most talked-about intervention came from Nigel Farage, who claimed 60 per cent of the 7,000 people diagnosed with HIV each year in the UK were not British nationals, remarking that treatment can cost up to £25,000 per patient per annum. 'What we need to do is to put the National Health Service there for British people and families who, in many cases, have paid into the system for decades.' Leanne Wood received applause from the audience when she shot back that the UKIP leader was 'scaremongering' and 'ought to be ashamed'. Nicola Sturgeon argued: 'When somebody is diagnosed with a dreadful illness, my instinct is to view them as a human being, not consider what country they come from.'

Among the 1,400,000 tweets prompted by the debate, Farage's comments were the most discussed. Sports presenter Gary Lineker tweeted: 'Always reluctant to offer a political view, but Farage is a dick!'

Seven million people on average watched the two-hour showdown, with a peak of 7.4 million viewers. Four snap polls – one each by ICM, ComRes, YouGov and Survation – were conducted immediately after. Ed Miliband came first or joint first in three of them, Cameron was joint top in two, and Nigel Farage came joint first in one. In all four polls, Nick Clegg came fifth, Green leader Natalie Bennett sixth and Plaid Cymru's Leanne Wood in seventh place. Meanwhile, Nicola Sturgeon was the clear winner in one poll, and fourth in the other three.

Yet for a politician with a limited UK profile, leading a party that only a tenth of viewers could vote for, and given she was not even a candidate at the election, this was a coup for Nicola Sturgeon. One of the most Googled questions in the debate was 'Can I vote for the SNP?', alongside 'What is a referendum?' and 'Who is Nigel Farage married to?'. Rupert Murdoch tweeted: 'Great performances by SNP Sturgeon and UKIP Farage, Cameron sort of ok, Miliband not, Clegg pathetic.'

On the evening of Friday 3 April, the *Daily Telegraph* published a story online that would appear on the front page of the next day's paper, with the headline: 'Sturgeon's secret backing for Cameron.' Based on the contents of a leaked UK government memo, it claimed that, during a meeting with the French ambassador, Sturgeon had said she would rather see David Cameron remain Prime Minister than Ed Miliband, who was not 'Prime Minister material'. The implication was that the SNP leader realised a Conservative UK government would be unpopular in Scotland and could drive more people to vote for independence in a future referendum. This incident was soon dubbed 'Nikileaks'.

'Your story is categorically, 100 per cent untrue,' Nicola Sturgeon tweeted at the paper's Scottish political editor, 'which I'd have told you if you'd asked me at any point today'. A Twitter storm was raging, and so was the First Minister.

Days earlier, Euan Roddin, special adviser to Scottish Secretary Alistair Carmichael, asked his boss if he should leak the document. When Carmichael approved disclosure, Roddin used his civil service mobile phone to call Simon Johnson of the *Telegraph* to tip him off about the story. A copy of the memo was also passed to the journalist.

It later emerged the memo had been written by a civil servant in the Scotland Office, after a confidential conversation with the French consul general in Edinburgh. The morning after the story broke online, speaking to a camera crew on his doorstep, wearing an open-necked white shirt, brown tweed blazer and circular-framed glasses, the consul general chose his words carefully. He denied that a preference for Prime Minister was mentioned. The Cabinet Office later confirmed the civil servant who had written the memo was 'reliable' and had 'no history of inaccurate reporting, impropriety or security lapses'.

Yet with the First Minister, French ambassador and consul general all denying the key comment, who was telling the truth? The *Telegraph* is a Conservative-supporting – and pro-UK paper – with a long history of criticising the SNP, but its Scottish political editor Simon Johnson is widely respected, seen as being fair and accurate, while regularly breaking original stories.

Stopping to speak to reporters at a Bairns Not Bombs – anti-nuclear weapons – rally in Glasgow's George Square, Nicola Sturgeon said: 'Anybody who knows me knows that's absolutely preposterous. I've spent my whole life campaigning against Tory governments.' Yet the First Minister avoided a question from ITV's Debi Edward as to whether Ed Miliband and David Cameron's names had been mentioned. She also dodged Sky's James Matthews's query as to whether she thought Ed Miliband was prime ministerial material. Instead, Sturgeon attacked the UK government: 'It suggests a Whitehall system out of control – a place where political dirty tricks are manufactured and leaked,' she commented.

But many could not believe that the careful, professional, constantly on-message Nicola Sturgeon would be so candid or even gossipy. Would she really confide in an ambassador who had only been in the job for seven months, and was on her first official trip to Scotland?

After admitting approving the leak, Alistair Carmichael – together with his adviser Euan Roddin – forfeited their severance pay after leaving government. Others with experience of Whitehall were perplexed with what they saw as a botched leak. 'What the fuck happened? Staffers are there to be thrown off the sled,' argued one experienced figure. 'Carmichael should have said: "I am bloody shocked by what my adviser did. I'll make sure he never works as an adviser ever again. He's fired." His handling of it was so amateurish.'

The *Telegraph* was later forced to apologise by the press regulator IPSO for breaching its editors' code of practice by not verifying the accuracy of the story with Sturgeon prior to publication.

In Labour HQ, Jim Murphy's chief of staff John McTernan had transformed the party's research and press operation, but, with unorthodox methods, he had secured few allies. 'He's the most divisive person I've met in my life,' complained one source. 'He tried to play up too much to the caricature.' At a meeting with researchers, when one junior member of staff was being critical of Murphy, McTernan interrupted: 'Your point, caller?' Another common interjection, according to colleagues, was to roll his eyes and say: 'Can I stop you there? You're wrong.'

'He has very poor manners,' another Labour source claimed. 'If you're sitting in a meeting with John, he's constantly on his BlackBerry, or on Twitter, or on the internet looking up a clip of a 1970s docudrama. He can't concentrate on anything for more than five minutes; his brain is on a different plane dealing with five or six things at once.'

Some suggest McTernan struggled to adapt to the different dynamics of the Scottish media. 'Let's put that press release out,' he would suggest at 8 or 9 p.m. at night. 'There's no point,' colleagues would reply. 'He didn't get there's no 24-hour media in Scotland. BBC News and Sky don't care about Scottish Labour.' Colleagues also argued McTernan was too focused on 'elite UK media' in London, once expressing delight that ex-Blair speechwriter Phil Collins had written 'a very helpful piece' in *The Times*. 'Nobody gives a fuck apart from us,' remarked one staff member, pointing out that the party's target voters 'primarily read *Metro* and the Sky News app'. When the team was having trouble with one journalist, McTernan suggested: 'Phone him up and tell them it's fucking bollocks and you can't fucking print it because it's a fucking lie.'

'John is a great writer with connections to the top of Miliband and Balls's teams, and to Gordon Brown,' explained a colleague. 'He was always fair to me, but a bastard to other people, and no amount of brilliance excuses that.' Another in the team – although impressed by McTernan's expert political analysis – concurred: 'He flies off the handle for no need, and at strange moments. When he loses control, he is very quietly aggressive.' At one particularly tense moment, he raged: 'I can't fucking believe this is fucking happening!'

Jim Murphy's preparation for TV debates was more low-budget than Miliband's. He had spent one morning with US presentation expert Michael Sheehan in London, but, after that, sessions were run by his director of communications Susan Dalgety. At least at first. 'It was a car crash, a catastrophe,' complained one senior figure, 'Jim didn't trust her judgement.'

There were four TV debates in Scotland – three with the

four main parties, and one with the Greens and UKIP as well. It did not help that Murphy was not interested in long sessions of debate preparation. 'It was always a low priority,' explained a team member. 'Jim wanted it done, and to be on to the next thing. He gets bored easily, he's constantly restless. He's interested in always moving, being on the go: "What's next? Let's power through this."'

Director of policy Blair McDougall, David Ross from the Scottish Labour press team, and policy whizz Nigel Anthony – all Better Together veterans – ended up being the core team, alongside John McTernan and Kezia Dugdale. McTernan had considerable experience in such TV encounters, and instructed the team to look into recent interviews and speeches Sturgeon had given in order to understand her key arguments. The three aims were to: (i) establish a clear difference between Labour and the Conservatives; (ii) expose the SNP's record in government; and (iii) avoid any boos from the audience.

In fact, in the first Scottish debate in Edinburgh, Nicola Sturgeon was the one to be booed, as she hinted at the possibility of a second referendum on independence. 'The Westminster election is not a re-run of the referendum campaign,' she insisted. But when questioned by STV's Bernard Ponsonby about what might happen after the next Holyrood election in 2016, Sturgeon admitted: 'That is another matter. We will write that manifesto when we get there,' attracting jeers from the audience.

Most attention, however, was paid to an audience member sporting a comedy moustache, who trended on Twitter and was soon dubbed 'Tache Man'.

At a hotel meeting room in Aberdeen, Murphy was getting frustrated. 'Jim was really annoyed so little work had been done. He'd hoped to have lines and answers crafted. He wanted new zingers.' The second debate came just twenty-four hours after the first, but, with basic groundwork not done by staff, the Scottish Labour leader was forced to undertake short bursts of preparation, with frequent breaks to allow his aides time to work. It was 'nonsense', according to one person involved: 'There was so little effort, it was embarrassing how little we did.' Murphy, however, had a 'remarkable ability to just read a brief, absorb it and deliver it well'.

At the University of Aberdeen's baronial Elphinstone Hall, there was no green room, so all six leaders were wedged into the same small space. This was the one debate in which the Greens and UKIP would make an appearance. 'You could see the difference between the Nats and Labour,' commented one observer, 'Jim was hyper, and turned up late with his team, just twenty minutes before the programme. The BBC staff were flustered he hadn't been through make-up. Nicola was sitting on a sofa on her own reading over notes, not being crowded by anyone. It was a symbol for the wider differences in style and approach.'

During the debate, Murphy pressed Sturgeon on the contentious issue of full fiscal autonomy – devolving all tax powers to Scotland – which Scottish Labour argued would equate to £7.6 billion of cuts.

'Would your MPs vote for it next year?' Murphy asked.

'I would vote for it, would you support it?' Sturgeon shot back.

UKIP's Scottish MEP David Coburn caused the biggest stir, accidentally calling Scots on low incomes 'the lowest people in society', and suggesting the UK government should 'wean Scotland off' the Barnett formula – the mechanism used to calculate how much funding each UK nation receives.

He received an onslaught of criticism from his fellow debaters. 'Stop demonising people!' Murphy shouted. Nicola Sturgeon branded Coburn 'absolutely disgusting' for previously comparing SNP minister Humza Yousaf to convicted terrorist Abu Hamza.

The next morning, Defence Secretary Michael Fallon used an appearance on the BBC's *Today* programme to launch a blistering attack: 'Ed Miliband stabbed his own brother in the back to become Labour leader; now he is willing to stab the United Kingdom in the back to become Prime Minister.' Fallon's argument was that the Labour leader was so duplicitous he might exchange the UK's nuclear deterrent Trident for a post-election deal with the SNP.

Fallon's comments provoked a flurry of responses. Even prominent Conservatives described them as 'far too personal'. Some suspected, however, that the intervention was a well-timed example of Tory election chief Lynton Crosby's 'throwing a dead cat on the table' strategy, whereby something so outrageous or alarming is said, everyone discusses that rather than whatever is causing difficulties for the party – which, in the Conservatives' case, was the issue of non-dom status for tax purposes.

That afternoon, Labour's shadow Cabinet met at the party headquarters in Westminster for their final gathering before election day. Ed Miliband and Harriet Harman were upbeat, as was shadow Welsh Secretary Owen Smith: 'All's well in Wales,' he beamed. 'I wish I was Welsh,' remarked shadow Scottish Secretary Margaret Curran.

Most of Miliband's top team understood the scale of the problem in Scotland: 'Caroline Flint had been up a lot,' explained a senior source. 'Chuka always had interesting stuff to say, and Ed Balls really got it.'

The unexpected flourishing friendship between Balls and Murphy was one of the election's surprises, with the shadow Chancellor regularly travelling up for campaign events. 'They spoke more in that campaign than in the two decades before,' remarked one adviser. 'It was the burying of the absurdity of the Blair/Brown splits – at least temporarily.'

With exactly four weeks before polling day, Miliband's team realised that, if the party won seats in Scotland, 'there was not just the possibility of being the largest party, but the hint of a majority'. This meant a 'shitload of money' was assigned to constituencies north of the border for direct mails.

Later that day, Jim Murphy, John McTernan and Brian Roy had the unenviable task of reallocating their campaigning resources to maximise the chances of holding on to seats. Choices were limited: 'The only option left was sandbagging,' explained one senior source, 'protecting what we could.'

More and more money was coming from the UK party – 'They knew they were fucked if we were wiped out in Scotland' – but there was very little organisationally to do or change. 'We took everyone out of Dundee, put more people in Fife,' one source remarked. In the grand scheme, however, it was a minor reallocation. MPs and candidates losing campaign staff would be given more leaflets: 'It was never presented in a "you're losing" way.' And, until polling day, the party was seriously resourcing twenty-eight seats, many in areas they were certain of defeat.

Jim Murphy's political relationships played a role in this. All evidence and polling said the constituency of West Dunbartonshire was 'fucked and fucked for a long time', according to one senior source. Yet Murphy refused to give up on his friend Gemma Doyle, the incumbent, as well as in other unwinnable seats held by his allies.

'He wouldn't pull their resources,' remarked a colleague. 'But, to be honest, where else would you put them? The trajectory was set. Why take away from somewhere you're doing really badly to put somewhere you're doing quite badly? And then have to deal with the fallout?'

Some in the team objected to Murphy's approach: 'He was not ruthless enough and needed to take tough decisions,' one campaigner suggested. 'We put resources into seats we'd never win, because we were so scared of candidates moaning to the press. There was no discipline with Westminster politicians.'

Aside from his Paisley constituency, Douglas Alexander only became closely involved with the Scottish campaign in the final four weeks. He secured 'loads more money' from the UK Labour pot, but on one condition: he got to decide how it was spent. A set of 'door drops' – addressed leaflets delivered by Royal Mail – for seats north of the border were designed by the party's team in London, leaving Scottish Labour's graphic designer with little to do.

The leaflet borrowed branding from the TV action series 24. It was black with red text. A digital clock displayed the time as '23.59', with the words: 'You only have 24 hours to stop a second referendum. The clock is ticking…'

This negative messaging underlined Labour's less-than-subtle strategic shift, highlighting both the supposed high cost of the SNP's plans for full fiscal autonomy, as well as the 'continuing threat' of independence. 'The SNP are known for spending eight months planning a consistent three-month campaign,' commented one Labour adviser, 'whereas in January we were trying to bring Yes voters in, and by the end of April we were trying to stop No voters leaving us, and threatening them with fear.' Some critics compared these last-minute negative tactics to the work of Better Together seven months before. 'It was Project Fear 2,' complained one nationalist.

Douglas Alexander and Patrick Heneghan – Labour's 'Mr Elections' – were, however, focused on trying to save seats with a high percentage of No voters, and research proved the threat of a second referendum was a powerful argument.

But, because Jim Murphy refused to take failing constituencies with a high proportion of Yes voters off UK Labour's list of key seats, they also received the 24-style leaflets aimed at No voters. 'They went down like a bag of sick with candidates and activists,' explained one of the team. 'They were furious about it. Threatening a second referendum in those areas was mad.'

Alexander's response to critics was: 'The evidence is telling us to do this.' There certainly was an abundance of research. In the final stages of the campaign, Greenberg Quinlan Rosner was holding two focus groups in Scotland every week. But the carefully crafted messages were being delivered to completely the wrong voters. 'In trying to look after his friends, Jim was screwing them even more,' admitted a senior Labour source. 'But he didn't realise it.'

One candidate – Glasgow South West MP Ian Davidson – did complain to the media, telling the *Telegraph*: 'We need to be playing down Jim because he is not a particularly stimulating leadership figure for us.' After losing his seat, Davidson wrote that the Labour campaign was 'one of the most blatant examples of cronyism ever seen in politics'.

In response, a senior figure claimed: 'Ian Davidson didn't have any organisers because he never did any door-knocking.' Another source argued Davidson's 'contact rate' with voters was 'the second- or third-lowest of any of our MPs in Scotland'.

Murphy, McTernan and Roy devised a three-point test when choosing where to send organisers and spend money. First, they would not reward failure – candidates who had not worked hard, would get no extra resources. 'We can only fight for people who fight for themselves,' argued one senior figure. Second, any change would have to 'add value'. No money would be spent on wealthy seats. And third, Murphy was keen to 'protect the future' and the next generation of MPs. Candidates in their thirties were likely to be far better funded than those in their sixties.

Coatbridge's 74-year-old MP Tom Clarke was among a group of older parliamentarians considered stuck in a different era, and whose majorities were so large they had never needed to campaign. 'Seven people were canvassed in Tom Clarke's constituency,' claimed someone in party HQ. 'And those contacts were made by [neighbouring MP] Gregg McClymont's team canvassing the wrong street, and putting it into the system.'

One younger candidate revealed: 'Colleagues who had been MPs for more years than I have been alive were coming up to me asking how to run a campaign. It was anathema to them; they didn't know what to do. One thought he was doing well because when he walked up the high street, the ratio of those smiling at him to ignoring him was seven to one. He lost by 18,000 votes.'

High-profile politicians were kept well-funded. Shadow Scottish Secretary Margaret Curran – who had little chance of winning – was among them. 'We couldn't cut her adrift,' argued one colleague, pointing out that none of Curran's fellow Glasgow MPs had their resources cut either. 'We moved no one in Glasgow. And the whole of Glasgow was fucked.'

Even considering the longstanding *froideur* between Murphy and Alexander, the Scottish Labour team was clear: 'We didn't want Douglas to be a Chris Patten.' (As party chairman, Patten ran the Conservatives' 1992 general election campaign. The party won, but Patten lost his seat.) 'We made sure he was fully resourced,' remarked one strategist, 'because, if it came to it, we wanted to keep the Scottish Labour leader and the shadow Foreign Secretary.'

Murphy and Alexander were further bolstered by secret 'phone banks' – telephone canvassing operations – in London. Labour supporters, especially Scots living in the capital, joined evening and weekend sessions phoning voters in the two politicians' constituencies. Others in the party claim Murphy and Alexander relied on further resources they managed to keep under wraps: 'We'll never know what, but both had other mechanisms and avenues to resource their seats.' Murphy was an effective fundraiser for both his constituency and the Scottish party. And, as chair of general election strategy, Alexander had a huge amount of power and money at his fingertips.

Scottish Labour's campaign machine was considerable: 'We had more literature than ever before, had never canvassed so many people, the data was consistent and in volume,' said one politician. There were fifty-five full-time paid members of staff working in the field – more than ever before. 'We had resources coming out of our ears, direct mail coming every second day: my recycling bin was overflowing,' joked another. 'It was the largest, most expensive election campaign in the history of the Scottish Labour Party.' But – despite all the money spent – it was not working. 'It was like the Prussian Army,' complained one MP. 'They had drones and nuclear bombs and we had nice uniforms.' Another politician remarked: 'Nothing was landing. I can tell when voters are lying to me; some were brave enough to tell me straight.'

'Ed Miliband is unfit to call himself a socialist!' The conference room at Labour's London headquarters near Victoria was scattered with takeaway boxes from Wagamama – Miliband's restaurant of choice – as he received another onslaught from 'Nicola Sturgeon'.

The Labour leader's unbalanced campaign diet had led – colleagues claimed – to him 'putting on 9lbs'. Miliband was 'feeling a bit podgy and unhappy in his own skin', according to one adviser. There was, however, no time for self-consciousness: his showdown with the SNP leader was just days away.

By the time the Labour leader was preparing for the second UK-wide TV debate, the 'short campaign' was in full swing, meaning he had scheduled visits in the morning, and debate preparation sessions started in the afternoon at One Brewer's Green. Yet the Labour leader still insisted on working full eight-hour sessions, starting at 2 p.m. and finishing at 9 or 10 p.m. Being based in party HQ also meant it was far easier for more people to be involved.

A problem, however, had been caused by Miliband's notes from the first debate being left in a dressing room at the TV studios. The *Sun on Sunday*'s political editor David Wooding published them under the headline: 'The secret behind robotic Ed.' Miliband's motivational notes included 'Happy Warrior' and 'calm never agitated'. However, aside from ten pages of handwritten – and almost illegible – notes, there were ten pages of carefully crafted and tested lines, including two pages of core arguments on key election issues, four pages of detailed statistics, and two pages of 'comebacks' and 'zingers'.

Frustratingly, four of these comebacks had been written to use against Nicola Sturgeon and three against Nigel Farage – both leaders were taking part in the second debate. Those aimed at the UKIP leader included: 'This is a man who blames traffic jams on the M4 on immigrants and blames bad weather on gay marriage. I'm not going to call him a racist; I am going to call him ridiculous.' Most galling for Miliband's advisers: few of the lines had been deployed but they were now unusable. 'We had to write loads more,' they complained.

David Cameron and Nick Clegg would not be taking part in this programme, dubbed the 'Challengers' Debate', meaning the Labour leader would need to be better briefed on likely attacks from the smaller parties. Baroness Bryony Worthington, who had advised Miliband on climate change as Energy Secretary, was recruited to impersonate Natalie Bennett. She had a better grasp of the Greens' policy platform and could provide detailed answers. Another peer, Baroness Eluned Morgan, joined the team to play Plaid Cymru's Leanne Wood. 'She was spectacular,' said one person watching on, 'She had absorbed her lines, came across so well and she's so bloody Welsh.' Answers regularly began with: 'In Wales, we have a saying for that…'

The real concern, however, was Nicola Sturgeon. Alastair Campbell joined the sessions and was keen for Miliband to get stuck into the SNP leader. 'She could cause him more damage than the good he could get out of the event,' argued one aide. 'If she looks more Labour-y and social democratic than him, it could be very bad for the party in Scotland,' added another. The Americans 'didn't have a clue' about the Scottish dynamics and seemed perplexed.

A tension also developed between Miliband's head of

strategy Greg Beales – who argued 'Scotland's fucked, let's focus on UKIP' – and Douglas Alexander, who was constantly pushing Miliband to engage directly with Sturgeon. Ignoring her, he believed, would seem like the Labour leader was ignoring Scotland, and would look bad.

Ed Miliband learnt to respond to 'statesmanlike Sturgeon', as well as the SNP leader in 'fiery First Minister' mode. The intense sessions were also taking their toll on Kezia Dugdale, who was impersonating Sturgeon alongside Harriet Harman's aide Ayesha Hazarika. One source joked she had almost developed Stockholm syndrome and was starting to think like the SNP leader: 'It was challenging for her brain to be in the head of Nicola Sturgeon for hours, as well as providing a critique of Ed's responses to her.'

Blair McDougall – key to the referendum debate preparation – was therefore more heavily relied on to provide feedback, although he was writing speeches and co-ordinating policy for Jim Murphy at the same time. Scottish Labour's manifesto launch was the day after the 'Challengers' Debate'.

Three days before the showdown, news came through that Ed Miliband would get the lectern on the left-hand side of the stage, which the Labour leader's team members were delighted with, as it allowed him to lean against his desk, look across at his opponents and make the key point: only one of us here can be Prime Minister and that's me.

There was, however, another 'big drama' with the lecterns, according to an insider. In both debates, the broadcasters had positioned them too low for Miliband, despite his team requesting a set height, meaning he could not execute his well-rehearsed lean quite as planned.

On the afternoon of Thursday 16 April, Ed Miliband was supposed to have finished his preparations. Yet timing ran over and the Labour leader was still practising after lunch, leaving him nervous. To cool down, Miliband and his adviser Ayesha Hazarika took a short walk around the streets surrounding Labour HQ, accompanied by the leader's Met Police security detail. 'He looked so anxious,' commented a colleague.

Later, the Labour team moved across to Methodist Central Hall in Westminster, where the debate was to be filmed. Fifteen minutes before the debate started, Leanne Wood was spotted slipping into the SNP's green room alone. It confirmed the suspicions of Miliband's team that the three female leaders were working closely together.

Highlights of the televised debate included Green leader Natalie Bennett's increasing frustration at not getting a word in, which culminated in her screaming into her microphone: 'It's my turn to come in now!' Nigel Farage also attracted attention for attacking the audience: 'This lot's pretty left-wing, believe me,' he argued.

And while Ed Miliband attempted early on to challenge the absent David Cameron to a one-on-one debate – which prompted a spike on social media – the Labour leader did not have a strong answer to the inevitable question from Nicola Sturgeon about joining with the SNP to keep the Conservatives out of government. 'Whatever differences you have with me,' Sturgeon said, directly to Miliband, 'surely they are nothing as to the differences both of us have with the Tories? I can help Labour be bolder; to deliver the change we really need.'

Ed Miliband responded that she had an 'odd approach', reminding the SNP leader of her call for people to vote Green in England and Plaid in Wales. 'You want to gamble on getting rid of a Tory government,' he argued. 'I can guarantee you I'll get rid of a Tory government.'

Sturgeon argued: 'If on 8 May, there are more anti-Tory MPs in the House of Commons than there are Tory MPs, then, if we work together, we can lock David Cameron out of Downing Street. So, tell me tonight, is it the case that you would rather see David Cameron go back into Downing Street than work with the SNP?' She received cheers and applause from the audience.

Given another chance, Miliband's response was again weak. 'I've fought Tories all my life,' he claimed, attempting to draw a comparison with the SNP's support for the Conservatives in 1979 and the Liberal Democrats' in 2010.

Sturgeon pointed out she was nine years old in 1979, and, speaking directly to Miliband, she argued: 'You have a chance to kick David Cameron out of Downing Street. Don't turn your back on it. People will never forgive you for it.'

In the Labour green room, there was an overriding sense of disappointment. 'It was a disaster,' said one of Miliband's team. 'He was out of sorts and had a lot more in the tank. We knew he could have done a lot better.' A Survation poll for the *Daily Mirror* suggested the Labour leader had narrowly outperformed Nicola Sturgeon, with Nigel Farage in third place. But Labour insiders knew Miliband had a phalanx of well-crafted lines he had never used.

In contrast, two SNP ministers accompanying Nicola Sturgeon – Humza Yousaf and Derek Mackay – were ecstatic at their leader's performance. They were also impressed by the buzz of the spin room: far busier and star-studded than the equivalent at Scottish broadcasts.

Stefan Rousseau, the Press Association's chief political photographer, captured the defining moment of the night with a shot of the three female leaders – Sturgeon, Bennett and Wood – hugging after the debate, Miliband awkwardly watching on.

Team Murphy was pumped up on the morning of 17 April 2015. They had spent weeks working on Scottish Labour's 'vision to make Scotland the fairest nation on earth', and now, at the Tollcross Leisure Centre in Glasgow, their general election manifesto was being launched.

At the core of their calculations was the figure of £2.5 billion. This was the amount predicted to be raised each year with UK Labour's mansion tax, and the party's pledge to clamp down on tax avoidance. With Scotland roughly constituting a tenth of the UK's population, this meant Jim Murphy had £250 million to play with – but only if there was a Labour government. 'I want to give people free stuff,' he announced in one policy meeting. And from this spirit of spending came a pledge for 1,000 extra nurses – the SNP accused Murphy of 'playing an arbitrary numbers game' – as well as a payment of £1,600 to eighteen- and nineteen-year-olds leaving school and going straight into employment, to help them advance their careers.

The manifesto, however, was missing some vital elements. 'It contained no childcare policy,' commented someone involved, 'because we were absolutely unable to agree whether or not to replicate the UK offer. In the end, it was just ignored, which speaks to a certain dysfunctionality.'

'It was a house of cards, built on nothing,' complained another in the team. 'Shall we do this policy? Yes. Can we get a visit sorted? Yes. It was very scattergun, with no theme to it all.' Scottish Labour's approach to getting other organisations to endorse their policies was also unconventional, according to a third Labour source: 'We made up a policy on Monday, phoned up the Scottish TUC or Barnardo's on Tuesday, and expected them to get behind the idea by Wednesday.' In any case, the manifesto was about to be swept off course.

'The launch was great, looked good, Jim's speech was good, the manifesto was good,' explained one senior figure. 'We were hyper and excited. Then Ashcroft came at 4 p.m. and killed it.'

The Conservative peer had published yet another raft of constituency polls, and Jim Murphy's East Renfrewshire constituency was among them. In February, Ashcroft's research suggested Murphy was one point ahead of the SNP. This time, he was nine points behind, and on course to lose his job.

Douglas Alexander, Labour's chair of general election strategy, was eleven points behind his nationalist rival Mhairi Black, a twenty-year-old politics student. David Mundell – the only Conservative MP in Scotland – was now two points behind his SNP challenger Emma Harper.

Back at the party's Glasgow headquarters, there had been a sudden collapse in morale. It was the first time the team realised it was possible that Murphy might lose his seat. 'The atmosphere was dead, deflated,' explained one person present. 'It was definitely the point we knew we were fucked.' Another remarked: 'We knew the game was up. If we were behind in East Renfrewshire, we were fucked everywhere else.'

Aside from Labour's manifesto launch, 17 April was when most postal votes would be sent out. Just twenty-four hours after Nicola Sturgeon's success in the 'Challengers' Debate', her party was flying high in the polls. 'It was the sweet spot, the dream ticket,' according to an SNP source, pointing out that most voters complete their ballots within the first two days after receiving them.

At the same time, SNP candidates who were 'selected but never expected' – including, nationalist insiders admit, 'a few crazies' – were instructed to cancel all holiday and tell their employers they might not be coming back to work.

For the final weeks, Murphy would begin each day with a campaign photocall, and record clips for broadcasters. He would then spend the rest of his time in his East Renfrewshire constituency. The area had a significant number of Conservative voters, and many had previously been keen to support the once Blairite Murphy. But his media appearances and left-wing rhetoric changed that: 'Jim was on telly every night kicking lumps out of the Tories,' complained one source, 'then he expected the Tories to vote Labour in his patch.' When setting out the merits of a mansion tax, Murphy's ability to persuade tactical-thinking Conservatives soon faded away.

STV's Stephen Daisley acidly commented on the Scottish Labour leader's seemingly fluid ideology: 'Murphy's shift from the right to the left is remarkable. As conversions go, it's Damascene – if Saul of Tarsus had found Christ and immediately become a Seventh-Day Adventist. Labour politicians used to discover socialism after reading Marx or Laski. Jim Murphy discovered it after reading the opinion polls.'

Labour colleagues claimed Murphy's constituency team ran a weak campaign and shifted tactics too late: 'They changed in the last two weeks to focus on getting Tory votes,' explained one colleague, 'but, by then, they'd all gone.' In the final fortnight, canvassing data suggested his local support could be as low at 20 per cent.

Murphy's personal poll ratings had been steadily decreasing at the same time. YouGov conducted four polls between February and May asking voters: 'Do you think that Jim

Murphy is doing well or badly as leader of the Scottish Labour Party?'

In February, 57 per cent of voters thought Murphy was doing fairly badly or very badly, with the rest deciding he was doing fairly well or very well. By May, the negative responses had grown to 70 per cent of those surveyed, with only 30 per cent of voters positive about Murphy's performance. Other research suggested he was more unpopular than David Cameron in Scotland.

'Jim was the sole face of the campaign,' argued one colleague, 'and there's a real Marmite reaction to him.' Many question the decision to return to the streets and speak on top of Irn-Bru crates – a reminder of Murphy's role in Better Together. 'How were we supposed to forget the referendum when he repeated what he'd done during the No campaign?' Others argue his deputy Kezia Dugdale 'should have been used much, much more'.

Nicola Sturgeon's brilliant personal poll ratings were also a source of frustration: 'If she was discovered drowning kittens,' one senior Labour figure commented, 'they would either blame it on MI5 or argue drowning is the most progressive way of looking after them.'

The Conservatives continued to campaign hard on the danger of a Labour–SNP deal. Former Prime Minister John Major suggested in a high-profile speech that Ed Miliband would be vulnerable to a 'daily dose of political blackmail' from the SNP, while Home Secretary Theresa May claimed such an eventuality would be Britain's 'biggest constitutional crisis' since Edward VIII abdicated in 1936.

Conservative peer and former Scottish Secretary Lord Forsyth later called the tactics 'short-term and dangerous', and Labour's Alistair Darling criticised the Tories for their 'destructive embrace of the nationalists'.

Meanwhile, in Scotland, the party's leader Ruth Davidson seemed to be enjoying herself with a series of wacky photo-calls. Keen to promote a fun, positive message for her party as their vote came under pressure from the tactical messages of Labour and the Liberal Democrats, Davidson appeared astride a tank, holding a fish, driving a steam train and even playing the bagpipes. Her team was irritated, however, when Nicola Sturgeon took to the skies in a helicopter. The Scottish Conservatives had planned a similar trip with a helicopter loaned for free – but it was called off due to fog.

As the outlook for many Liberal Democrats looked increasingly bleak, one figure brought a smile to those working at the party's Edinburgh headquarters. Sir Menzies Campbell's wife Elspeth – tough, *Coronation Street*-loving, immaculately dressed – would sit in the corner and assist the small overworked team. One evening, as Campbell was about to leave, a staff member politely asked: 'Are you going to have a glass of wine or a gin when you get home, Elspeth?'

She replied: 'Oh, I've got bottle of champagne I just nip away at.'

On Sunday 26 April, appearing on the BBC's *The Andrew Marr Show*, Ed Miliband ruled out a confidence and supply agreement with the SNP, in addition to his previous commit-ment to not enter a coalition with the nationalists. Miliband had first been asked about deals with the SNP fifteen weeks before, on exactly the same programme, and refused to rule out anything. Now, just eleven days before polling, this com-mitment was a significant moment.

A few days later, on another BBC programme, Miliband went further: 'It's not going to happen. I couldn't be clearer with you … If the price of having a Labour government was coalition or a deal with the Scottish National Party, it's not going to happen.' With just a week until election day, after more than four months of questioning, many in Labour thought it all far too late.

'Stur Wars: Another Hope' was the *Scottish Sun*'s headline, along an image of Nicola Sturgeon as Princess Leia from *Star Wars* holding a lightsaber. On 30 April, *The Sun* published their UK and Scottish editions endorsing two different parties. The UK version depicted David Cameron as a newborn baby and urged readers to back the Conservatives to 'stop the SNP running the country'. The *Daily Record* – a Scottish competitor to *The Sun* – accused the 'downmarket tabloid' of being 'two-faced'. *The Sun* pointed out their two editorial positions came from two editorial teams in two different countries. Either way, it was bad news – as expected – for Labour. Kezia Dugdale tweeted the two front pages side by side with the comment: '2 papers, 1 objective.'

One week before polling day, Labour's campaign chief Douglas Alexander was at the party's Westminster headquarters gathering papers on his desk, before leaving London to travel up to his Paisley constituency. It would be his last time at One Brewer's Green, where he had, according to colleagues, 'put his heart and soul into the general election campaign'.

As Alexander made to leave, the whole campaign staff spontaneously stood up and began to applaud and bang their desks in the old Fleet Street tradition. There were no thank-yous, no speeches, no fond farewells – yet, for Alexander, doing his best to suppress tears as he slipped away, it was an incredibly moving moment.

The next day, Michael Ashcroft published yet another

set of constituency opinion polls. After nearly 250,000 telephone interviews, this would be the final raft of data from the Conservative peer.

David Mundell was now on course to lose his job; the SNP candidate had seemingly surged ahead, eleven points clear. Jim Murphy's team felt some hope when the SNP lead in East Renfrewshire appeared to have reduced from nine points to just three – within the margin of error. Were tactical Tory voters backing Labour to keep out the SNP? Might Murphy be able to save himself in time?

When an earlier Ashcroft poll suggested Labour's Ian Murray would lose his Edinburgh South seat to the SNP, his exhausted staff burst into tears. But, as polling day approached, he was the one MP who seemed likely to just about survive. The 38-year-old had a majority of just 316 votes in 2010. Because his seat was so marginal, with significant numbers of Liberal Democrat, Conservative and SNP voters, he had spent the parliament building up a reputation as a hardworking local MP, instead of developing his profile outside the constituency. He had set up systems to ensure all correspondence would be answered within twenty-four hours, every constituent was offered a home visit, and he would hold more open surgeries than any other MP in the UK – he worked out who did most, and then did more.

After five years as an MP, Murray had so much data on his constituents that he could target different groups with difference messages, including anti-Tory literature to Labour No voters, and the threat of a second referendum to No-voting Liberal Democrats and Conservatives. Unlike many Labour colleagues, his constituency was diverse enough to allow Murray to use a tactical voting message. He was even spotted canvassing in The Grange, an exclusive neighbourhood home to disgraced RBS chief executive Fred Goodwin. Murray christened Fairmilehead, which boasts some of Scotland's most expensive homes, 'FairmileRED'.

He also benefited from journalists uncovering his SNP opponent Neil Hay as the author of controversial tweets under the pseudonym 'Paco McSheepie', calling No voters 'quislings' and saying elderly people 'barely remember their own names'.

In the final week, as SNP support stayed solidly just short of 50 per cent in opinion polls, with Labour in the mid-twenties, the mood among senior politicians and advisers was one of quiet despair. 'The sky was coming in, we knew it would be a horrific night,' admitted one politician.

Among Labour activists, however, not everyone recognised the disaster that would soon befall their party. Head office staff describe the 'disconnect' between the central campaign and supporters on the ground. 'Some really didn't see it coming,' said one well-connected figure. 'I spoke to people in Edinburgh who were still saying, "We'll hold Mark Lazarowicz [Edinburgh North & Leith] and Fiona O'Donnell [East Lothian]." They had no idea what was coming.' Coatbridge MP Tom Clarke even told one colleague, apparently seriously: 'It's 1997 again. We'll sweep the board.'

In fact, an SNP tsunami was about to hit. 'We thought the high-water mark would be twelve MPs, and five the low-water mark,' explained one senior figure. 'We had strategised for hanging on to twelve, five and zero seats.' However, no one on Team Murphy believed there was a real possibility of losing everything. 'We didn't believe it was possible – it was too ridiculous to comprehend – so we spent no time planning for zero.' Yet even if the party were to retain just five seats, it would still mean Jim Murphy losing his.

Senior aides found it hard to comprehend that their boss could be defeated. 'It was a suspension of disbelief,' claimed a source. 'A room full of highly intelligent people can see the writing on the wall, but don't want to see it. There was no desire to get to grips with reality.'

One explanation for this lack of rationality was that many staff employed in the team had – as one source described it – 'bought into the cult of Jim'. They were 'all die-hard Jim Murphy fans'. Many staff had JimMurphy.scot email addresses and considered themselves working for Murphy, not the Labour Party. It rubbed many outside the clique up the wrong way. But when Messiah Murphy looked likely to be defenestrated, 'there were no tears, just despondency', explained one adviser. 'We were blankly staring into a pit of doom.'

On Wednesday 6 May, the day before polling, Jim Murphy decided that he would stay as leader if – as seemed highly likely – he lost his seat. Lawyers had already been consulted and had confirmed there was nothing in the party's constitution to prevent him staying on – though such an eventuality had, of course, never been considered. That evening, Blair McDougall began to draft two versions of a speech for the two eventualities.

In the final fraught weeks of the campaign, Murphy's mood had darkened. 'He started to get despondent more than anything,' explained one colleague. 'It didn't change how he operated: he's a strong leader, he knows how to behave.'

For all his life, Jim Murphy had been a star: an MP in his twenties; a minister in his thirties; and in the Cabinet by his early forties. His charisma and sheer force of personality had led to some touting him as a future Labour Prime Minister.

Such conjecture now seemed fanciful, almost absurd, for Murphy had come to the bitter, bleak realisation that, despite his determination, charm and ferocious energy, no amount of money, no clever tactics and no creative photo opportunities could change his fate. Privately, he told his closest advisers: 'This is really bad. I thought I could fix it and I can't. What have I done?'

CHAPTER 15

TSUNAMI

Even on polling day, Jim Murphy's team was preparing for protests. At 10.30 a.m., as the Scottish Labour leader travelled to vote in the village of Busby, knowing that, that night, he would be ousted as an MP after eighteen years, there was still an expectation he would be confronted at the polling station by demonstrators. Inveterate agitator Sean Clerkin, who had regularly attempted to disrupt Labour events in Glasgow, lives with his parents in nearby Barrhead and was a constituent of Murphy's. Labour activists were ready to take up position around the Scottish Labour leader, police were present and a car was on standby to whisk him away if needed. But there were no protests. His detractors had made their point. Their job was done.

Murphy spent much of the day touring the polling stations in his patch and phoning undecided voters. He kept in regular contact with Scottish Labour headquarters in Glasgow, where the General Secretary Brian Roy was monitoring turnout – a key factor in calculating how many seats his party could cling on to. Roy lists his date of birth on Facebook as 3 May 1997 – the day after Tony Blair became Prime Minister and his father, Frank Roy, was elected to Parliament. This seems to be a political point: he is far older than eighteen. His team of organisers had been sent to monitor two polling stations in each held seat: one in a traditionally Labour-supporting area and one in a neighbourhood where the SNP was strongest. The plan was then, through a complex series of algorithms, to calculate a likely result.

Early on, the signs were surprisingly positive. Turnout in Labour-supporting areas was far higher than in those favourable to the nationalists – in part due to the activity of early rising older Labour loyalists.

'But then, between 5 and 6 p.m., it all changed,' explained one senior party source. 'It was like flicking a switch.' Turnout in SNP areas suddenly surged. 'White-collar workers came home from work, went to vote and they all voted SNP.' Roy stared at his computer screen as, over the course of an hour, the horizon was transformed, and Labour's hopes of holding on to even its safest of seats evaporated.

As the evening wore on and the close of polls drew near, exhausted staff and weary cagoule-clad activists returned to HQ. 'We knew early on that things were bad, really bad,' remarked one senior Labour figure. Massive majorities were not just wiped out, but completely overturned. As the scale of Labour's looming defeat in Scotland became apparent, Brian Roy could be heard being physically sick in the toilets at party HQ.

Labour's national campaign team always knew Scotland would be difficult, but they remained confident that governing at Westminster was in their sights. For the past year, former Lord Chancellor Charlie Falconer had been leading the party's transition team, preparing for a Labour administration. Alongside Miliband's chief of staff Tim Livesey, Falconer had been liaising with the civil service about a

Labour government's priority bills, an emergency Budget to be held within weeks, and plans – reported by *The Times* – to reinstate a 'delivery unit' to guarantee key outcomes.

At 9 p.m., bookmakers Betfair announced that Ed Miliband was odds-on favourite to be the next Prime Minister at 10/11, with David Cameron on 11/10. As Miliband and his closest adviser Lord Stewart Wood worked on his victory speech in the leader's constituency home near Doncaster, they were blissfully unaware of the earthquake about to destroy their well-laid plans.

In a secret London location, a team of five political scientists had spent all day poring over data collected from 22,000 voters in 141 locations across 133 constituencies. At 10 p.m., they would release the official exit poll, jointly funded – at a cost thought to be over £100,000 – by ITV, Sky News and the BBC. Researchers from the pollsters Ipsos MORI and GfK NOP had been standing outside polling stations asking people not how they *intended* to vote, but, for the first time in the contest, how they *had* voted.

The methodology, based on surveying the same places year after year, had largely been focused on the Conservative/Labour battlegrounds. This time, other parties – principally the SNP and UKIP – were likely to play a far greater role. In Scotland, the number of polling stations monitored was doubled from five to ten, to pick up trends north of the border. Convening the all-male team was the distinguished psephologist Professor John Curtice – a regular fixture in the general election exit-poll room since the 1970s.

The first data sets had arrived just after 11 a.m., but were used merely to ensure the system was working and to monitor the rates of voter participation. Serious analysis started after lunchtime, and the story in Scotland remained the same thereafter. As for the whole UK, the Conservatives were consistently ahead, and close to being able to form a majority government. 'We knew for hours,' said one person involved. 'It always shifts a little at the start, because Tory voters are more like to vote early, but, from mid-afternoon, the story did not shift.' For over six hours this group kept the details secret. 'It's illegal for anyone to leak,' explained one of the team. They knew, however, that, as soon as the numbers were released, it would set off a frenzy in the four-hour news vacuum between the close of polls and the rush of results after 2 a.m.

As 10 p.m. approached and broadcasters were given details of the exit poll, most candidates in Scotland had gone home to rest, get changed and have a cup of tea. As kettles boiled and as Big Ben struck ten, ITV's Tom Bradby, Sky's Adam Boulton and the BBC's David Dimbleby relayed the astonishing figures to the nation.

The poll predicted that the Conservatives would win 316 seats, just ten short of a majority, with Labour on 239 and the Lib Dems on ten. A defiant Paddy Ashdown – a former Liberal Democrat leader – dismissed the findings, telling the BBC's Andrew Neil: 'I can tell you that is wrong. If these exit polls are right, I'll publicly eat my hat.' According to the exit poll, Nicola Sturgeon's Scottish National Party was likely to secure fifty-eight of Scotland's fifty-nine Westminster constituencies. The SNP's communications chief Kevin Pringle texted his party's key spokespeople: 'Play down expectations. It can't translate into seats.' Alastair Campbell didn't believe the figures either, declaring on the BBC: 'I will eat my kilt.'

While the early prediction could prove to be wide of the mark, it stunned MPs across Scotland. 'I said "fuck".

Just one word: "fuck". My wife said exactly same thing,' remembered one. 'It made me feel physically sick,' admitted another Labour candidate. 'Part of me was disbelieving, but I recognised the story we'd been hearing day in, day out.' A third prominent name recalled: 'I was with my election agent at his house. We'd just had fish and chips, and I just said, "I'm gone." It was numbing.'

At Ed Miliband's cottage in South Yorkshire, the room fell silent. Just 20 miles away in Sheffield, Nick Clegg was in his constituency flat with his wife, Miriam. 'That can't be right,' he said. The Lib Dems were predicted to retain just ten seats – a crushing collapse. This meant forty-seven of Clegg's MPs would lose their jobs, leaving their party back at their most paltry level of representation for forty-five years. Clegg's pitch that the Liberal Democrats would add 'a heart' to a Conservative government and 'a brain' to a Labour one had failed spectacularly.

In the Liberal Democrats' Scottish headquarters, shattered staff members were distraught: 'In that moment, we could do nothing else,' explained a member of the team. 'No leaflet could be sent out to change it. Nobody saw it coming. Nobody could believe it was that bad.' The campaigners were not sure if they had kept even their safest seat, Orkney & Shetland, as exit-poll predictions reflect a sum of probabilities, and cannot readily be extrapolated to seat-by-seat analysis.

In BBC Scotland's election studio, Conservative leader Ruth Davidson and Willie Rennie from the Lib Dems were sitting alongside Labour's deputy leader Kezia Dugdale and SNP Transport Minister Derek Mackay. Each member of the panel questioned the accuracy of the polls. 'We were all in complete and utter disbelief,' said one of the panel. The four politicians, from then on, were glued to their phones and iPads, grasping for any idea of what was really happening across the country.

Labour's deputy leader Harriet Harman was sitting with a group of advisers outside Crussh, a cafe in Four Millbank – which houses the Westminster studios of ITV, Sky and the BBC – preparing to go on air. When the exit poll popped up on their phones, there was shock on their faces. 'Fucking hell,' spluttered one aide. Another had her head in her hands. Harman looked white 'like she'd seen a ghost', according to someone present. The team spent the next ten minutes trying to work out what line to use during TV interviews.

The problem for Harman and every other Labour politician on air was that their detailed media briefings were completely unusable. Written on the assumption that there would be a hung parliament, there were two pages of bullet points on 'The Constitution', with details of Ramsay MacDonald's appointment as Prime Minister in 1924 – he had fewer seats than Stanley Baldwin – as well as Winston Churchill's victory in 1951, and Ted Heath's resignation in February 1974. Quotes from constitutional experts Robert Hazell and Michael Pinto-Duschinsky were even included, as well as a reference to paragraph 2.12 of the Cabinet Office manual, which states that an incumbent government 'is expected to resign if it becomes clear that it is unlikely to be able to command' the confidence of the House of Commons 'and there is a clear alternative'.

Fascinating as it all might be for political anoraks, this detail was, for the moment at hand, utterly useless.

A separate YouGov survey had less dramatic findings. It put the Tories on 284 seats, Labour on 263, the SNP on forty-eight and the Lib Dems on thirty-one. However, it was not a true exit poll. Instead, over 10,000 people had been asked how they intended to vote in the three days immediately prior to polling. YouGov president Peter Kellner later admitted: 'We got the election wrong,' adding: 'So did the other ten polling companies who produced eve-of-election voting intentions.'

When Labour's 10.30 p.m. election-night script was emailed out twelve minutes late by Tom Hamilton, Labour's head of briefing and rebuttal, it recommended politicians remain optimistic about the party's chances of forming a government. 'We're sceptical of this exit poll,' the document read. Labour took comfort in the fact that the YouGov figures were 'very different' from the broadcasters' poll. 'It looks wrong. Exit polls have been very wrong in the past.'

Jim Murphy was one of the few politicians not at home as polls closed. His daughter was sitting a Higher exam the next morning, and Murphy did not want to disturb her. Instead, he chose to lie low at the Busby Hotel in Clarkston. Murphy guzzled Irn-Bru as his adviser Lynsey Jackson and press officer David Ross sipped cups of tea.

Murphy had been booked into one of the hotel's honeymoon suites, but his honeymoon had ended long ago. By 11.30 p.m., the confirmation came: he would lose his seat by at least 2,000 votes. The Scottish Labour leader had long prepared himself for a bad result, 'but not quite this bad', a colleague admitted. One aide recalled repeatedly thinking: 'Well, at least we'll hold onto … oh, no.'

Murphy was calm, not sad or emotional. He was worried for his colleagues and blamed himself. 'I'm sorry I couldn't fix this,' he said again and again on the phone to losing candidates as the results came through.

Blair McDougall had drafted a concession speech, which

Murphy, Jackson and Ross spent the next hour editing. The team was focused on getting their leader to the count and out with dignity, and ensuring that his speech gave the clear message that he would remain as leader.

Advisers had, however, foreseen problems if Murphy's deputy Kezia Dugdale was live on TV when his leadership came into question. 'We were worried Jim would lose his seat while she was on air,' explained a member of the team. This prompted a dash to get Dugdale out of the studio. She was swiftly replaced by Gordon Matheson, leader of Glasgow City Council.

For the Scottish Conservatives, early signs were not good in the two seats they hoped to gain. 'The SNP were doing too well in our areas,' one strategist explained. The party's focus quickly switched to retaining the sole Conservative MP north of the border and avoiding a repeat of their 1997 wipeout. David Mundell had survived against the odds in Dumfriesshire, Clydesdale & Tweeddale for the past ten years, and, from the count, his team was sending details box by box to both Scottish Conservative leader Ruth Davidson in Glasgow and the party's headquarters in Edinburgh. 'We knew if any of our areas didn't perform, he was out,' said one of the team. 'And we were reliant on the Labour mining areas holding up and not switching to the SNP.'

At 1.30 a.m., Scottish Labour's most senior politicians and advisers joined a conference call. By this point, they were aware that very few of their MPs would survive. 'We knew we were about to get absolutely fucking annihilated,' explained one person on the call. With Murphy's seat almost certainly lost, it was looking like Edinburgh South's Ian Murray and shadow Foreign Secretary Douglas Alexander would be the only two left.

'I'm heading to the count right now,' Alexander told his colleagues. 'They're telling me it's 100 votes either way. Whatever happens there'll be a recount.' He seemed energised and optimistic. With the weight of Labour's UK-wide campaign on his shoulders, Alexander had been under huge pressure for months. Yet, after it seemed his chances of fulfilling his long-held ambition of becoming Foreign Secretary were slipping away, there was still a glimmer of hope that he might just hold on to his seat.

Yet, after arriving at Paisley Lagoon Leisure Centre, Alexander would soon find out he had been cruelly misinformed. His campaign team had run a clumsy sampling operation. 'How Douglas coped was just amazing,' said a friend. 'He was laughing going in. Then there was this realisation': he had been defeated by a twenty-year-old politics student. And her majority was not 100, but 5,684. There was no need for a recount. It could not have been clearer: Labour's seventy-year run in Paisley was over.

Later, as flashbulbs flickered at this most difficult of personal moments, Alexander congratulated his opponent, and said: 'Scotland has chosen to oppose this Conservative government, but not place that trust in the Labour Party. It will be our responsibility to re-win that trust in the months and years ahead.' Former Labour strategist Paul Sinclair told the BBC he was 'deeply sad' to see his ex-boss beaten: 'I think it is bad for Scotland, as well, because he was a big figure.'

As Alexander stepped off the stage, Scottish Liberal Democrat leader Willie Rennie was driving himself back from Glasgow. As he approached Edinburgh, he received a call on his hands-free from his party leader. Nick Clegg revealed that he would resign the leadership later that morning. 'It's just dreadful,' he said. 'There's no way I can stay.'

As Rennie reached the Lib Dems' Scottish headquarters at Clifton Terrace, he knew he would soon have to start the same painful exercise of ringing round colleagues to apologise. He went to the office's meeting room, away from staff and activists, and spoke in turn to defeated colleague after defeated colleague.

This was the moment Rennie realised that all the polls and predictions in Scotland had been right. The experience of losing was not a new one for Scottish Liberal Democrats, who had suffered in council, Holyrood and European elections. Yet, on his watch, towering figures like Charles Kennedy, an MP for all of Rennie's adult life, had gone. Talented media performers like Jo Swinson and dogged local campaigners like Alan Reid had been wiped out. And, in three hours, Danny Alexander, at the centre of the coalition government for five years, would be out of government, out of Parliament and out of work.

'We did everything we could,' Rennie told one colleague. 'Don't torture yourself.'

Not everyone was sympathetic about the Liberals' predicament. 'There is a personal pleasure in seeing Lib Dems lose in so many seats,' grinned one Scottish Conservative.

Jim Murphy arrived at Williamwood High School in the wealthy Glasgow suburb of Clarkston just before 3 a.m., surrounded by a scrum of TV cameras and photographers. His campaign team greeted him, many in tears.

Within fifteen minutes, he was on stage shaking the hand of Kirsten Oswald of the SNP, who had beaten him with a majority of 3,718. The Conservatives had secured a substantial 12,465 votes – clearly very few Tories had chosen to vote tactically to keep out the SNP.

Murphy congratulated his opponent, but added a note of

caution: 'No one, of course, should ever confuse nationalism with our nation, no one should ever mistake their party for our country, because our history, our streets, our flag have never and will never belong to one political party or one political cause.'

He pledged to 'continue to lead Scottish Labour', before concluding: 'The party that had traditionally been the tireless champion of the underdog now finds itself in the position of being the underdog. But the Scottish Labour Party has been around for more than a century and, 100 years from tonight, we'll still be around. Scotland needs a strong Labour Party, and our fightback starts tomorrow morning.'

There were cheers from Murphy's emotional supporters before he swiftly left the building, followed by TV cameras. The BBC and STV had both been promised interviews, but Murphy's team decided his speech summed up his message.

At 3.33 a.m., Ruth Davidson was with Eddie Barnes, Scottish Conservative director of strategy and communications, in a room at the Hilton Garden Inn. Its location, across the River Clyde from the BBC and STV studios, meant the Scottish Conservatives' leader could be on air in minutes if required. Looking at her Twitter stream, Davidson spotted the news she had been dreading. An STV reporter wrote that, 'judging by the piles of votes being stacked up, the SNP have indeed won' David Mundell's seat. This shock revelation sent Davidson into a panic and she immediately rang party HQ in Edinburgh. At that point, all ballot boxes had been accounted for, allowing the number crunchers in the capital to confirm to their leader that her friend and colleague would, in fact, just hold on. Mundell would later win by 798 votes.

Over in Glasgow, a jubilant Nicola Sturgeon told the media at the city's Emirates Arena that 'the tectonic plates in

Scottish politics have shifted', describing her party's performance as 'a historic watershed'. The SNP had never before won a Glasgow seat; this time, it was to be a clean sweep of all seven. The First Minister's predecessor Alex Salmond claimed the 'Scottish lion has roared', describing the results as an 'extraordinary statement of intent from the people of Scotland'.

Among those defeated was Scottish Labour MP and shadow Scottish Secretary Margaret Curran, who had long joked that, if ousted, she would move to Tenerife and open a gay bar called Margarita's (her political adviser Martin McCluskey would be in charge of marketing, with Curran working front of house).

William Bain, the Labour MP for Glasgow North East, had first been elected in a 2009 by-election. (His name had been changed to 'Willie' after focus groups decided the more informal Scottish version would be electorally favourable.) Bain told friends a few weeks before that he could be 'the last man standing' in Scotland. And yet – despite once enjoying a majority just shy of 16,000 – he, too, was swept away with a UK record swing of 39 per cent, so large it broke the BBC swingometer.

Back at Scottish Labour's Bath Street office, staff were crowding around a television screen on one side of the room. Blair McDougall was alone on the other side, at his computer with headphones on, watching coverage on Twitter. He was silent and dismayed.

'It was like a funeral. Lots of people were crying,' described someone in the team. 'It was the full horror; truly morbid.' Murphy's loss had been the most difficult moment, with gasps among those watching. Party stalwart Annmarie Whyte told a colleague: 'This is it. This is the end.'

Murphy soon arrived to cheers and applause. Among those in tears were Susan Dalgety and Blair McDougall. 'Blair's so big that when you see him crying, you think, "Fuck,"' remarked one colleague. Brian Roy – having watched his father lose his job more than an hour before – was 'calm, quiet and despondent'.

Jim Murphy gave what one person watching described as an 'amazing off-the-cuff speech'. He told colleagues: 'One bad night does not kill 100 years of Labour history. We shouldn't underestimate what has happened to us, but don't exaggerate it either.'

The team immediately went into a meeting to develop the details of the speech Murphy was to give the next day.

Ian Murray was at the Edinburgh count at the city's International Conference Centre. He had, by this point, re-alised he would be Scotland's sole remaining Labour MP. Murray spent an hour trying to concentrate enough to write a speech on the back of conference centre notepaper, utterly devastated at the defeat of his two hardworking local col-leagues, Sheila Gilmore and Mark Lazarowicz. The junior press officer sent to accompany him was of little use, and the only direction he received from director of communications Susan Dalgety was: 'Do what you want to do.'

In the background, supporters of defeated SNP candidate Neil Hay were 'incredibly bitter and angry', according to one activist, as this was one of the very few unsuccessful SNP campaigns in the country.

At 5.19 a.m., as the sun was rising, Nick Clegg won his Sheffield Hallam seat with a greatly reduced majority. The shell-shocked Liberal Democrat leader was blunt about the catastrophe his party was now facing: 'This has been a cruel and punishing night for the Liberal Democrats.'

Minutes later, Ed Miliband admitted in his acceptance speech in Doncaster: 'This has clearly been a very disappointing and difficult night for the Labour Party.' He was 'deeply sorry' for MPs who had lost their seats in Scotland, and hinted that his leadership would soon be over. 'The next government has', he told supporters, 'a huge responsibility in facing the difficult task of keeping our country together. Whatever party we come from, if we believe in the UK, we must stand up for people in every part of our united kingdom.'

As he swiftly left to join a four-vehicle convoy back to London, Ed Miliband would rapidly need to make a decision about his own future. Staying as leader was untenable. Watching TVs on the second floor of the One Brewer's Green open-plan office was the other half of Team Miliband. Labour staff, who had been sure of victory, were inconsolable. 'People were in tears all through the night,' admitted one weary staff member, 'mainly in shock.' But there was little time to discuss the defeat as 'resignation speeches needed to be written'.

One historic defeat among the mêlée was that of former Liberal Democrat leader Charles Kennedy, who had been an MP from the age of twenty-three. He had been expecting to lose since Christmas, and would soon fly down to London to start packing up his parliamentary office. One Liberal Democrat adviser texted Kennedy: 'Really gutted. It's been a privilege to work with you.' He replied simply: 'Amen to all that.'

At 5.39 a.m., Labour politicians across the UK were sent an updated media script. In a Q&A section, under the question, 'Who won the election/have the Tories won?', Labour was still insisting that their representatives trotted out the line: 'It looks likely that no party has won a majority.' At that exact moment, Labour was thirty-one seats down on their 2010 result, and the BBC was forecasting that David Cameron would end the night with enough seats to form a majority. Out of a list of ten possible gains from the Tories on the Labour media briefing, the party was to win none.

At 5.40 a.m., security was tight at Windrush Leisure Centre in Witney where David Cameron had just arrived with his wife Samantha and director of communications Craig Oliver to hear the result of his constituency count. Officers from the Metropolitan Police Counter Terrorism Command were dotted around the hall, in case any of the eccentric candidates – one was dressed as the *Sesame Street* character Elmo, another as a 'fake sheikh' – got out of hand. Cameron welcomed the strong showing for his party, but said it was 'too early' to say what form the next government would take.

Standing alone, watching the speech on a flat-screen TV in Macclesfield Leisure Centre, 150 miles north of Witney, was George Osborne. Just after 7 a.m., it became clear that the Chancellor had held the Tatton constituency, increasing his majority by 3,754 to 18,241. 'I remember standing on this stage five years ago and I made a commitment to work with the British people to try to turn Britain around,' he said. 'And we've made great progress. Tonight, the British people have asked us to finish the job, and that is what we'll now set about doing.'

Confounding all expectations, and even with just a 0.8 per cent increase of the national vote share, the Conservatives had won 331 seats and a majority of twelve in Parliament.

But the real revolution had happened in Scotland, where the SNP had secured an astonishing 50 per cent of votes, and all but three seats. Labour support, meanwhile, had collapsed. The Scottish electoral map, once a multicoloured mix, was now yellow – with a dash of orange, a splash of blue and speck of red.

EPILOGUE

THE PAST

In the immediate aftermath of the general election, many of the defeated candidates were preoccupied with purely practical considerations. One recalled having to catch an 8 a.m. train to London – just three hours after losing his job of eighteen years – to empty his Westminster office. Another wistfully remembered having to sit his children down and tell them, 'Daddy's lost his job,' with tears ensuing and concerns about playground teasing. A third newly former MP worried about being able to pay the mortgage and having to sell their home.

Many Labour and Liberal Democrat candidates in Scotland also mentioned the relative comfort of collective defeat. Losing did not seem to be a reflection on their personal abilities, rather the result of a wider shift towards the SNP, one without parallel in modern British political history.

What underlay this wider tectonic shift? There is no doubt that there was an existing narrative of increasing openness to the idea of independence and of Labour and Liberal Democrat decline. But this may have gained further leverage from the divisive language of the referendum debate, the temporary alliance of pro-UK parties in the Better Together coalition, the absence of a generous and collaborative post-referendum narrative from the winning side, the avoidable proximity in time of referendum and election, and the leadership transition and membership boost of the SNP.

Despite the rejection of Scottish independence by a clear margin, the referendum itself was, beyond the predictions of any of those involved, a catalyst for far-reaching change. The vote's closeness to the general election – largely the result of a David Cameron mistake three years before – ensured that voters were still immersed in the emotions and judgements of the independence debate when they went to the national polls. Among the currents at play was a desire of those who voted Yes – and lost – to re-emphasise their position, while many of those who voted No wished to add a 'devo max' rider to the outcome. Many in both groups would vote for the SNP, who promised to 'stand up for Scotland'.

Perhaps the party's general election success would have been less pronounced if Scots had reached their decision on independence a year earlier, in September 2013, with a longer period for its consequences to play out before they made their second decision in 2015.

There is little doubt that the opportunity to define the No campaign victory was almost casually discarded. This was partly the result of David Cameron's 7 a.m. speech on 19 September 2014, which immediately moved the focus onto the contentious issue of EVEL. The Prime Minister's decision to conflate the two issues seemed to many – including prominent Conservatives – to be unnecessarily framing the referendum outcome in divisive terms. It allowed the

SNP – pro-UK sources suggest – to continue its 'betrayal narrative'. And losing the referendum became not a setback for the independence movement, but progress towards its central aim.

Yet the argument for apportioning most of the blame to David Cameron only follows if he had diverged from a carefully considered and agreed post-referendum plan. This was not the case: there was no plan. 'We were only interested in crossing the finishing line,' complained one senior source. Another likened Better Together's behaviour to 'a bride focused on her wedding day. Whereas Yes Scotland was focused on the marriage, and planning life afterwards.' A third pro-UK source argued: 'They had a full [general] election strategy and we were surviving Heath Robinson style, just about keeping it together.'

This was indicative of a campaign that had a solid strategy sustained – to its credit – through a barrage of criticism. But it was arguably flawed in its execution. 'I'm a stout defender of the strategy,' argued one experienced figure, 'but the campaign was shambolic.' By focusing so relentlessly on persuading undecided voters, Better Together seemed to lose track of how the campaign was perceived more widely.

The starting point for the pro-UK parties was, however, one where many Scots were already open to the idea of independence, more so than many in Better Together had, until that point, expected. One senior strategist claimed: 'A really good campaign could have got to 60/40, but all the way through the prediction was 55/45.'

After the referendum, the line 'Labour was hand in glove with the Tories' was regularly picked up on the doorsteps. However, Electoral Commission guidelines for the 2014 referendum meant there could only be one lead No campaign, and that was Better Together. If there is a next time, Scottish Labour might consider being less involved in this and putting more time and money into its own efforts.

Similarities can be drawn between the No campaign and the Conservatives' general election campaign. Both were much criticised, both had ruthless strategies based on strong evidence, and both were ultimately successful.

And while 'Project Fear' succeeded in securing a No vote, winning was far from all that was at stake, as became immediately evident in the days after the referendum result, when polls showed Scottish Labour support in decline as SNP support soared. The Labour dip seems to have happened in late September, and continued on a similar plane for the next eight months, suggesting that Jim Murphy could have done little to arrest his party's decline during his short spell as leader – although, in practice, polls suggest he may have made it worse.

Ninety per cent of Yes voters in the referendum backed the SNP at the general election, according to research from Professor Ed Fieldhouse of Manchester University. This correlation persisted, whether Scots agreed with Nicola Sturgeon's central anti-austerity election message or not.

Other polling suggests a significant proportion of Scots will continue to back the SNP, whether the party's record in government is strong or not, implying the party currently possesses a Teflon quality, because their many supporters have a broader aim. Jim Murphy likened the SNP's campaign to 'a quasi-religious rock concert'.

Nicola Sturgeon is an extremely polished political performer, seemingly far less divisive than her predecessor and arguably more authentically left-wing. By the time she took part in the ITV leaders' debate, Sturgeon had had eight years of experience in government – more than any of her rivals at Westminster. Being afforded a national platform for the first time was an opportunity for the First Minister to demonstrate her talents, without being challenged on her own record in power. And her opponents in Scotland were, by the very nature of the national media process, denied a similar level of exposure.

The SNP also had a consistency of message that the three pro-UK parties were unable to compete with. 'They managed to effectively line up their party-political offer with their referendum offer; ours was a compromise,' admitted one prominent unionist politician. 'For the Euros in 2014, we had three different offers, then one offer for the referendum, then we diverged for 2015, and we'll do the same in 2016, too.'

Unlike the professionalised operation of the SNP (which had learnt lessons, rather ironically, from New Labour), Scottish Labour has had – with eight leaders in fifteen years – glaringly inconsistent leadership. Much of this has been a consequence of the party's 'brain drain' to Westminster, combined with a striking absence of succession planning.

The possibility of a coalition with the SNP cemented Labour's troubles in Scotland, setting off a twin attack from both nationalists and Conservatives, each leaping on this vehicle for winning votes from Labour. Ed Miliband and his advisers did not seem to realise the damage this would cause in England until it was far too late.

Most Labour politicians and advisers argue that, if a cross-party deal had been categorically ruled out much earlier in 2015, it would have changed the course of the election and prevented some of the party's electoral damage on both sides of the border.

Various Labour luminaries also believe that 'the price we paid for the referendum was the general election'. This claim, that by uniting with the Conservatives they allowed themselves to be sacrificed for the future of the United Kingdom, does not seem to tally with the sustained trajectory of Scottish Labour's decline. Or, indeed, with Better Together's own research, which suggested a substantial shift had taken place in attitudes to independence in the decade since the Scottish Parliament was established. Some argue: 'The seeds of Labour decline were sown long before the referendum.'

Jim Murphy's role in the election was mixed. His strong identification with Better Together may not have helped with key swing Westminster election voters. He remains a charismatic media performer, but his sanctioning of repeated changes of strategy, as the general election campaign progressed, blurred the definition of Scottish Labour and disseminated – some of his colleagues felt – a sense of desperation.

Murphy was also semi-detached from his MSPs and allowed resentment, particularly among left-wingers, to fester. Even towards the end of his leadership, he did not know the names of all his Holyrood politicians. 'Who's that again?' he asked, after passing Jayne Baxter, one of his own MSPs. 'At least I don't have to come here again,' he joked, after announcing his resignation.

The Liberal Democrats, by contrast, had been in steep decline since their broken tuition-fees promise, and ended up almost completely devoured in the political cannibalism of coalition. This was compounded in Scotland by how the 55/45 referendum result played out in the first-past-the-post electoral system. As one Liberal Democrat complained: 'Forty-five divided by one is always going to be more than fifty-five divided by three.' Nicola Sturgeon recognised the irony of her party – always opposed to first-past-the-post – benefiting so starkly from that selfsame system.

THE FUTURE

On 2 February 2016, David Cameron was at the Siemens factory in Chippenham, Wiltshire, making an important speech. In it, he repeated the phrase 'best of both worlds' four times and stressed the importance of 'keeping the pound' on multiple occasions. For a few advisers and journalists, there was an eerie sense of déjà vu. Because, this time, the Prime Minister was not arguing for Scotland to remain in the UK, but for the UK to remain in the EU.

The parallels between the Scottish and EU referendums are striking and the EU In and Out campaigns are striving to repeat the triumphs and avoid the disasters of Yes and No in Scotland.

Two of the more respected advisers from Better Together – Andrew Cooper from Populus and ex-London 2012 strategist Greg Nugent – are already on board the Britain in Europe campaign. Many others involved in the Scottish referendum have been approached for advice. Much of this guidance has been conflicting, as there are divergent views on the lessons of the Better Together experience. Some veterans defend their roles and decisions with defiance. Others involved in the pro-EU agenda are convinced that the only lessons learnt from the Scottish referendum are the mistakes: 'It's going to be nothing like Better Together.'

Yet, on the basis of their experience in Scotland, Cooper and Populus have been commissioned by 'Britain Stronger In Europe' to carry out thousands of pounds' worth of research, including detailed focus groups and extensive private polling.

In Scotland, the pro-Europe campaign has been rebranded

'Scotland Stronger In', eradicating the word 'Britain' – a potentially divisive term post-indy ref. Two experienced political operators from opposing sides in the independence referendum have united. Better Together veteran Frank Roy has been recruited to run the In campaign's ground operation north of the border, while former SNP strategy and communications chief Kevin Pringle will look after media. And while, publicly, the Scottish nationalists refuse to formally join this cross-party campaign (seeking to avoid any perception of standing 'shoulder to shoulder with the Tories'), Peter Murrell, the SNP chief executive and husband of Nicola Sturgeon, has met with Britain Stronger In's executive director Will Straw.

The Leave side, in contrast, is a more complex mix of separate campaigns, reflecting not only the rival interests of UKIP, Conservative Eurosceptics and the small Labour Leave group, but also the differing ideologies behind their arguments for Out.

Both sides identify the big lesson from Scotland as 'Negativity'. The term 'Project Fear' has already been resurrected by the Eurosceptics, who have launched accusations of 'scaremongering', in an attempt to frame David Cameron and his fellow Remain campaigners as prepared to say anything to worry voters into backing their cause. That is because the Leave side believe negative campaigning was dangerously successful. 'Obviously Project Fear was effective,' argued one senior figure. And they worry that their opponents will deploy the same tactic with a persuasive emphasis on the risks of Brexit.

In contrast, although pro-EU strategists realise the potency of highlighting the risks and uncertainties of a Leave vote, they are desperate to avoid being seen as negative:

'We'll do anything to establish a positive frame for the argument,' said one heavily involved. But Stronger In also believe that the very reason anti-EU campaigners are on the attack is 'because they want us to stop – they know focusing on the risks of leaving works'.

At their heart, both EU campaigns are faced with comparable strategic challenges to Better Together and Yes Scotland: the importance of swing voters and the limited opportunities to influence them. Stronger In are already using a risk-based argument; the 'positive case for staying' may remain an elusive aspiration.

As we saw in Scotland, both sides in the EU referendum know economic arguments are key. 'All the early research says that overwhelmingly people are weighing this up as an economic judgement,' said one campaigner. And therefore the currency and jobs are likely to be key battlegrounds once again.

As per the Scottish experience, many undecided voters believe the burden of proof lies with the Leave campaign. 'Many are hoping they'll get the reassurances needed to vote with their hearts,' explains one pro-EU strategist, 'but it won't happen. It again comes down to a leap of faith and the evidence is that not enough people are willing to make that leap.' Eurosceptics have the challenge of explaining what Out would look like, but with no way of knowing until it has happened – the very same challenge Scottish nationalists had to grapple with. Pro-EU figures hope a vote to leave remains inherently too big a risk for people to take.

The similarities with the Scottish poll are so strikingly resonant that one group of undecided voters identified in the Stronger In segmentation analysis are called 'Hearts Versus Heads' – a phrase rehearsed ad nauseam in 2014.

Both sides in the EU referendum realise voters are far more likely to listen to and, crucially, trust the views of business leaders over those of politicians. 'As with Scotland, there are two dug-in campaigns with irreconcilable versions of the truth,' explained one senior figure. 'Voters want information from trusted third parties, and campaign messages are much more convincingly communicated via business people.' Former M&S CEO Lord Stuart Rose is chairing the Britain Stronger In campaign, while insurance businessman Arron Banks is bankrolling the Leave.EU group, and the board of the rival Eurosceptic campaign Vote Leave is full of prominent figures from business, such as restaurant entrepreneur Luke Johnson.

David Cameron takes great care to stress that the European Union is 'not perfect' and will not even necessarily be so in the future. But, as with his Scottish strategy, the Prime Minister will not be campaigning for the status quo.

In Scotland, it was 'The Vow' – a package of further devolution measures promised by the three pro-UK parties to sweeten a No vote. This time, it is Cameron's renegotiated terms of EU membership. On both occasions, the Conservative leader knows he must present himself as being on the side of change. 'It is always easier to argue "Ours is better change" than "Vote for us and nothing will change",' remarked one veteran campaigner.

Focus group participants like the idea that the UK has renegotiated powers and attempted to address their concerns. But when asked what specific powers they want back from the EU, 'they just don't know, except something unspecific about immigration', according to one involved. The same research suggests that Brits think the EU does not adequately recognise the unique interests of the UK.

Leave campaigners argue that David Cameron's renegotiation was more appearance than meaningful change. And,
privately, pro-UK sources admit there's some truth in that.
'For the voters, it's about knowing the EU have heard our
concerns and given some ground,' explained one strategist.
'People find the details so mind-numbingly boring and confusing that it's more about the big picture.'

With polls suggesting Scottish voters are far more pro-
Europe than their English counterparts, and with all four
Scottish party leaders supporting a Remain vote, links
between the various Leave campaigns and those with experience from the Scottish referendum are rare. Aside from
the potency of their opponents' negative campaigning, Leave
strategists have noted one key weakness of Yes Scotland.
'Too many of the Yes campaign's claims were countered
by external sources,' argued one prominent Eurosceptic.
'Salmond said, "We'll keep the pound," and then Mark
Carney implied it might not be so simple. Yes said Scotland
would get EU membership, then Barosso said, "You won't."'
Eurosceptics have therefore been briefed to be more cautious when talking about what might happen after a vote to
leave the EU: 'We are careful. We're not going to rely on the
generosity of others.'

However, there are some differences between the two
referendums. First, although the British electorate's voting
intention can roughly be split into thirds – Remain, Leave
and Undecided – it is clear that their Euroscepticism is to
the fore, and the polls are much closer earlier in the campaign than in Scotland's indy ref. According to focus groups
carried out by the pro-EU campaign Stronger In, 'Negative
things about Europe are at the front of people's minds, tum-
bling out; they can't think of the benefits.' When participants

are pressed on the advantages of the EU, they genuinely hit a blank. 'There must be some benefits,' said one voter, 'but I just don't know what they are.'

This provides a challenge to the Stronger In campaign, who are desperately trying to reset perceptions of the status quo. 'If it's a referendum about how much we don't like the EU, then the In campaign in is trouble,' said one activist. 'If the question is: "What does Out mean?", then the In campaign is on far stronger ground.'

Whereas Scots had to endure two and a half years of debate, the length of the EU referendum is much shorter: just over four months. The view of Downing Street is: now the renegotiation is over, why delay? A short campaign minimises the chance of the fissure in the Conservative Party turning into a chasm. It also reduces the chance of external events – such as the 2015 (and continuing) refugee crisis – influencing the result.

In Scotland, one of the many reasons the Scottish independence issue is still alive is the generational factor. A large proportion of older voters chose to stay in the UK and, in a decade, far fewer of them will be around to vote for the Union. With Europe, the demographics work the opposite way around: a strong commitment to vote Leave does, according to private campaign polling, correlate strongly with being older (as well as being less well educated and less well off). Therefore, if the UK does not vote to leave the EU this time, some argue it never will.

Yes Scotland had the Scottish civil service to help build the SNP-led government's case for independence. The EU Leave campaign will not have similar support, although the backing of the UK print media should cancel out this weakness.

Scottish Labour's new leader Kezia Dugdale has far more pressing concerns than the future of the EU: an upcoming Holyrood election in May 2016 for which every opinion poll suggests support for her party will decline yet further.

The 34-year-old has also had to contend with Jeremy Corbyn's controversial leadership of the UK Labour Party, something she did not expect. 'I don't want to spend my whole life just carping from the sidelines,' she told the BBC in August 2015 when questioned about Corbyn's candidacy. 'You have to convince me that he can be Prime Minister. Here's a guy that's broken the whip 500 times. So how can the leader of the party enforce discipline with that record?'

Dugdale was forced to perform a less than subtle reverse ferret when Corbyn was duly elected with a landslide 59.5 per cent of members' votes, telling journalists, 'It's an absolute delight to work with Jeremy.'

Relations between London and Edinburgh seem to have changed since the days of Johann Lamont, with the Scottish party now enjoying something close to autonomy north of the border. 'The branch office is not just closed,' explained one involved, 'the windows are boarded up and there's a "For Sale" sign out front.'

However, what appears to be autonomy could be disinterest. With just one Scottish MP at Westminster – the relatively junior Ian Murray – is anyone making a strong case for Scotland at Labour's top table? There is also a concern, north of the border, that Labour's Cabinet is worryingly London-centric, with the shadow Chancellor, Chief Secretary, Health Secretary, Defence Secretary and International Development Secretary all representing constituencies in the capital.

Some UK Labour Party figures privately believe Scotland is a 'lost cause'. Others recognise the Labour Party cannot

win again in Westminster without some form of Scottish revival, especially if boundary changes go ahead, with the loss
of up to twenty Labour constituencies in England.

There is limited evidence as to Scottish voters' perceptions
of Jeremy Corbyn, but what does exist is far from positive.
One poll in January 2016 suggested support for Labour has
fallen by a third since he took over as UK Labour leader.
Other research suggests that he is more popular with those
who vote SNP than with Labour supporters. 'He's a marginal
asset in working-class communities in industrial Scotland,'
explained one Labour source. 'But he's killing us in middle-
income Scotland.'

Some Labour activists believe it is not Corbyn's economic
plans but his views on the monarchy, shoot-to-kill and the
Falkland Islands that worry middle-class voters. 'It's fucking
madness,' argued one. 'Jeremy Corbyn is like a series of lapel
badges on a sixth former's blazer: pick your lost cause.'

Yet on the perennially divisive issue of Trident nuclear
weapons, which are based on the west coast of Scotland,
the UK leader is more in touch with Labour members in
Scotland than those in the rest of the country. Corbyn is anti-
Trident, unlike the UK party, which is officially pro. And
since November 2015 the Scottish party (and its one MP)
is officially anti-Trident, although its leader supports the
renewal of the system.

This confusing set of contradictions has not been helped
by Corbyn's sometimes farcical monthly visits to Scotland.
During one walkabout in the grounds of the Scottish
Parliament, TV crews and photographers surrounded the
Labour leader as he was guided by his Scottish counterpart:
'It was like Kez was navigating her granddad round the
Boxing Day sales,' said one attendant MSP.

The real challenge for Scottish Labour is that a third of their voters backed independence, and much of that referendum support has crystallised into votes for the SNP. Scottish politics post-referendum 'is ever so slightly less heated', explained one involved. 'People have calmed down, but the referendum still defines their politics.'

In September 2015, Kezia Dugdale announced that in any future referendum, Scottish Labour MSPs would be allowed to campaign for independence, in the hope it will encourage Labour Yes voters to return. It attracted headlines, but not everyone is convinced that the tactic will succeed. 'There is a state of denial within the Scottish Labour Party,' said one rival politician. 'The Yes Scotland voters are not coming back.'

And in an attempt to reposition Scottish Labour, Dugdale announced proposals for a 1p income tax rise under new powers devolved to Holyrood. The justification: reverse SNP cuts to education by using the new powers of the Scottish Parliament, thus highlighting that these cuts are a choice. The campaign slogan 'kids not cuts' has echoes of the SNP's anti-Trident 'bairns not bombs' rhetoric.

Dugdale has received plaudits for kick-starting a much-needed public debate on taxation and spending. But suggesting tax rises so soon before an election was seen as a 'kamikaze move' by some. There was also criticism that Scottish taxpayers would be worst hit, paying more than those in England to mitigate Westminster austerity that very few north of the border had voted for. Furthermore, Scottish Labour had explicitly campaigned during the referendum that an independent Scotland would lead to higher taxes. Scottish Labour had failed to commission any private polling or focus groups to see just how the policy would go down with voters.

The move, although popular among MSPs and party members, was a calculated risk, and made on an assumption that those voters who would be turned off by a tax hike had already left Labour because of Jeremy Corbyn. It also exemplifies a different – though not necessarily superior – party strategy. In contrast to the previous attention on short-term electoral success, Labour sources claim they are now focused on a longer-term effort to rebuild and reposition the party to the left of Scottish politics. 'Jim Murphy was the embodiment of a scattergun approach,' argued one senior source. 'The metrics of success for Kez are different: giving the party a purpose, bringing in new blood, and making sure it is fit for the future – not caught in a 1997 tribute act.'

This may, however, be irrelevant if the 2016 Holyrood elections don't go to plan. Scottish Labour spent just under £2 million during the 2015 general election, and will be lucky if there is £800,000 to spend for the 2016 Holyrood fight. The times when the party could post targeted direct mail to every house in Scotland are long gone.

With much of the party's support already haemorrhaged to the Scottish nationalists, there is a new potential threat: the Scottish Conservatives, who see the 'perfect storm' of Corbyn, tax, Trident and a seemingly weaker unionist stance as providing a vulnerable underbelly for assault. And in the forthcoming elections they plan to spend more than ever before.

Nicola Sturgeon and the SNP seem sure to win an increased majority at Holyrood, meaning most media coverage has been devoted to the battle for second place, with the Scottish Conservatives keen to talk up the possibility that it could be them.

'How far Labour fall is the unknown,' argued one senior Tory. 'They have started the death spiral and I don't see how they get out of it. What lever can they pull to stop the plane from crashing?' Another Conservative points out: 'It took fifty years for us to hit rock bottom in Scotland; it's taken Labour a matter of months. They're in a position we know well: completely reliant on the support of old people, and it takes years to break out of that.'

Ready and willing to exploit Labour's myriad problems is the energetic Scottish Conservative leader Ruth Davidson. The 37-year-old, openly gay, former Territorial Army signaller is optimistic about her party's chances, with their private research showing many months ago that there was a realistic chance of beating Labour and pushing them into third place.

Much of this is due to Davidson: an impressive communicator who has steadily gained in confidence in her four years as leader. She was one of the stars of the referendum and now boasts high personal approval ratings in Scotland, second only to Nicola Sturgeon. Why? In part, it is because she is not seen as a 'typical Tory'. 'Ruth doesn't fit any of the stereotypes,' insisted one close colleague. 'She's not a landowner, she didn't go to private school, she doesn't speak posh, she doesn't own a grouse estate, and she's not 104.'

Davidson has gained the respect of Downing Street and worked hard to transform her party, 'encouraging' many of her rather elderly group of parliamentarians (half are over sixty, one is over seventy) to retire. Publicly this has been characterised as a gentle 'changing of the guard' but in reality it was a more Machiavellian process and one in which Davidson did not act alone. 'It was a bit like *Murder on the Orient Express*,' remembered one Scottish Conservative with a smile. 'Quite a few of us had a hand in it. One MSP tried to bargain a knighthood or peerage for stepping down, but was firmly told, "No chance."' 'There's no point getting them out of this Parliament and then into another,' one insider explained.

Even with such a high proportion of new candidates, Davidson has failed to recruit many women. Just 15 per cent of those standing in constituency seats and on regional lists are women – the lowest proportion of all parties. In contrast, Labour and the SNP boast 51 and 43 per cent respectively. The Conservatives' current level of 40 per cent female representation looks set to drop.

Ahead of the Holyrood election, some speculate that Davidson's longer-distance sights are not set on becoming Scotland's next First Minister, but the UK's first female Defence Secretary. With a deep interest in the armed forces and foreign affairs, a few colleagues expect she will stand for Westminster in the next general election, and possibly gain a Cabinet seat.

And although it could be argued that Labour's splits over Corbyn, its policies on Trident and tax-raising, and its relaxed position on independence will all benefit the Tories with their proudly unionist, security-focused pitch, others are sceptical: 'We've been promised a Conservative revival in every election for a decade. Ruth Davidson's biggest problem is she's a Tory.' Another doubter claims: 'People want an opposition which can challenge the SNP to be bolder on bread-and-butter issues, not to cut taxes. There just isn't an appetite for that in Scotland.'

And while the smaller parties scrabble for second place, Nicola Sturgeon continues to ride high, with polls suggesting she can be confident of receiving the support of over half the Scottish electorate. She rarely makes a political error, determinedly avoids complacency and shows no sign of slowing down her punishing schedule any time soon.

The First Minister has no obvious successor. Unlike Alex Salmond, Sturgeon manages to stay across the portfolios of many of her senior ministers. 'She's a voracious reader of briefs; she likes information,' explained one close colleague, 'but is aware she needs to be less involved in absolutely everything.'

As with Scotland's other political parties, the SNP lacks a depth of talent at Holyrood. One unintended consequence of the stunning general election victory was that much of the SNP's most promising talent was shipped down to Westminster, to the very Parliament from which they seek to declare independence.

Rivals hoping Nicola Sturgeon will soon come a cropper look likely to be disappointed. Despite high-profile scandals concerning her MPs – including two cases involving the police – so far there has been no impact on the party's opinion poll ratings.

One Sturgeon-doubter predicts it will be her very work ethic that could cause her downfall: 'She is a robot – she is so disciplined in her message that she has lost her own personality. And she works so incredibly hard and does such long hours there really is nothing else in her life. Eventually people will see that.'

It is widely accepted that the SNP will win and win big. But with so many votes already sewn up, there is now a more limited pool from which the SNP can seek to further grow its support. Some claim the nationalists are already carrying out a 'black widow' strategy of cannibalising Green-supporting Yes-voters, similar to the Lynton Crosby-led destruction of the Liberal Democrats. 'If Nicola's "Both Votes SNP" argument is successful,' argued one source, 'the Greens are completely screwed.'

A glance at the colours of the electoral map of Scotland and those of the rest of the UK demonstrates vividly the marked differences between the two – something unlikely to change in the near future. A surprising number of pro-UK politicians and advisers I spoke to said something along the lines of: 'There's going to be a second Scottish referendum, and we'll lose it.' This sense of defeatism and of the inevitability of independence is perhaps surprising so soon after the decisive referendum victory.

The line that the vote on independence was a 'once in a generation' opportunity was mentioned ad nauseam by Salmond, Sturgeon and even the Scottish government White Paper. Yet, soon after the No vote, Salmond claimed a second referendum was 'inevitable'. Nicola Sturgeon has avoided the 'r' word ahead of the 2016 elections, but her significant resources – in both the SNP and the Scottish government – will likely be manoeuvring in preparation for the next attempt at securing independence.

One proposal – never acted upon – was for the Better Together core team to evolve into a think tank with a skeleton staff, continuing to present the case for maintaining the union, and remaining on standby for a second referendum. Research from Professor John Curtice emphasises the importance of economic arguments in Scots' voting intentions, as well as their own personal economic circumstances, meaning whichever side is most convincing on this will be likely to win next time.

The United Kingdom's future is not as secure as some assumed, and Labour's recent decline in Scotland will continue to affect the dynamics of Westminster politics in the coming years. Nicola Sturgeon is now faced with the quandary of whether to call for a second referendum in future election manifestos. A vote for Brexit, however, could make that decision for her: the First Minister believes a Leave result will 'almost certainly' trigger another indy ref. If the UK votes to Remain, some believe she may be minded to call for the devolution of the power to hold a vote on independence, which, if granted, would leave her in an influential position to put the question to Scots at a time of her choosing.

In any case, more tax, borrowing and welfare powers will be transferred from Westminster to Holyrood in the coming years. The challenge for the SNP will be to prove they can use them effectively to improve the lives of Scots. This devolution could gradually continue over the coming years until there's little left to transfer. As the former Welsh Secretary, Ron Davies, famously suggested: 'Devolution is a process, not an event.'

ABOUT THE AUTHOR

Joe Pike is a political reporter based at the Scottish Parliament, from where he covered the Scottish independence referendum and the 2015 general election. Prior to this, he was a reporter for LBC and Classic FM. Joe studied politics at the University of Edinburgh and journalism at City University London. He splits his time between Edinburgh and London. *Project Fear* is his first book.

INDEX

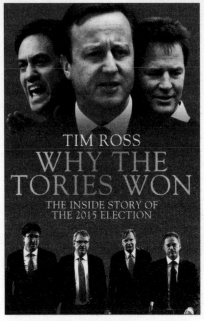

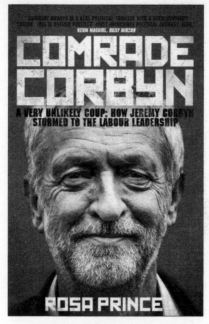

400PP HARDBACK, £20

"This is British politics' most incredible political journey. Ever."

KEVIN MAGUIRE, *DAILY MIRROR*

He is a most unlikely revolutionary: a middle-aged, middle-class former grammar schoolboy who honed his radicalism on the mean streets of rural Shropshire. Until recently, Jeremy Corbyn was barely known outside political circles, yet last summer he rode a wave of popular enthusiasm to win the Labour Party leadership by a landslide, with a greater mandate than any British political leader before him.

From Corbyn's cosy rural upbringing, through three marriages – including his decision to divorce one wife for sending their son to grammar school – and his long espousal of contentious causes, from Irish Republicanism and a free Palestine to opposition to military action in Syria and Iraq, *Comrade Corbyn* tells the intriguing story of the most unexpected leader in modern British politics.

— AVAILABLE FROM ALL GOOD BOOKSHOPS —

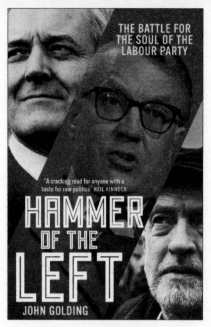